# Fannish Folklore

German Studies in America

No. 77

PETER LANG
Oxford • Bern • Berlin • Bruxelles • New York • Wien

Jaime W. Roots

# Fannish Folklore

## Feminist Fan-Fiction Retellings of Germanic Fairy Tales

**PETER LANG**
Oxford • Bern • Berlin • Bruxelles • New York • Wien

**Bibliographic information published by Die Deutsche Nationalbibliothek**
Die Deutsche Nationalbibliothek lists this publication in the Deutsche Nationalbibliografie; detailed bibliographic data are available on the Internet at http://dnb.ddb.de.

A catalogue record for this book is available at the British Library.

Library of Congress Cataloging-in-Publication Data

Names: Roots, Jaime W., 1988- author.
Title: Fannish folklore : feminist fan-fiction retellings of Germanic fairy tales / Jaime W. Roots.
Description: Oxford ; New York : Peter Lang, (2022) | Series: German studies in America, 0721-3727 ; vol no. 77 | Includes bibliographical references and index.
Identifiers: LCCN 2022001675 (print) | LCCN 2022001676 (ebook) | ISBN 9781800793330 (paperback) | ISBN 9781800793347 (ebook) | ISBN 9781800793354 (epub)
Subjects: LCSH: Fan fiction--Germany. | Feminist fiction, German--History and criticism. | German fiction--21st century--History and criticism. | Fairy tales--Adaptations--History and criticism. | Digital storytelling. | LCGFT: Literary criticism.
Classification: LCC PN3448.F36 R66 2022 (print) | LCC PN3448.F36 (ebook) | DDC 398.2082--dc23/eng/20220324
LC record available at https://lccn.loc.gov/2022001675
LC ebook record available at https://lccn.loc.gov/2022001676

Cover image: ToniAnne Wong, "Artists of Today." Reproduced with permission.
Cover design by Peter Lang Ltd.

ISSN 0721-3727
ISBN 978-1-80079-333-0 (print)
ISBN 978-1-80079-334-7 (ePDF)
ISBN 978-1-80079-335-4 (ePub)


Published by Peter Lang Ltd, International Academic Publishers, Oxford, United Kingdom
oxford@peterlang.com, www.peterlang.com



This book has been peer reviewed.

# Contents

# Figures

# Acknowledgments

I gratefully acknowledge the many people who have contributed to this book by either reading the entire manuscript, offering comments on various sections, or helping me develop ideas into full-fledged chapters. The feedback and suggestions from Laurel Plapp and the anonymous reader have helped invaluably to produce this book in its present form. I am ever grateful to Gail Hart for her encouragement to pursue the topic of fan fiction as an area of study as well as her feedback along various forms of my manuscript. I am grateful as well to my partner Daniel Stapleton and his patience in listening to and helping me work through many of my arguments before they were developed enough to be committed to paper and for providing feedback on many of them once they were.

My dear friend Crystal Carney provided her copywriting expertise as well as her mutual love of the topic; from childhood we have been writing stories and giving each other feedback. My great thanks to Morgan Morales for reading through several chapters and helping me refine my ideas. Finally, I must acknowledge two students of my students, Joey Dickinson and ToniAnne Wong, for their contributions to this book. Joey Dickinson helped with the painstaking categorization of fan fiction works and comment thread discussions as well as coding our data into graphic visualizations. ToniAnne Wong produced the marvelous cover image in fan art style with her interpretation of the contents of this book.

INTRODUCTION

# Storytelling and the Role of Fan Fiction

## The Art of Storytelling

Storytelling is ever-present in our lives, and yet it is often taken so much for granted that we are scarcely aware of it. We tell stories to pass the time, for entertainment, and for sympathy, understanding, and persuasion. Humans are so inclined to tell stories that, given the opportunity, we opt to connect events and rationalize what has taken place rather than let them sit unconnected in isolation. Take, for example, this simple exercise:[1]

> The man meets the woman. I walk her dog. The boy visits with flowers.

Looking at these three simple sentences, our minds quickly begin to draw connections between them. Am I walking the woman's dog so that she may meet up with the man? Is the boy bringing flowers the man has ordered for the woman? In truth, there is no inherent connection between these three sentences: they have been selected at random and yet our brains are already working to create connections between them—to tell a story.

The human brain, above all, likes to make sense of things even if, as with this example, it needs to make it up. It is also important to note that we are often completely unaware that we are creating connections where none previously existed: our brains want to make sense of the world—to explain our surroundings—and drawing connections and conclusions (telling stories) is how this is accomplished. Stories are our means of understanding

1 This exercise has been adapted from Jonathan Gottschall's *The Storytelling Animal.*

the world. Folklorist Bruce Jackson describes the phenomenon of making connections which may not exist: "People are very good at making sense, even if they have to create it. That's one of the jobs our stories have" (44). He indicates further that this phenomenon appears already in early youth as soon as children understand the concept of a story. Children learn through stories that events should lead to a sensical conclusion and will often create non-existent connections to draw even extraneous details together.

It is of course not just children who like to link situations together for a sensible progression of events. Everyone is a storyteller. This does not mean that everyone is a skilled storyteller, able to enchant audiences and weave monumental epics, but rather that everyone tells stories, even if it is something as seemingly inconsequential as describing one's day. Storytelling helps us define ourselves and make sense of the world. Storytelling is such a part of us as humans, that human experience and storytelling are inextricable. John D. Niles describes the importance of storytelling in the role of human development:

> Through storytelling, an otherwise unexceptional biological species has become a much more interesting thing, *Homo narrans*: that hominid who not only has succeeded in negotiating the world of nature, finding enough food and shelter to survive, but also has learned to inhabit mental worlds that pertain to times that are not present and places that are the stuff of dreams. It is through such symbolic mental activities that people have gained the ability to create themselves as human beings and thereby transform the world of nature into shapes not known before. (3)

Stories permeate society and we as a species are "addicted to story." Folklore has long been seen as a means for communities to pass their traditions and views of the world to new members and generations, and it is still a means by which we identify ourselves and our place in our communities. Even now in the twenty-first century we "still hew strongly" to folklore passed down through the ages (Gottschall xiv). No matter the technological, political, philosophical, or other advancements to human society, folklore remains a fixed part of our lives. "Cut from the marrow of human experience" (Wilson 149), folklore is constantly around us in myriad forms.

Folklore and folk practices, in the colloquial use of the term, are often associated with times long since passed: the "old-timey stuff" of vanishing cultures and traditions (Blank, "Introduction: Towards a Conceptual" 4). The broad term "folklore" encompasses folk expression such as material culture, belief, and ritual, among others, though throughout this book I will focus specifically on one type of folklore: folk stories. In the West one often thinks, for example, of folk stories which were written and collected in now-famous anthologies largely during nineteenth-century Europe such as the Grimms' *Kinder- und Hausmärchen [Children's and Household Tales]* (1812–1857) or Hans Christian Andersen's fairy-tale publications (1835–1852). Yet Whitney Phillips and Ryan M. Milner note that there is "no inherent rule that folk expression must consist of 'old stuff.' " What is of more importance is that folklore expresses consistencies which allow a group to perceive their folklore as "traditional, locally derived, or community generated"—everyday expressions by everyday people (23–24). Folklorists study folklore to "understand the nature of human cultural history and expression" (Toelken 31) and that certainly includes contemporary, everyday expression. The evolution of folk stories is often characterized as a "multifaceted process involving the production, institutionalization, definition, acceptance, rejection, transformation, revision, and interpretation" of traditional versions of tales (Haase, "Introduction" *The Reception* 12). These stories which evolve and shape as they are retold and refashioned allow participants to personalize stories while still maintaining ties to the traditional versions of tales. Put quite simply, then, folklore is "the study of the living performance of tradition—for better and worse and for everything in between" (Phillips and Milner 25).

Folklore is such a crucial part of our lives that it is represented in all media. The human connection can be so strong and multifaceted that folklore is not contained within just one media form but reaches across all genres to help represent and authenticate human experiences in diverse ways—such as the themes and characters of oral fairy tales which exist in textual form, in film representations, song, performance, and fine art. While folk stories may be told through media as diverse as text, film, song, stage, and image, the Internet has expanded the space of storytelling, and opened a space for amateur writers to collaborate and share their stories with people around the world—allowing the emotional and personal connection to these stories to continue to flourish and be shared broadly. Jack Zipes, for example, writes that technological innovation, in particular, has enabled folk stories to expand in cultural domains. The availability of more widespread dissemination and discussion enabled by technology such as the Internet has helped folklore to spread to wider audiences. And folk stories, in particular, continue to spread, "embracing, if not swallowing, all types of genres, art forms, and cultural institutions" including the Internet (*Irresistible* 22). Technology makes this diffusion of stories much easier and more readily available than ever before, as technology at its most effective helps give us new and more effective ways to do what we had been doing anyway.

The Internet has also affected these stories in other ways. The Internet has expanded the space for storytelling. It has offered new options for storytellers to share "'classic' small-scale stories" across the globe (Lundby 3). While published books may be distributed throughout the world, the rate at which online stories can traverse the globe is instantaneous. Feedback, editorial work, publication, distribution, and audience commentary and feedback on the work, which can sometimes take years to accomplish with published works, can happen within seconds online. Indeed, "like nothing that has come before, accessibility puts the everyday expressions of everyday folk collectives right at users' fingertips" (Phillips and Milner 49). Technological innovation has allowed folklore to flourish and spread to audiences in ways which, until recently, were unimaginable. In my study, I focus on a particular technological innovation which amplifies the power of folklore: the digital storytelling of fan fiction. Henry Jenkins has defined modern media fans as "the most passionately engaged consumers of mass media" ("Fandom"). While many media fans never engage in transformative works such as creating artwork or writing stories based on the media they consume, here I discuss the fans who are "active participants in the construction and circulation of [...] meaning" (Jenkins, *Textual* 24). All fans discussed in this book are fans who *do* create transformative works based on the media they consume. Though fan fiction (also abbreviated as *FF* or *fic*) is certainly more nuanced and will be discussed in more detail later, it may be simply defined as unpublished, amateur stories based on other (usually published) works such as film, television, and books.

In my investigation, I focus on one of the largest strictly German-language sites *FanFiktion.de* and its stories classified under the category of "Grimms Märchen" or "Grimms' Fairy Tales." This collection is also of particular interest in relation to studying the evolution of folk stories in German-speaking cultures, since fans directly engage with the Grimms' tales, treating them as central to an established fairy-tale canon. These fans acknowledge this canon while simultaneously rewriting and critiquing the tales, often engaging in metadiscussions of the genre. Fans at times discuss not just the Grimms' role in defining the genre, but their own active engagement in redefining the fairy-tale tradition. I likewise narrow my focus to discuss this specific treatment of the genre because, as Kristina Busse and Karen Hellekson note, it is impossible, even perhaps dangerous, to speak of all fan fiction as a single genre; fan fiction revolving around different media are often part of online communities which have strikingly different rules and expectations ("Introduction: Why a Fan Fiction" 6). Below I introduce the genre of fan fiction, though for the sake of clarity I first define terms key to the discussion of online fan fiction as well as provide a description of the site *FanFiktion.de*.

## Key Terms

The fan fiction community has many terms and acronyms that members employ. Not all terms belong specifically to fan fiction communities—some are taken, borrowed, and even repurposed from various sources such as general Internet slang or even literary criticism. These terms are nevertheless widely used within fan-fiction communities on a globalized scale. Even on *FanFiktion.de*, a site exclusively in German, nearly all terms have been adopted from English with only a select few being translated. While there are hundreds of terms, I will briefly discuss those most pertinent to my investigation.

Fan fiction is often discussed in terms of fandoms. *Fandom* itself refers to the fan community surrounding a specific form of media such as a book, movie, TV show, or game. Fandoms refer to "the social structures and cultural practices created by the most passionately engaged consumers of mass media" (Jenkins, "Fandom, Participatory"). A fandom, then, is not just individual fics within a category or individual fans, but a reference to the fan community surrounding a particular form of media—all fans whether they write fics, comment on them, participate in discussion threads, or otherwise actively and passively participate within the community. The "Grimms Märchen" fandom, then, includes all fics, fans who post and comment, as well as the group norms established and enforced within that community.

All works of fan fiction are based on the *canon* or the official background of the specific fandom. For the *Lord of the Rings* fandom, the canon is generally considered to be the *Lord of the Rings* trilogy published by J. R. R. Tolkien. There can be debate as to what constitutes canon, however. For example, in the *Lord of the Rings* fandom it may be debated as to whether the ancillary book *Silmarillion* is considered canon, and likewise whether the Peter Jackson films should be considered. For a fandom such as "Grimms Märchen," the majority of the fics on *FanFiktion.de* follow either the 1857 version of the Grimms' tales or Disney film versions. If a fic writer creates a fic where they ignore or change certain parts of the story established within the canon and considered essential, such as ignoring the death of a character, they are said to "break canon." Though even when fans do stray significantly from the canon, the author usually clearly labels the fic as "alternate universe" or "constructed reality" to signal significant changes which maintains the source text as a "discursive referent" (Stein and Busse, "Limit Play" 196).

Two common genres of fan fiction are crossover and slash. A *crossover* fic is one which contains a mix of two or more series. An example would be creating a story which contains characters from both *Star Wars* and *Star Trek* or has characters from one series enter the universe of the other. In the "Grimms Märchen" fandom,[2] a crossover would be a fic which has

2 For the sake of clarity, from this point forward in this book, the word "fandom" will refer specifically to the "Grimms Märchen" fandom unless otherwise stated.

characters from multiple tales interacting with one another such as Little Red Riding Hood and Little Briar Rose/Sleeping Beauty meeting. A *slash* fic is one which contains same-sex romantic relationships, though it does not necessarily need to contain sexual relations. Typically slash fics depict male same-sex relationships, and depictions of female sexual relationships are relatively rare, to the point where they are often labeled specifically as *FemSlash*. The term "slash" comes from a shorthand developed in the 1970s which would denote same-sex relationships as male/male or m/m and came to be shortened to just "slash" ("Fan Fiction Terms").

A *Betaleser* or "Beta reader" (often shortened to just "Beta") is a crucial part of fan fiction. A *Betaleser* is someone other than the fic writer who reads and edits the fic for various reasons such as grammar and spelling, plot, and general cohesiveness of the story itself. A Beta is a member of the fan-fiction community and almost always a fic writer themself. A writer can have more than one Beta, requesting Betas for specific purposes such as one to read for spelling and grammar, and another for plot. Betas will advertise themselves on the site and will typically cite their strengths and weaknesses. A Beta might note that they are good at helping to develop plot, but not as strong fixing grammatical mistakes. Betas are an integral part of fan fiction, and many sites, including *FanFiktion.de*, suggest that all pieces of fan fic be read by Betas before being posted. There is an obvious connection here between Betas and professional editors as well as peer reviewers. Fan-fiction communities often incorporate or modify professional literary practices. All writers and Betas are community members who may both interact with one another as writer and Beta in turn. "Betaleser" is not a title that one retains; rather fans serve as Betas for various fics and directly discuss the work and their suggestions together—thus the power dynamic between writer and Beta is less structured than in professional writing and editing and it is more transparent than the practice of anonymous peer reviewers. Importantly as well, there is no monetary exchange between writer and Beta, rather an exchange of time and energy which will be detailed in Chapter 3.

Finally, many fics contain an A.N. (also written A/N), or Author's Note, often before the beginning or at the end of a fic. They also frequently appear at the end of individual chapters in multi-chapter fics. In an A.N., the writer speaks directly to other fans within their community, often giving a short introduction to their fic, noting their specific state of mind while writing (e.g., noting that they have been busy lately and have not had very much time to devote to writing) or thanking specific Betas or users for leaving commentary. In an A.N., writers will typically ask their readers direct questions or request that people leave comments. As an example, one fic writer leaves an A.N. describing her inspiration and motivation for writing her fic:

> Die Idee zu diesem Text kam mir, als wir "Gender" in Englisch durchgemacht haben und uns eine politisch korrekte Version von "Rotkäppchen" angehört haben. Mir kam der Gedanke, wie "Rotkäppchen" ablaufen würde, wenn der Wolf eine Wölfin, die Großmutter ein Großvater und der Jäger eine Jägerin wäre.
>
> [The idea for this text came to me when we were going through "Gender" in English and listened to a politically correct version of "Little Red Riding Hood." The idea came to me how "Little Red Riding Hood" would turn out if the wolf were a female wolf, the grandmother a grandfather, and the hunter a huntress.][3] (dreamycato)

## Description of Site

As of August 2020, *FanFiktion.de* had over 400,000 texts written in ten different categories: Anime & Manga, Books, Cartoons & Comics, Computer Games, Crossover, Theater- & TV-Films, Musicals, Celebrities, Tabletop- and Roleplaying Games, and TV-Series. These categories are then broken down further into subcategories. Under the category of "Films" one can find the subcategory of "Star Wars," and under "Books" one can find the subcategories of "Harry Potter" and "Grimms Märchen." *FanFiktion.de* describes itself as a site dedicated exclusively to fics written in German and explicitly forbids fics written in English. Under the bans and restrictions (*Verbote und Einschränkungen*) listed on the site it states,

3 All fan-fiction translations are mine.

> FanFiktion.de ist ein deutschsprachiges Archiv, weshalb wir unserem Grundsatz, für deutschsprachiges Publikum eine Lese-/Autorenecke zu sein, mit englischen Geschichten widersprechen würden.
>
> [FanFiktion.de is a German-language archive, which is why we would contradict our principle of being a reading- and writing nook for a German-language public with English stories.]

The site also identifies strongly not only with the German language but with Germany itself as it follows the laws set forth in the *Bundesdatenschutzgesetz* (Germany's Federal Data Protection Act) which is cited multiple times on the site. Some of the largest fan fic websites have large numbers of fics in English such as *fanfiction.net* which, as of July 2020, had over 800,000 fics for *Harry Potter* alone. *FanFiktion.de* prides itself as a corner of the web for strictly German-language fics. As will be discussed in Chapter 2, this language exclusivity fosters a sense of community that fans express they have difficulty finding on sites with large numbers of English-language fics from around the world.

Access to the site is not limited to registered users, though if one chooses to register, profiles are generated for each user as a space for personal expression of identity and interests. Here users have the option to provide details about themselves as well as a short biography. Users typically list their username, gender, country, or city of residence as well as their age. Here one can find a list of all fics the user has written with links to each one. Some users will also link to outside personal pages such as Facebook, Instagram, or LiveJournal. Upon opening a given fic, there are also links to reader reviews where feedback is posted by other users for individual fan fics or individual chapters. Fan commentary and feedback is a crucial component to the fan-fiction genre, and the website makes navigation between fics and feedback readily accessible to both registered and unregistered readers.

*FanFiktion.de* contains a rating system which details to users how they should rate their fics. Fics on the site are rated on a provisional scale denoted by a "P," since users are rating their own fics, followed by a number to denote the suitability of the fic for a given age range. A "P6" rating is acceptable for an audience of 6 years or older and so on. Likewise, each rating above P6 has an equivalent "slash" rating to mark when the main character(s) or important secondary characters are involved in a same-sex relationship—though there is currently debate in various forums of the website that "slash" should be separated from age restrictions since some users rightfully find using "slash" as a part of the rating system discriminatory toward L.G.B.T.Q.+ relationships ("Warum wird FemSlash"). It is explicitly stated on *FanFiktion.de* that "die reine Existenz eines irgendwo in der Geschichte erwähnten homosexuellen Pärchens rechtfertigt jedoch noch kein Slash-Rating" [the pure existence of homosexual pairing which is only referenced in the story, however, does not justify a Slash-Rating]. According to the website, the relationship needs to be an integral part of plot or character development to warrant the "slash" rating. The ratings are as listed below:

- P6: stories without negligible use of expletives or insults and without sexual content.
- P12: stories with low to extensive use of expletives and insults with low to moderate descriptions of violence, without graphic descriptions of sexual practices.
- P16: stories with low to extensive use of expletives and insults with low to moderate descriptions of violence and sexual tones without graphic depictions of sexual practices.
- P18: stories with low to extensive use of expletives, low to extensive descriptions of violence, or with graphic descriptions of sexual practices ("Rechtlinien").

*FanFiktion.de* positions itself as a place for users of all ages to comfortably read and participate in conversations with other users, and as such, the rating system is obligatory to post a fic on the site.

## Internet Fan Fiction

Fan fiction is not a genre that is entirely new, but the Internet has profoundly affected its scope and distribution, causing a recent, revolutionary change. Though the term "fan fiction" did not come into use until the 1960s, there are many different interpretations of when fan fiction began to be written. Some estimations state that it began as early as John Lydgate and Robert Henryson's extensions of Geoffrey Chaucer's work in the fifteenth century, whereas others argue that it did not begin until fan extensions of *Star Trek* TV series which began airing in 1966 (Black 11). Yet, what we see in fan fiction, no matter where its origins lie, are changes, adaptations, and reinterpretations of published material. As fan Sionon Klingensang describes it,

> Fanfiction ist vielleicht so gewissermaßen das "Comfort Food" der Literatur [...]. Fanfiction ist wirklich das, was die Leute lesen wollen, während hochoffiziell verlegte Literatur oft das ist, von dem Verlage denken, dass die Leute es lesen wollen, oder das, was die Leute vor zehn Jahren lesen wollten.
>
> [Fan fiction is probably to a certain extent the "Comfort Food" of literature [...]. Fan fiction is really what people want to read while very officially published literature is often what the publisher thinks people want to read or rather what people wanted to read ten years ago.]

If folkloric expression is a mirror of societal and cultural values (Blank, "Introduction: Towards" 4), then fan fiction, as a representation of what different communities "really want," can give deep insights into both society and culture.

As fan fiction has moved to the Internet from its earlier home in print magazines, such as the fics examined by Camille Bacon-Smith in her seminal work *Enterprising Women* (1992), the space for fannish storytelling has been expanded. And while *FanFiktion.de* (since it boasts of itself as a place for the German language) may not have as large or diverse a reading audience as a site which has fics in English, the availability of these fics to speakers of German is much more immediate than that of print tales. Fans note the smaller user-base of *FanFiktion.de* as something positive because it allows them to feel a sense of community with fellow German-speakers. These stories can come from anyone with access to a computer and the Internet—vastly increasing not only the number of perspectives and interpretations of media but also vastly increasing their distribution throughout the world. Not only is everyone a potential storyteller, but with new technologies such as the Internet, everyone has more of a chance to be read by a wider audience.

Stories are continually retold because they have some sort of resonance in the storyteller's life. They can be updated so that they remain relevant to the present time, the present audience, and the storyteller. And while this aspect of retelling is certainly important and valid, there are additional reasons that stories are continually rewritten and retold—especially within the realm of fan fiction: fascination and frustration. Henry Jenkins writes that fan fiction, "after all, is born of a balance between fascination and frustration: if media content didn't fascinate us, there would be no desire to engage with it; but if it didn't frustrate us on some level, there would be no drive to rewrite or remake it" (*Textual* 247). With frustration, Jenkins refers to aspects of media content which did not live up to the expectations of fans. Whether these be plot holes, unsatisfactory relationships, untimely deaths, or perhaps fringe elements of stories which were not given much attention in the canon, fans are left with a feeling of dissatisfaction. It is out of this sense of frustration and dissatisfaction then that fan fiction comes to be. A "good" story that is continually retold does not necessarily need to be well constructed or even well told, but it likely does need an interesting plotline that leaves ample room for interpretation. Fan fiction writers express aspects of the story which were not expressed in the canon, rather than seeking to tell the same story over and over again.

While this type of writing may be seen as something which is freeing or liberating to the fans, allowing them to participate in a conversation about their favorite stories, it also has limitations and restrictions since fans write based on previously established characters and universes. There is not total freedom in what a fan may or may not do, as their story must ultimately come back and be in some way in conversation with the canon. Yet within the world of fic, these versions are accepted as being able to exist alongside one another offering potentially infinite possibilities. In fan fiction, the ever-adapting fairy tale is developed in a medium which flourishes on adaptation, revision, and reinterpretation.

Fans imbue their fics with meanings which are "grounded in [their] lived realities and social worlds" (Black 13–14). Communities learn how to tell their stories by absorbing stories and histories which seem relevant to them, and this is exactly what the fan fiction writers are doing. Yet fan writers see the canon as incomplete, somehow frustrating in its incompleteness, and thus the writers and fans adapt and change their tales to fit with their ideas and expectations for the canon. The fans challenge the canon by altering endings, placing emphasis on different characters, and adding depth to existing tales. However, they are also reaffirming that the canon has a place in their community and an impact on their lives. Fan writers, while they may see the canon as somehow lacking, acknowledge its continued importance in their lives. They discuss their adaptations to establish meaning within their community and determine the role the narratives should play in their lives.

Fan-fiction writers can be said to be "transformative fans"—individuals who are critical of the media they consume (Hellekson and Busse 4). Fics generally expand on existing knowledge of the canon, seek to explain character motivations, or bring minor characters into the foreground. Yet while fan fiction has the ability to alter the original narrative into something unrecognizable, the fics that are most favored by other fans are those which stay true to the canon. Fic writers often seek to test the absolute authority of the media they are based on in order for these stories to remain relevant to contemporary readers. As one fan explains, she writes fics "weil mir oft nicht gefällt, was die Autoren […] präsentieren. Ich schreibe dann gerne alles um oder erfinde neue Sachen dazu" [because I often don't like what the authors […] present. I then gladly rewrite everything or invent new things] (MonaGirl). Rather than treating the original published media as absolute and untouchable, fans seek to bend, change, and reinterpret.

## My Study of *FanFiktion.de*

At the outset I must acknowledge that my own background and identity will inevitably influence my reading and interpretation of the study that follows. Being an American, white, Millennial, cisgender, heterosexual, educated, middle-class woman will both include and exempt me from certain life experiences. My lived experiences both inform the way I see the world as well as my interest in and relationship with all topics covered in this book. Likewise, my experiences as both a Germanist and a folklorist will inevitably inform my interdisciplinary work with fan studies and Internet studies. Discussing fan studies, Cornell Sandvoss writes that "fan studies has indeed eroded the boundaries between audiences and scholars, between fan and academic more than any other field" (30). Myself an "academic fan" (or rather, an "aca-fan"), I have long been interested in fan fiction and folklore before I ever came to formally study them.

As a pre-teen and teenager in the late 1990s and early 2000s, I wrote, rewrote, shared, critiqued, discussed, rewrote again, and edited many pieces of writing (some original works, others which I would later learn would be classified as fan fiction) within a small group of friends. The point of our extremely informal discussions was to imagine new characters, plot lines, plot twists, and relationships between characters we already knew and loved. We would read published stories and books and then eagerly discuss various "what if?" scenarios. Questions ranged from broad, overarching discussions such as "if this particular side character were more prominent, how would that change the overall story?" or discussions of the appropriate balance of action and dialog to some more decidedly weird like "what's the most dramatic and niche way I could kill off this character I don't like?" But no matter what the questions were, it was about reimagining, reframing, and changing loved stories and challenging perspectives.

Beginning here, and continuing throughout my eventual studies, I have been most interested in how stories adapt and change through various reworkings and retellings. My own personal interests only encouraged this focus in my scholarly studies. Inevitably there will be some blurred boundaries between my academic study and personal experience with fan fiction. When I approached the primary website of my focus for this study, *FanFiktion.de*, I opted to study and investigate the site merely as an observer. I specifically chose a site I had never used for my own stories. The large influence the presence of an interviewer or folktale collector has on how stories end up being told has been importantly documented by many folklorists (see Bauman, Lord, Niles, Toelken, among others). Yet the Internet gives scholars a unique opportunity to investigate and analyze folklore in its authentic form without any interviewer/observer influence and bias. The Internet can provide a greater "paper trail" for folklorists to follow and analyze the ways attitudes within communities change and how different cultural attitudes are expressed—the good, the progressive, the altruistic, as well as the bad, the bigoted, and the ugly. The Internet gives us new and different opportunities to study folklore and its transmission.

For the purposes of my investigation of the fandom, I have unavoidably removed the tales and fan comments from their original context. Likewise, I have had to make decisions on which fics and comments to amplify and which to ignore. I recognize that inevitably voices and opinions will be left from the conversation. It is, however, clearly impossible to give voice to all members of the community, nor would that necessarily be beneficial since fics within a fan community are not meant to be read in their entirety by every member; rather fans select various fics to read and comment on. Thus I have focused on fics and comments which highlight measurable trends and are intended to serve as representatives of the fandom community to those who are unfamiliar. In part due to my own background and relationship with fan fiction, I strove to include as many fan voices as possible throughout this book—allowing fans to speak for themselves and define their own community. Some fan quotations may be analyzed, some add to my own analysis, and still others might serve as just chapter or section headings. It is crucial, though, in a study of fans to ensure that the fans themselves and their works stay in the foreground; as well as to highlight fan conceptualizations, critiques, and analyses of themselves, their communities, and their own work. Likewise, by including a wide variety of fan voices, I aim to give voice to individuals with life experiences different from my own.

As I began studying the fandom on *FanFiktion.de*, I noticed several significant trends in the types and subject matter of fics users were posting as well as the types of interactions taking place among fans. It appeared as though the majority of fans both writing and commenting within the fandom self-identified as women. This matched with other studies of fan fiction communities which, even (if not especially) since pre-Internet times, have been comprised nearly entirely of women writers. Although this gender statistic has been slowly changing, many fan communities still remain a space dominated by female-authored transformative works (Hellekson and

Busse, "Fan Identity" 75). To investigate trends across the fandom, in the summer of 2020 I undertook a project together with my German and Data Science student Joey Dickinson to compile information in two data sets to quantify findings about both the authors and fan fiction pieces themselves as well as the comments taking place within the fandom. Due to the size of the fandom (161 fics written by 106 unique authors with 291 unique commenters as of August 2020), we were able to read every fic and every comment to compile the data sets. Additionally, we scoured through over 50 general comment threads on *FanFiktion.de* itself to find fan comments on various topics. This was, at times, a very painstaking process which revealed several enlightening and sometimes surprising statistics.

According to user profiles within the fandom, 87% of those who self-reported their country of residence lived in Germany, while 96% lived in a predominantly German-speaking country. Fics ranged anywhere from less than 100 words to over 40,000 words in length. Though there was no place to specify race or ethnicity in user profiles, in order to gain an understanding of the treatment of race and ethnicity within the fandom, I investigated character descriptions within fics. The majority of fics (63%) had no description of character appearance or a description that was so vague that race/ethnicity could not be determined, such as a simple explanation that a character had brown hair, or that an elderly character had white in their hair. Of all stories, 26% contained characters who were described as identifiably white (i.e., either specifically noting that the character had white skin or describing the character as having blonde hair, blue eyes). That is, though fans do not identify their own race or ethnicity either in their profiles or anywhere in commentary left on fics within the fandom, through investigation of character descriptions, there does appear to be an assumption of whiteness[4] with respect to expectations within the fandom and the types of social justice issues fans tackle in their fics.

Of these authors, 12.4% did not specify gender on their user profiles, but 1.9% of fics were written by authors who self-identified as "diverse" (i.e.,

4 There was only one fic in which a character was described as an identifiable person of color which was done by inserting a celebrity. This topic will be covered in detail in Chapter 6.

nonbinary), 6.8% self-identified as "male," and 78.8% of all authors self-identified as "female"—showcasing the overwhelming majority of people identifying as women in this online space (see Figure 1). Throughout this book I refer to any fan who self-identified as "diverse"—as well as those who did not specify a gender—either with the fan's username only or with the pronouns "they/them/their" so as not to presuppose any gender identification. Likewise I use "they/them/their" as a general pronoun for unknown and hypothetical persons rather than the binary "he or she" / "him or her" / "his or hers" for similar reasons.

While the real identities of each writer cannot be verified, this women majority should not be discounted. As Phillips and Milner note, "[d]igital media scholars [...] have pushed back against any stark divide between 'online' and 'offline,' particularly in the context of identity expression" (66), and here in the case of the online fan fiction, I would like to specify expression of gender identity. Online and offline experiences are so fundamentally intertwined that it has now become impossible to distinguish where the embodied experience ends and the digital begins. They sustain and contextualize each other. Even deliberate deception, which is often presumed to be a much higher risk in digital spaces (such as a heterosexual,

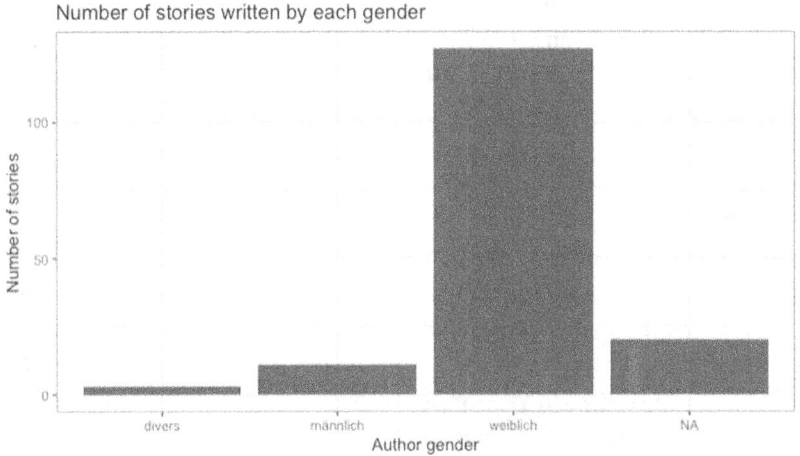


Figure 1. Graph: Number of stories written by gender.
Divers: *diverse* (nonbinary), männlich: *male*, weiblich: *female*.

cisgender man taking the online persona of a woman or a member of the L.G.B.T.Q.+ community), plays out both online and off (albeit in different ways). As Nancy K. Baym argues, "it would be as naive to imagine that people do not deceive online as it is to think everyone is always honest offline" (quoted in Phillips and Milner 67). Likewise, "identity tourism," or the practice where people switch identity online, such as their gender or race, functions largely as a "heuristic device for thinking about gender and race" rather than being an actually prevalent online practice (Daniels 111). And, unfortunately as much as early cyberfeminist theorists (see Daniels) discussing the Internet in the early- to mid-1990s had sincerely hoped that the Internet would become a disembodied utopia where gender, class, race, sexual orientation, or disability would no longer play a role in interaction, we see that these identity markers remain largely salient (Kendall 319).

Identity tourism or identity deception has long been a subject of interest in Internet studies (see, for example, Bromseth and Sundén, and Buchanan). Yet reports of identity deception have now taken a nearly mythical quality with the same stories being told over again and used as cautionary tales "inoculate the unwary" (Kendall 318). We see then that tales of Internet deception have also reached our human need to tell and retell stories. Identity tourism or deception certainly *does* take place online, yet researchers have found that in long-standing communities, deception has been minimized since community formation depends on consistent and trustworthy identities (Kendall 319). People's lived experiences are directly encoded in everything they do online, whether their true identity is known or not. Their online identities represent them as they would like to be seen, what they value, and with which groups they identify.

I have devoted separate chapters to the discussion of fan fiction as folklore, interpreting the fairy tale, new media storytelling, misogyny online, and how fan fiction (re)interprets the past as well as personal and community identity through critical analysis of the canon. The reader is asked to remember that no one of these aspects of fan fiction can be described completely independently of the others without seriously misrepresenting the complex nature of fan fiction and the storytelling process.

CHAPTER 1

# New Media Folklore

With the advent of the Internet, new means of reinterpreting and distributing fairy tales have developed, notably including fan fiction. Written by media fans for other fans, fan-fiction versions of fairy tales challenge traditional notions associated with the genre, such as gender roles, the stark contrasts between good and evil, or even the possibility of fairy-tale figures living "happily ever after." With the migration of fandom from printed magazines to the Internet, no longer do writers need to rely on physical distribution of their fics within relatively small groups of fans; instead, the Internet offers the option to instantly share "small-scale" stories to various corners of the globe (Lundby 3). Often engaging in bold speculation, fan fiction engages with the canon material, imagining what could happen to characters if circumstances were different—if actions and events are reinterpreted or shown in a different perspective.

With the reinterpretation and transposition of familiar stories and tales, writers and tellers of fairy tales create and transform them to serve contemporary needs. Reinterpreting classic tales allows them to be "defamiliarized" which opens opportunities for a shift in perspective or new critical responses. This allows storytellers and writers as well as their audiences to reflect anew on these stories which serve as foundations for cultural narratives (Greenhill and Matrix 12). No fairy tale is sacred or free from reinterpretation as one can see by the numerous revisions of fairy tales and their themes. These themes are evident not only in published editions, but in film, television shows, music—even appearing in commercials and advertisements. The fairy-tale genre has the remarkable capability to be retold, manipulated, and passed down with an ease like hardly any other. The diversity of fairy-tale interpretations highlights the genre's remarkable potential for meaning.

The fairy-tale genre has been described as multifaceted and characterized by "diversity and dissonance" (Haase, "Introduction" *The Reception* 12); it is a genre that "resists a definitive reconstruction of 'original' meaning and even invites contradictory responses" (Haase, "Introduction" *The Reception* 16). Likewise, both fairy-tale and fan-fiction cultures have been described as offering "key critical alternatives to mass-mediated storytelling in their ability to undermine the coercive inevitability of any one ending" (Kustritz, "They All Lived" 6). Bringing fan fiction and fan studies together with fairy-tale studies allows for the merger of two volatile and fluid genres: fan fiction and the fairy tale. In fan fiction, the "diversity and dissonance" already inherent in the fairy tale is actively exploited by fans.

We are reminded that to understand folklore is to "understand the nature of human cultural history and expression" (Toelken 31). Scholarly studies show how fairy tales have been manipulated, rewritten, and retold to serve in processes such as socialization or gender constructions. While this scholarly reception and analysis is certainly valuable and offers critical insights into the genre, small-scale interpretations and revisions such as those discussed between family and friends and by non-professional writers and filmmakers, among others, likewise demand our attention. Amateur responses can inform our understanding of the living meanings of fairy tales and their continued role in society, providing critical insights into the genre's influences on attitudes and behaviors, and likewise the influence of societal changes on the reinterpretations of fairy tales. Small-scale versions of these stories, however, are much more difficult to document due to the more intimate and personal spaces in which they are told. The study of fan fiction and the online communities these stories are produced in give us an opportunity to investigate small-scale transmission of folk stories.

It can be dangerous to generalize, stating that all fan fiction follows the same rules and patterns, since each fandom may have significantly different norms and expectations depending on the canon media it revolves around. Rather, I will focus on one of the largest strictly German-language sites, *FanFiktion.de*, and predominantly on its stories classified under the fandom of "Grimms Märchen" to both explore the fandom itself and the fans' metanarrative engagement with the fairy-tale genre. Fans' metanarration showcases not only that fans are actively participating in the fairy-tale genre, but that they are aware of their own interventions in the transmission and reinterpretation of fairy tales. To understand and document the role of online fan fiction as folklore, I first situate fandoms as online communities where fans form community ties while sharing and exchanging stories. After all, what is important to folk stories should be the mode of transmission rather than its existence only within specific, traditional forms of media. Of primacy for folk stories is that they come from "dynamic interactions among human beings" rather than the "rigid channels and fossilized structures" of formal editions which hold pre-industrialized oral storytelling as the prime examples of folk storytelling (Toelken 32). Though the medium might have changed with time, the communal storytelling aspect of online fan fiction is crucial to discussing fan fiction as a continuation of the folklore tradition.

I then situate fan fiction as folklore and analyze it as such, highlighting fans' metanarration of the fairy tale while actively discussing their roles in folkloric tradition. Folklorists must follow where folk expression within communities leads, and the impact of the Internet becomes increasingly important as folklore evolves toward new media—or media delivered using digital technologies. The fairy-tale genre is built inextricably upon participatory storytelling and has continually inspired numerous interconnected reinterpretations across multiple media. Traditionally, fairy-tale storytelling cultures place a precedence on all people being potential storytellers, inserting themselves into the ongoing narrative flow which seeks to make sense of the surrounding world. Modern fan-fiction cultures are similar in their shared assumption that everyone can be a storyteller, fitting stories into their own narrative framework with social purpose. At different points in time both the fairy tale and fan fiction have been belittled as "low culture" and not worth serious study, yet as a part of the folkloric tradition, fan fiction accomplishes various social functions for writers, readers, and tellers in multiple contexts and serves as a place to negotiate community wants, needs, and desires.

With their reevaluation and reinterpretation of source material, fan fiction and fairy-tale studies come to a united front. Fairy-tale revisions have been often described as works that are not just influenced by pre-texts but continually reflect back on them even as they offer critical responses

(Joosen 10). That is, they make new by reusing the old to put forward new perspectives of the media on which they are based. While fan fiction texts themselves, if taken in total isolation are not necessarily wholly unlike other professionally published transformative fairy tales, they are markedly different in their foregrounding of "communal and intertextual performativity" which caters to the community's reading desires (Busse 57). Continually creating these tales anew adds to the rich storytelling tradition of various versions existing alongside one another.

## Online Community Formation

Early in the advent of the World Wide Web, the Internet was described as an alien-like "strange new world" ("The Strange New World"). While there is often an inclination to view new media as somehow substantially different from previous means of connection, new media rarely if ever produce entirely new forms of communication. Rather, they produce affordances for us to do the communicating we were already doing. The advent of new media does not suggest that we need entirely new theories and explanations to discuss them, rather that we should investigate similarities in addition to questioning the possible differences from existing media. One can say that the Internet provides both a "strange new world" with exciting new opportunities, but also that despite online influences, what and why we communicate has remained relatively unchanged. The Internet does not create a fundamentally new form of communication, but it does create spaces where new communicative techniques and possibilities may be explored.

New technologies often cause moral panics and dystopian ideas of how they will change society for the worse. New genres of media continually incite fearful commentary; yet it is primarily misunderstanding which prompts these moral panics. Fan Lexila writes of her personal experience with such moral panics:

> Man hört es heutzutage doch immer wieder, wenn man zugibt, sehr viel im Internet zu surfen und in vielen Forengemeinschaften aktiv zu sein: "Du hast doch gar kein echtes Leben mehr, wenn du nur am Computer sitzt!" oder "Du hast doch gar keinen Kontakt mehr zu Menschen, wenn du nie rausgehst!"
>
> [You hear it constantly nowadays if you admit to surfing a lot on the Internet and being active in many forum communities: "You don't have a real life anymore if you just sit at the computer!" or "You don't have any contact with people anymore if you don't go outside!"]

Captain Trips, after acknowledging that they too have received similar comments from others, responds "Ich kenne solche Sprüche hauptsächlich von der älteren Generation." [I'm familiar with such sayings mainly from the older generation] ("Das Internet"). Throughout more of the discussion, it becomes clear that when fans discuss the "older generation" they specifically refer not just to those who did not grow up with technologies such as the Internet, but mainly to people who are technophobic and seem to assume that new technologies will inherently lead to disconnection. Such comments do not stem from seeing an actual disconnection from the outside world, these fans write, rather it is an outsider's inability to perceive such behavior as real community formation and connection. Yet despite the fear that new technologies will fundamentally disturb community and togetherness—leading to isolation—time spent with friends and family has not been found to decrease. Though use of the Internet has become more easily accessible, it does not "steal time" from our sociability or our willingness to communicate with others, even in person. What we can see is that people largely opt to use new technologies that add to their social repertoire rather than reduce it (Miller, Michelle 55) which reflects just how social the human species is.

The emergence of digital technologies such as the Internet certainly pose both new possibilities as well as new challenges to the understanding of what constitutes meaningful connection with others and the formation of "communities." Traditionally, the term *community* has referred to neighborhoods, religious centers, and nation-states. Though today we often speak of "global communities" which are only made possible through new technologies as specific geographical locations become less important. These physical distances are "disrupted by the possibilities of the digital" (Avance

63) when people in various locations around the globe come together digitally to form what they call *communities*. Yet since this social interaction takes place using a new form of media, it is often perceived negatively by individuals unfamiliar with it. Often, as is heavily implied by the comments Lexila and others have received, a distinction is made between an "online" and an "offline" or "real" world, as if the two are mutually exclusive. The "online/offline" or "online/real world" divide both suggest that what happens online is less real and therefore less meaningful or impactful than when we physically meet with others, as well as that a truly "computer free" world exists. To avoid this dichotomy, when discussing interactions when we meet with people face-to-face versus interactions on the Internet, I instead use Tom Boellstorff's term "actual" world to discuss face-to-face interaction. The actual world consists of the "places of human culture not realized by computer programs through the Internet" (Boellstorff 20–21), though it does not presume that this is a world entirely detached from these technologies.

It has now become impossible to suggest that the actual world can be entirely separated from the digital as online services become increasingly a part of our everyday lives. One fan notes that for their university studies, there are numerous events and appointments in the actual world that they can only register for online ("Das Internet"). Application processes for jobs—and even for tickets to movies, museums, and sporting events—are increasingly moving to online spaces. The boundary between the online and the actual worlds has become increasingly blurred. In the actual world I might meet up with friends at a coffee shop, but we might also be periodically texting or searching for information online with the small but powerful computers many individuals now carry on their person at all times: the cell phone. This blurring has become increasingly visible during the lockdowns and physical distancing necessary during the COVID-19 pandemic—meetings and conferences, classrooms, and even doctor's visits and theatrical plays have all moved to entirely online formats to both the relief and frustration of many.

While there have been many new phrases and terms coined or repurposed to describe what happens when people come together online such as "affinity spaces" (Black), "virtual worlds" (Boellstorff), and "networked virtual economies" (Burdick et al.), I term the fandoms on *FanFiktion.de* "communities" not only due to theoretical descriptors, but importantly because fans use the term "community" to describe themselves. Communities are distinguished by the style in which they are imagined (Anderson 6), and it becomes clear through fan commentary that fandoms are imagined as communities. Fan TonicWater touches on the topic of community formation as well as the blending of the online and actual world:

> Wenn es diese Seite nicht mehr gäbe, würde ich durchdrehen, weil hier wirklich einige User mir richtig ans Herz gewachsen sind, obwohl ich sie nicht kenne [in the actual world].
>
> [If this site didn't exist, I would go crazy because there are some users here who I've really grown to care about even though I don't know them [in the actual world].] ("Das Internet")

When discussing what constitutes a community, we should keep in mind that the origin of the term referenced a quality of fellowship before it ever referred to an aggregation of people (Avance 68).

Community is then a "performative process" (Thorne 305) where fans, though not physically present, actively maintain their communities through interaction and participation. Community formation is a process where individuals use communication to forge and advance common goals and aspirations and there is a collective interdependence and feeling of belonging. Some fans even state that their online community provides an even more real or authentic connection than allowable in the actual world. A number of fans expressed that their fandom was important to them because they cannot find the same sense of understanding in the actual world, noting that actual-world friends and family can be bigoted and unsupportive once the topic of fan fiction enters conversation. Katzelin writes:

> Ich habe bereits erlebt, dass Leute, mit denen ich mich vorher sehr angeregt unterhalten habe und die offensichtlich etwas mit mir gemein hatten, ganz plötzlich sehr wortkarg wurden. Klingt dämlich, ist aber so. Mag sein, dass diese Leute oberflächlich sind, schön ist das Gefühl dann trotzdem nicht.
>
> [I have already experienced that people with whom I had previously very excitedly discussed things with and who I obviously had something in common with suddenly

> became very reticent. Sounds stupid, but it's true. It might be that these people are shallow, but that doesn't make the feeling any better.] ("Ist euch FanFiktion.de")

Katzelin describes that she has come to the online community on *FanFiktion.de* to communicate with like-minded others without the judgment she has been met with in the actual world.

Fans stress the importance and strength of their online communities, specifically noting lockdowns due to COVID-19 when people have been more isolated from physical social contact than ever. Fan Vicktoria writes that fan fiction and her online community has become "wichtiger denn je" [more important than ever]. And Severin Sesachar responds noting that people who already have established online communities and use the Internet for social interaction have fared through COVID-19 lockdowns and the resulting physical isolation better than those who did not have established online social networks. They write, "was […] Menschen in Corona-Zeiten machen, liest man ja auf Facebook und Co. Verschwörungstheorien ohne Ende" [you can read what […] people do in Corona-times on Facebook and Co. Conspiracy theories without end] ("Anonym unterwegs"). These fans state that the strength of their online communities were able to provide the social interaction that they require.

Fan-fic sites allow fans to communicate directly with others with whom they would not normally be able to communicate. Compared to previous media forms such as television or even the telephone, the Internet holds the potential for "more widely dispersed and differentiated forms of social and cultural innovation" (Jensen 44). Thus the Internet affords the opportunity to converse with more people with different experiences and opinions and form wider-reaching communities than previously possible. Likewise, since much interaction on *FanFiktion.de* takes place in discussion forums and comment sections which are visible to anyone who accesses the site, more people have a chance to see and participate in conversations. This helps the development of social solidarity as well as norms of helping others (Faraj and Johnson 1,468) since all conversation forums are open to all users of the site at any time. The asynchronous nature adds to this as well since people can enter, leave, and rejoin conversations when they have available time.

The slower pacing of asynchronous interaction can allow for more time for reflection. And while it is certainly not always the case (which will be covered in detail in Chapters 2 and 6), connecting with an online community such as the fandoms on *FanFiktion.de* can help individuals exchange information with like-minded individuals. Fan fiction, often described as the "literature of the subordinate" (Derecho 71), can likewise serve as an opportunity for members of historically excluded groups to share and normalize their stories and experiences, creating opportunities for support and reflection. In some online communities "the mutual sharing of empathy, support, and personal narrative may happen by design" (Hammond 179). That is, sharing sensitive personal information can prompt others to likewise open up and seek as well as give advice.

Fan Usaria explains that she began hiding her hobby of writing fan fiction after her parents continually told her that fan fiction was an embarrassment. After she explains she needed to put her writing away whenever company came over to avoid embarrassing her parents, MonaGirl enters the conversation:

> Wirklich traurig, dass deine Eltern so wenig Verständnis für dein Hobby aufgebracht haben. Mein jüngster Sohn schreibt auch [...]. Ich finde es schön, dass du nie aufgegeben hast und deinem Traum weiter verfolgt hast.
>
> [Really sad that your parents had so little understanding for your hobby. My youngest son writes too [...]. I think it's great that you never gave up and continued to follow your dream.] ("Anonym unterwegs")

MonaGirl first normalizes Usaria's situation, as both she and her youngest son write fan fiction, and then offers encouragement for Usaria to continue a hobby that she so thoroughly enjoys. In this way, social norms are outlined and re-enforced within online fandom communities.

Fans often come to comment threads and discussions looking to both receive and share advice. Studies have found that in online communities where there is an expectation of direct reciprocity between community members, these actions were strongly expected to be returned (Faraj and Johnson 1,466–1,467). Reciprocity helps to build and maintain the community that exists on *FanFiktion.de* where interaction is overwhelmingly positive. Within the fandom, I classified 90% of all comments as positive or helpful. Whether fans commented on specific sections they enjoyed, asked encouraging questions, or left critical but constructive criticism, within the fandom there seems to be a strong sense that comments and discussion remain helpful and supportive and that fans are not alienated even if users disagree with one another.

Since it boasts of itself as a place for the German language, *FanFiktion.de* may not have as large or diverse a reading audience as a site which hosts fics in English. Yet fans note that the German language is a contributing factor to their sense of community on the site. Fans stress the importance of language in community formation noting that predominantly English-language sites such as *Archive of Our Own* and *fanfiction.net* have no German-language community. Fan Des-C-Kudi laments:

> Allerdings sind da einfach zu wenig deutsche Leser unterwegs. Ist blöd, wenn man gerne Feedback haben oder einfach mal eine Story auf Deutsch lesen möchte.
>
> [Admittedly there are simply too few German readers out and about there. It's stupid when you'd just like to have feedback or would simply like to read a story in German.] ("Auf welchen")

Certainly, language itself is strongly rooted in community formation. Little connects people together more than language (Anderson 145).

While it may seem obvious that the ability to speak the same language binds people together, fans on *FanFiktion.de* specifically note the longing to read and speak with other German-language speakers despite being fluent in other languages. Fans comment that large fan-fiction sites such as *fanfiction.net* have become more and more English-language focused, and while they can certainly read and respond to others in English, the same sense of community that they feel on *FanFiktion.de* seems to be lacking. Thoronris writes that

> ich vermute, die deutschsprachigen Leser dort sind abgewandert [...]. Die Community und das Interagieren mit anderen Lesern und Autoren ist allerdings hier [FanFiktion.de] bedeutend besser.
>
> [my guess is that the German-speaking readers have migrated from there [...]. The community and the interaction is significantly better here [FanFiktion.de].] ("Auf welchen")

Language is strongly tied to tradition, and it is often tied to specific stories that are told and passed down. Fans note the feeling of community, comfort, and shared vulnerability when they communicate in German, and the ways that this binds them closer together.

That fandoms should be classified as *communities* is crucial to seeing fan fiction as part of the folklore tradition. Folklore functions as a unifying element which reinforces values as well as strengthens ties of culture (Gottschall 137). It helps define communal identities and unite people around common values: folklore contains and expresses a community's worldview. The privatization of the fairy tale, like those circulated in modern times by media giants such as the Disney corporation, violates the communal aspects of folklore since folklore comes directly from common experiences and beliefs (Bacchilega 7). By reclaiming the tales as their own, fans insert themselves in the folklore tradition of taking communal rather than individual ownership of the tales. These transformative fan activities follow the multi-authored history of fairy-tale storytelling. Fairy tales owe much of their longevity to their ability to be continually told anew and reinterpreted as befits a given worldview.

## Fan Fiction as Folklore

Broadly, fan fiction has been noted to share similarities with fairy tales and folklore (see Black, Kustritz, McNeill). The fact that online fan fiction inherently uses new media often leads interpretations of fan fiction to stop with descriptions of the similarities, rather than fully classifying it as a kind of folklore. Fan fiction is described as a new tradition which borrows elements from folklore rather than a continuation of an age-old practice. The advent of new media requires that we view it in the light of existing theories and explanations, while simultaneously investigating the possible differences from existing media which do not involve digital technologies. New media does not *replace* or create fundamentally different forms of communication; what it does do is give a "new social existence to older media" (Baetens et al. 102). Humans rather use all available means to communicate and share information with one another; and the Internet is an efficient means to that end.

What often hinders fan fiction from being classified as a form of folklore has partially to do with (often subconscious) prejudices about how folklore is defined. As folklorist William Wilson points out, a hindrance to the study of folklore in general is "a persisting romantic, or antiquarian, view that recognizes the artistic and humanistic worth of folklore but values the creations of the past much more than those of the present" (17). After the emergence of the concept of folklore in the late eighteenth century, folk stories in Western traditions have often been colloquially viewed as oral tales that fill collections by great collectors such as Jacob and Wilhelm Grimm, Hans Christian Andersen, and Charles Perrault. This leaves folk stories to appear to have a life of their own, to exist in a pristine state with "original" versions, and somehow separated from everyday people and their experiences. This past-oriented view, one which is often intensely invested in the study of ostensibly vanishing traditions, is one which detracts from the value of folklore as an embodiment of current cultural values and beliefs. We should not, of course, ignore the past or older traditions, and we can learn much about past societies by studying their folklore. Yet folklorists should also follow how these stories, traditions, and beliefs change with time and new technology, giving rise to new forms of folklore.

Discussing the impact of these preconceived notions about what constitutes "folklore" necessitates a brief discussion of the massive influence that Jacob and Wilhelm Grimm have had on Western notions of folklore and the fairy tale. Various definitions, including one by André Jolles, in his influential book *Einfache Formen* [*Simple Forms*] explicitly define the fairy tale as a story told in the fashion of the Brothers Grimm (219). The Grimms and their conception of folklore and the fairy tale have forever changed the Western notions of which form stories from the folk should take.

The Grimms believed that they had found the ideal storyteller in a woman named Dorothea Viehmann. They viewed her as such a powerful representative of what they conceived to be the traditional, peasant storyteller that a drawing of her, done by their brother Ludwig Emil Grimm, adorned every edition following the second in 1819. The significance of the Grimms choosing Viehmann to be the ultimate representation of folklore should not be understated. In their prologue, the Grimms stress Viehmann's age, making sure to portray her as an older, German peasant woman, one who spent a life working—a woman far removed from the carefree life of the upper classes—despite the fact that Viehmann was considered middle class and was fluent in both German and French. Importantly, she is described as a "peasant" from a "village" (iv). They provide the reader with a vivid textual image, which is later supplemented by an actual drawing of the woman with a wrinkled face gazing off into the distance.

Viehmann's was the image readers were to carry with them as they read the tales. Then as now this image has influenced the perception of readers, including those in scholarly circles, as the authentic origin of the Grimms' tales. With her picture, the Grimms began to effectually construct the perception of the folktale and its antiquity from the very first pages of their collection. The Grimms take pains to note that the tales in *Children's and Household Tales* are rooted in an imagined Germanic past ambiguously described as having taken place sometime during the medieval period. The folktale is portrayed as supposedly ancient, undying, and passed down with care and only slight alteration. According to the Grimms, folktales only stop being told because their tellers die out. The folktales themselves live on forever, simply waiting to be discovered again (vii).

The Grimms not only used the image of Viehmann at the beginning of their collection to persuade readers that they were reading tales from just such a storyteller who seemingly acted as a conduit for ancient knowledge; it was also sent to many of the men and women who aided them in their collection. The pictorial conveyance of a peasant storyteller—which worked to firmly root their collection in an uneducated, "folk" tradition—was deemed so important to the Grimms that they sought to convince even their own storytellers of its supposedly ancient, peasant origins. They pushed for this portrayal even though the majority of their storytellers were highly educated. Yet because they believed folktales to spring from the lips of uneducated peasants in the Golden Age of the Germanic Middle Ages, the image of Viehmann—as a representation of *all* peasants—was chosen and used as a marker of authenticity for the collection. Though the Grimms were certainly not alone in their belief that the folktales of the common people originated in what was perceived to be the simple life of the Middle

Ages, the Grimms' lasting influence on the fairy-tale genre still influences conceptions of the folktale and fairy tale today.

The establishment of *Children's and Household Tales* as a part of Western cultural memory is certainly secure. In 2005, the collection was cataloged in the United Nations Educational, Scientific and Cultural Organization's (U.N.E.S.C.O.) "Memory of the World" project. U.N.E.S.C.O.'s "Memory of the World" website declares *Children's and Household Tales* to be part of the "world's documentary heritage" which should be "preserved and protected for all and, with due recognition of cultural mores and practicalities, should be permanently accessible to all without hindrance." Though what does it mean for something to be a part of a "Memory of the World"? Or rather a part of a public, cultural memory? Cultural memory refers to the handing down of meaning which feeds tradition and communication by external conditions imposed by society and cultural contexts (Assmann, Jan, *Cultural Memory* 5–6).

I will explore this connection with folklore in more detail in Chapter 6, but for now it is enough to say that cultural memory represents cultural mores and traditions. It embodies or encapsulates them while consistently changing and updating in order to stay relevant to contemporary society. The incredible staying power of folklore and with it, the fairy tale, can be attributed to its role as a part of cultural memory. Stories and events which are a part of cultural memory are ones which are understood right away and without any hesitation or interpretation of its significance (Casey 19) by members of a particular culture. Cultural memory within a group focuses on the relevance of a tale being told that revolve around the question of "what we must not forget" relating to a group's perception of itself (Assmann, Jan, *Cultural Memory* 16). Though the answers to what must not be forgotten and why groups may arrive at this conclusion are multifaceted, there can be little denying that certain fairy tales have become a part of cultural memory through their incredible ability to be recognized, and flexibly modified and retold throughout time.

Despite the very successful efforts of the Grimms to convince their readers that folklore consisted of ancient knowledge passed down by an unlettered "folk," there is no inherent rule that folk expression must consist of "old stuff" saved from the oblivion of dying traditions. What is of more importance is that folk stories communicate consistencies which allow a group to perceive stories as "traditional, locally derived, or community generated" (Blank, "Introduction: Towards" 6). Even when colloquially speaking of the Grimm tales, one usually is not referring to the tales themselves as published in 1857, but is rather referring to the cultural responses and revisions provoked by them.

However, constraining folklore as an abstracted concept, and defining folk stories by what appears in the polished forms that fill volumes collected by individuals such as the Grimms is an injustice to what folklore is at its core. Folklorist Richard Bauman writes that "we must recognize that the symbolic forms we call folklore have their primary existence in the action of people and their roots in social and cultural life." The texts we find in folktale collections are but a scant record of "deeply situated human behavior" (2). In our published editions, we often have profoundly edited and refined versions of folk stories. Being simply everyday expression from everyday people means that much of folklore is raw and unpolished. It is this rawness that can also lend to folklore being incomplete, inconsistent, filled with coarse language or even just downright disturbing.

The divisions often made between folktales and literature, or folk art and "high" art are more than just a division in terms, they show clear prejudices of class, gender, and race and ethnicity. These divisions persist and are evident in the clear preference for edited, literary volumes of folktales and fairy tales curated by collectors such as the Grimms, Andersen, and Perrault. Well-intentioned though they may be, comments by scholars noting that folklorists should study scholarly critical responses to folktales and fairy tales as well as the ostensibly "irresponsible responses" of the masses (Haase, "Response and Responsibility" 239) continue to enforce an established, elitist hierarchy. Sorting reactions and adaptations into "responsible" and "irresponsible" categories still prioritizes expert, scholarly interpretations and creates a division between who is allowed to interpret folk stories and who is perceived to be fumbling around in their irresponsible play.

Fan fiction is often disparaged as being of "negligible cultural value," or a part of "low" culture. William Shatner, the actor who played Captain Kirk in *Star Trek*—the series that many argue prompted the beginning of fan fiction as we know it today (Black xiv)—famously yelled "get a life!" to a staged crowd of devoted *Star Trek* fans during a 1986 sketch on *Saturday Night Live* (Siegel). His outburst gave voice to an accepted cultural attitude that participation in fandom is not only of no value, but an utter waste of time. Additionally, comments like Shatner's presume that fannish activities are somehow not a part of "life." This presumption relegates activities such as attending conventions, creating fan art, writing fan fiction, cosplaying—or fans dressing up as their favorite characters—as a type of fantasy rather than meaningful forms of creativity, personal expression, and community building. Though fan fiction is increasingly studied and given credence by scholars, the assumption that fan fiction is produced by "nerds" and societal outsiders—often with connotations of the writing as pre-pubescent or childish "girl stuff" (Panthera)—with no real lives still abounds. Even if one *does* view fan fiction as having negligible cultural value, it is still a form of folk expression. This habit of dismissing fan fiction because it may not fit with established norms or conform to high literary standards is not proof that it is unworthy of respect or a justification that it is an "irresponsible" response; only that it does not appeal to our personal tastes. Fan-fiction interpretations do, however, likely conform to the cultural expectations and folklore produced by a given community.

Folklore is "the study of the living performance of tradition—for better and worse and for everything in between" (Phillips and Milner 25). And the "living performance of tradition" includes fan fiction. Being highly communal, folklore helps define community norms and expectations as well as how communities view themselves. Certainly not all communities have the same norms and expectations. What might be offensive in one community might be just another common saying or story in another. It is *because* folkloristic expression is the everyday expression of everyday people that it is quite often, to use the Internet term, "nsfw."[1] Folk stories are not always the perfected and edited versions found in folktale and fairy tale anthologies.

Like fan fiction today, folklore and the fairy tale were previously degraded and dismissed as not being worthy of serious study. Even the

1 "not safe for work" or containing explicit language or images.

Grimms, as influential as they have been to the fairy-tale genre, were openly criticized for failing to make their tales more literary in their first edition. Clemens Brentano, fellow collector, friend, and mentor to the Grimms, wrote a scathing review of the first edition of *Children's and Household Tales* stating that

> wollten die frommen Herausgeber sich selbst genug thun, so müßten sie zu jeder Geschichte, ein[e] psychologische Biografie des Kinds oder des alten Weibs, das die Geschichte so oder so schlecht erzählte voran setzten.
>
> [if the pious editors wanted to do themselves a favor, at the beginning of every story they would have put a psychological biography of the child or the old woman explaining why the story had been somehow or other badly told.] (Arnim and Brentano 674)

Unaltered folk stories were simply not up to the bourgeois society's literary standards. Also of note in Brentano's critique is his dismissal of bad form with the association of children and women—one could even say his critique is a dismissal of unaltered folktales as childish "girl stuff."

As scholars began to study folklore, many critics believed that folktales which had not been rewritten as a literary tale were a waste of time to read and even offensive to bourgeois sensibilities. Dr. Franz Joseph K. Müller, a psychiatric doctor, wrote a response shortly after the publication of Franz Xavier von Schönwerth's folklore collection *Sitten und Sagen aus der Oberpfalz* [*Customs and Sagas from the Upper Palatinate*] (1857–1859). In his response, he accused Schönwerth of having put together a collection of "abergläubischem Unsinn" [superstitious nonsense] (Drascek 32). Others, such as Friedrich Nicolai (1733–1811) argued that folksongs and tales belonged to the peasantry while the educated classes should look to retain their more sophisticated culture (Loges 348).

There is certainly an ethnocentric and elitist bias which privileges the classics of Western written literature over the supposedly "less-refined" stories of the folk. Critics of folk stories are often unaccustomed to the vernaculars used and the language is often perceived as "simple, formless, lacking in artistic quality and complexity" (Bauman 7). Language use can even be, like in fan fiction, nsfw. Only popularly viewed as moralizing tales for children toward the mid-nineteenth century, folktales were previously kept away from young ears, and instead reserved for adults, after the children had been put to bed. They could then, as now, be violent, sexy, raunchy, and crude just as often as they could be hopeful, empowering, uplifting, and beautifully told. And though statements that both the fairy tale and fan fiction are seemingly uneducated "girl stuff" are certainly dismissive, intriguingly, both fan fiction and the fairy tale often have strong associations with women storytellers in Western culture.

Back in 1992, Camille Bacon-Smith wrote that "almost without exception the women fans have complained that their interests are trivialized at least, and are often criticized by family and workmates" (285). While there is more acceptance of fan fiction writing today than there was in the early 1990s, 30 years later her statement is still a reality for many fans. Fairy tales and fan fiction have both been described as bearing markers of "low culture with little artistic or political potential" (Kustritz, "Fan Fiction" 508). The fact that they are both associated with women storytellers only intensifies these views. Adult fan Zuckerspinne speaks on this issue, writing that

> ich hab, als ich elf jahre alt war, meiner mutter meine erste geschichte gegeben [...]. ich war also elf, und meine mutter liest es und lacht laut darüber. dann läuft sie damit zu meinem vater und liest ihm laut lachend ein paar stellen vor [...] solange bis ich komme und es ihr wieder abnehme [...]. ich glaube meine mutter wüsste sie [, dass ich noch ff schreibe], würde es als zu kindisch abtun. für sie war ich ab meinem vierzehnten lebensjahr alles was irgendwie danach aussieht als wäre es für kinder gedacht.
>
> [i had, when i was eleven years old, given my mother my first story [...]. so i was eleven and my mother read it and laughed out loud about it, then she ran with it to my father and read a few parts to him laughing out loud [...] until i came and took it from her [...]. i believe if my mother knew [that i still write ff], she would discount it as childish. for her after i was fourteen years old everything that somehow resembled it was thought of as for children.] ("Anonym unterwegs")

We can see here in this modern example that Brentano's description of folklore persists along with its negative association with women and children.

In the realm of fan fiction, like with many fairy-tale storytelling cultures, it is indeed often the act of finding stories, reading, writing, and collaborating which is of the most importance rather than creating a literary or refined version. What can cause fan fiction to appear unpolished (just as we have seen previously in criticism of the fairy tale) is that often the texts able to be read online are products left behind from the performative act of communal storytelling. Kristina Busse notes that while fandom does produce objects which we can investigate (such as fan fiction texts) "we miss large sections of fannish creation and its effects if [textual investigations] were the only criteria we employed" (56). It is the community building and communal storytelling aspects of writing and creation which makes fan fiction a part of the living folklore tradition, and so different from other creative interpretive endeavors such as published fairy-tale variants or films. Different fan-fiction versions live alongside one another in these online communities. While not everyone within the community may agree with every version, they are seen as equally valid even if entirely contradictory. They serve different social functions within the community and represent their current wishes, worldviews, and desires. As fan Sionon Klingensang writes, "Fanfiction ist wirklich das, was die Leute lesen wollen" [Fanfiction is really what the people want to read] ("Umfrage—Was ist"). And folklore shows how different communities make sense of the world and their circumstances.

## "Geschichte wird von den Gewinnern geschrieben" [History is written by the winners] (Farfalla 91): Fan-Fiction Metanarration

In traditional modes of writing within the literate Western world, books and stories are authored and published by individuals who are, more or less, professional writers. One of the major differences between fan fiction and more traditional modes of writing is that the means by which fan fiction is being created and produced, that is, being posted on the Internet by using a computer, has become increasingly affordable and widespread throughout the West. Writers of fan fiction are able to more easily write and share their fics with a much wider audience than before rather than leaving the space for the written and published word to be dominated by professional writers and editors. These stories are not all "written by the winners," (farfalla 91) but from anyone with access to a computer and the Internet—vastly increasing not only the number of perspectives and interpretations of media, but also increasing their distribution throughout the world. Fans are likewise producing stories and versions that they see as better addressing their community norms and beliefs. Fan Melina Evergreen, for example, comments on a fic: "auch wenn das jetzt vielleicht etwas komisch klingt mag ich deine Version sogar noch etwas mehr als das Original" [even if that sounds maybe somewhat silly, I like your version even more than the original]. Her comment shows that fans often find stories that have been modified to better fit within the community norms and expectations are more easily relatable, and therefore perhaps also "better" to a modern reader than the canon Grimm versions.

In living folklore tradition, folktales and fairy tales often serve an emancipatory function, even more than they do in popular culture because they express problems and desires of the communities who tell them. In modern times, the fairy tale has been frequently instrumentalized and commercialized to support bourgeois and conservative interests (Bacchilega 7). The domination of Disney in the fairy-tale genre has only solidified the values purported by Perrault and the Grimms with their emphasis on domesticity and patriarchal authority (Duggan 115), though this has slowly begun to change with more recent Disney fairy-tale adaptations. In their writing, fans reclaim the communal and often emancipatory function of the fairy tale. For fans, the canon media is used as a springboard for discussion and interpretation. As fan Andauril writes, "Fanfictions schreibe ich, weil ich von etwas, dass ein anderer erschaffen hat, mehr will. Mehr von den Charakteren, der Welt, den Hintergründen, der Geschichte" [I write fanfictions because I want more from something someone else created. More from characters, the world, the backgrounds, the story] ("Fanfiction Schreiben"). They may love the media on which their fics are based, but fans also view it as somehow lacking and in need of change or expansion.

While fan fiction is a format where writers could easily alter the original media into something unrecognizable, the fics most favored by other fans are those which stay true to the canon, much like traditional retellings of tales. In the fandom community, for example, one member leaves a comment stating that when they read certain fics, they feel as though they have opened "das dicke Märchenbuch [ihr]er Oma…" [[their] grandma's thick fairy-tale book] and that already in the first sentences they feel that the story is "wie im Märchenbuch" [like a fairy-tale book] (Countess of Shadow). Another fan writes

> bin gerade auf deine Rotkäppchen-Version gestoßen und muss sagen: wirklich ausgezeichnet! Ich mag deinen Schreibstil, es war wie ein richtiges Märchen verfasst. Die Abwandlungen, die du zum Original gemacht hast, waren gut durchdacht.
>
> [just stumbled on your Little Red Riding Hood version and have to say: really fantastic! I like your writing style, it was written like a real fairy tale. The changes that you made to the original were well thought through.] (isabella1994)

Fan texts are in constant contact with the canon media. While what "staying true to the canon" actually means can vary widely from fandom to fandom, what we can see here is that the fics in the fandom follow what appears to be an unwritten but established group norm to mimic the writing style of the Grimm tales.

Fan writing displays a creativity within boundaries (Stein and Busse 197) as fan writing by its very definition is based on already established themes and characters. Yet, fans often use these same boundaries to foster explicit discussion of what they have altered in order to open up the possibility of multiple, even contradictory narratives. It is a genre that exists to play with narrative. And while I noted previously that fairy tales continue to serve an emancipatory function in communities, new interpretations of the tales are not simply emancipatory. Even with changes which are sometimes dramatic, they are continually retold, reinforcing social norms and ensuring that the tales function purposefully within the community. Those fics which fit the canon standards receive high praise, comments, and are favored by fellow fans. Those which make drastic or what fans have found to be distasteful changes such as graphic depictions of sex or violence that do not advance the plot, are shunned by the fandom community. This is often communicated via little or no fan interaction with the offending fic, or comments detailing dissatisfaction. While fan fiction writers can and do critically analyze and complicate the canon, they are also conservative, evident in their continual references to the past and the canon material.

It is important to note that this community assumes its members are already familiar with the referenced media and thus that fans within the community will be aware of any embellishments and deviations from the canon. A fic must always go back and reference the canon; by definition, it does not exist as a stand-alone piece of writing: the canon delineates the fan writing (Stein and Busse 196). Here fan fiction and fairy-tale studies come to a united front, as fairy-tale revisions have been often described as works that are not just influenced by pre-texts but "reflect back on them, coloring our view of them" (Bacchilega 32). Fan fiction writers do not claim to tell an entirely new tale. The point of writing fan fiction is not to create a new, original story, but to add a new perspective, a new slant, a new interpretation to a story that is already known—using much of the same characters, the same motifs, and often the same setting. Fans, however, do not view these restrictions of the canon as something which hampers their creativity or ability to interpret stories anew, but rather as something which is liberatory. This is a space where they can freely ask "what if?" about the canon material as they imbue it with new meanings. As one fan succinctly writes, "Was wäre wenn Cinderella mal ganz anders aus geht? [...] Was passiert?" [What if Cinderella turned out entirely differently? [...] What happens?] (NoBelieveNoTrust). Within this succinct question is actually the basis of all fan fiction: the answer to "what if?"

Apart from exploring new possibilities for their favorite media, within the fandom, fans also discuss the role of fairy tales in their lives and communities, often detailing their complex relationship with the genre. Fan Perscitia begins discussing her own complicated relationship:

> Meine Beziehung zu den Grimm'schen Märchen ist nicht ganz einfach. Einerseits liebe ich die Welten, die sie aufbauen [...] aber an anderen Stellen [...] werden mir Menschen und Handlungen unangenehm glorifiziert, ohne, dass ich den Grund dafür sehe.
>
> [My relationship to the Grimmian fairy tales isn't entirely simple. On the one hand I love the worlds that they build [...] but in other parts [...] people and plots are uncomfortably glorified without a reasoning I can see.]

She continues by writing that due to these complex feelings, in her fics, she enjoys altering fairy tales and showing that the "good" characters can be bad, or that she tries to show the decisions and motivations of the "evil" characters in the Grimm versions. Fics are a place where fans can question, extend, and critically reflect on the fairy tale genre.

Far from the static stories often thought of as "traditional" folk stories, as a part of cultural memory, folk stories need to adapt to changing cultural circumstances in order to be kept alive in communities. If this adaptation or interpretation does not take place, the meanings of the stories are lost within three or four generations (Assmann, Jan 74) because they can seem no longer relevant to community members. Canonical texts may embody "normative and formative" values of a community, but it is because of this that these stories need ongoing interpretation rather than simple recitation (Assmann, Jan 79). They are part of a living tradition which changes as communities change and evolve. These stories are shaped to allow participants to personalize them while still maintaining ties to the traditional tales. As fan Pterano Dante puts it, "Das Erzählen von Märchen ist ein gewichter Teil der Alltagskultur" [the telling of fairy tales is an important part of everyday culture] ("Rumpelstilzchen"). It is because of this influence of the fairy tale on his life that he sees his stories and revisions as taking part in the fairy-tale storytelling tradition.

Due to the influence of communal storytelling, members of the fandom feel a sense of ownership over the material. This feeling of ownership is not viewed in the same sense as an author who owns the rights to a published novel, but rather that fans have collectively claimed ownership of the characters and stories within their fandom. This feeling of communal ownership allows fans to feel justified suggesting changes and even entirely new ideas to other authors within the fandom. Fan TARA describes the feeling of belonging that comes with fan fiction writing as such:

> Dass ganz normale Leute einfach mal zu Autoren werden können und selbst ein Teil einer Welt werden, die sie so lieben und [...] nicht mehr nur [dar]über lesen, sondern auch selbst darin leben können oder aus der Sicht eines Charakters schreiben können, der dort spannende Abenteuer erlebt. Denn das sind Fanfiktions.
>
> [That completely normal people can simply become authors and themselves be part of a world that they love so much and [...] not just read more about it, but can live in it themselves and write from the perspective of a character who has an exciting adventure there. That's what fanfictions are.] ("Fanfiction-Sachbuch")

This feeling of belonging contributes to fan authors viewing characters, worlds, and plots as "theirs." As TARA writes, they inhabit these worlds and can "live there." They can see through the eyes of characters and even experience adventures themselves through their writing. Within the fandom, the role of the author is entirely reimagined since everyone within the fandom has an equal stake in writing, commenting on, revising, and posting fics rather than viewing the authors of the canon tales as the only authority.

It might be easy to forget while we silently read novels with an author's name printed large on the outside cover that until the past few centuries, telling stories was always a communal activity to varying degrees (Foley, *Oral Tradition* 185). The fan fiction concept of authorship and owned commodities is a profound decolonization of knowledge in a participatory environment where fans are enabled to express their thoughts and ideas through social means of cultural and community formation. This decolonization can lead to greater representation of members of historically excluded groups. Fan PanicMoon, for example, notes her reasoning for writing her fic with a same-sex relationship. She sees herself as adding to the fairy-tale corpus: "mir ist heute Morgen aufgefallen, dass mir spontan kein Märchen mit LGBTQ+-Inhalt einfällt [...]. Auf jeden Fall dachte ich, es ist Zeit, mal ein bisschen mehr vom Regenbogen in der Märchenwelt unterzubringen." [This morning I realized, that I couldn't spontaneously think of any fairy tales with LGBTQ+ content [...]. In any case I thought it's time to add a little bit more rainbow in the fairy tale world.] Her thoughts, opinions, and ultimately, fairy tales are accepted as valid additions to the genre.

## "Aber davon haben die Grimms mal wieder nix mitbekommen" [The Grimms didn't catch any of that again]. (DieLadi): Fan Fiction and Authenticity

The Grimms note on several occasions throughout the introductions of their editions of *Children's and Household Tales* that they have changed and altered their tales in order to preserve what they determined to be the "Inhalt," or the true "content" of the tale. In their introduction they write that throughout their years of collection, they have honed their abilities in determining what was truly a part of the folktale and what had simply been added on or distorted by storytellers. They claim to have only made changes in order to differentiate the simple, pure, more complete tales from what they termed the "Verfälschten" [falsified/fraudulent] ones (18). They do not specify in their introduction exactly what they have added nor what they omitted or changed. By investigating the versions of these tales as they develop across multiple editions, it is clear that what they found most important was simplicity in language use and plot, as well as maintaining the innocence, purity, and presentation of Germanic traditions with clearly identifiable notions of nineteenth-century bourgeois Christian morality.

The many changes the Grimms made to their tales have been importantly and thoroughly described as due to guiding the tales in their collection toward entertaining, but didactic tales for children (see Zipes, "Changing Function"). These changes also served to adapt the collected tales to Christian bourgeois sensibilities as the bourgeoisie ascended to power in the nineteenth century (see Zipes *How Fairy Tales Stick*, Tatar *Hard Facts*). Changes are likewise connected with the process of National Romanticism and the creation of a national image (see Gunnell). The Grimms attest that medieval sources had left them with the bones and joints of an ancient mythology (see Battles). It was up to them, then, to reassemble the skeletons and put flesh on them. In fannish interpretations, fans often take issue with exactly how those skeletons were reassembled and fleshed out. Fans note their familiarity with (and disapproval of) the changes the Grimms made to their published tales. In the beginning of her fic, fan Zulixe writes from the perspective of a character in her story, "Es geht um Grimms Märchen. Uns ist zu Ohren gekommen, dass dort etwas ganz falsch lief" [It's about Grimms' fairy tales. It has come to our attention that something went entirely wrong there.] This specifically refers to what Zulixe details as the incorrect documentation of a fairy tale.

In the same spirit as comments made by the Grimms regarding the importance of remaining true to the content of tales rather than wording or expression, the notion of remaining faithful to content seems to play a fundamental role in fic writers' conception of fidelity to the canon. Interestingly, some fic writers in the fandom, who have taken issue with the changes and adaptations collectors made two centuries ago, make a bold claim: their fics are more true to the supposed content of the folktales than the canon. In a comment to DieLadi's fic collection "Habt ihr euch immer schon mal gefragt..." [Have you guys ever asked yourselves ...] Knallkeks 007 writes, "alles ziemlich selbsterklärend. Sehr logisch. Also deine Erklärungen, nicht das Märchen selbst." [Everything's pretty self-explanatory. Very logical. I mean your explanations, not the fairy tale itself.]

DieLadi's responses to fan comments are quite telling in that many of her responses echo the same sentiment which underlies the premise of her fic collection: "davon haben die Grimms mal wieder nix mitbekommen" [the Grimms didn't catch any of that again]. In response to comments like those from Knallkeks 007, DieLadi references her fic based on "Frau Holle" [Mother Hulda] (ATU 480) and notes "In der Variante, die ich kenne, war [die Protagonistin] dumm und faul. Aber wie wir gesehen haben: alles nur Propaganda!" [In the variation that I know, [the female protagonist] was dumb and lazy. But as we've seen: all just propaganda!] Thus, she claims, her tale could be a version from which the Grimms' tale had been derived—not the other way around. In her comments, DieLadi has taken on the responsibility to determine the true content of the canon rather than assuming it has been authentically portrayed in the Grimms' collection. For DieLadi and many fans like Knallkeks 007, the Grimm tale is not the definitive version, it is just one variation. DieLadi likewise does not position herself as telling a definitive version, but she does posit her role as telling one of many versions of the tale from which the Grimms' tale could have originated. By adding complexity in plot and ambiguity of human action into her tale, and evidenced by her comments regarding tale origins, DieLadi expresses that she sees the Grimms' tales to be inaccurate representations of the tales' true content—whatever that may be.

It is a documented phenomenon that fans see themselves as the rightful interpreters and heirs to the canon material, at times even reacting with anger at the canon writer(s) for what fans see as not properly interpreting character motivation and plot patterns. Fans can consider the *fanon*, or non-source material substance matter which is widely accepted by fans, to be truer to the content than the originally published material (Jenkins, *Textual* 107). Responding to a fic version of "Little Red Riding Hood" (ATU 333), moe-rikyou writes an analysis of the changes the Grimms themselves made to the tales in their collection:

> ich finde es besonders gut, dass es immer noch "realistisch" ist [...]. Ich habe übrigens mal gehört, [...] dass die Gebrüder Grimm wohl noch einige andere Versionen von Rotkäppchen hatten, wo Sex und Verführung eine viel größere Rolle gespielt hat, ähnlich wie bei dir, sie aber aufgrund der prüden Gesellschaft, die harmlose Version veröffentlichen mussten... ;D
>
> [I find it especially good, that it's still "realistic" [...]. By the way, I have also heard [...] that the Brothers Grimm certainly had a few different versions of Little Red Riding Hood where sex and seduction play a much larger role, similar to your story, but that they had to publish the harmless version because of the prudish society... ;D]

Certainly the Grimms were widely criticized in their time due to their collection containing versions of tales that suggested characters had sex before marriage, such as the criticism of their 1812 version of "Rapunzel" (ATU 310). This first version contained dialog which revealed that Rapunzel became pregnant before marrying the prince. This defilement of bourgeois sensibilities was deemed as not only immoral, but supposedly had the capability to corrupt children (Rölleke 1170). As moe-rikyou notes, the tale was indeed altered because of the "prudish society." Knowingly or not, many fans take it upon themselves to undo some of the changes made by the Grimms, as well as to update the emphasis and priority of certain characters, plots, and lessons of the tales.

Fan writers in the fandom are renegotiating the canon's presentation of cultural memory through folktale and fairy tales as fans' expectations and priorities have shifted from those expressed by the collectors of the nineteenth century. Fan versions of folktales are often repurposed to serve new functions within the communities in which they are told. In the comment section of a fic version of "The Devil with the Three Golden Hairs" (ATU 930), fan Fledermaerchen writes:

> ich hab' doch schon immer gewusst, dass die bekannte Fassung des Märchens wohl eine kastrierte war ;-) DAS HIER scheint mir die wahre Geschichte zu sein, also

> das, wie es wirklich ablief [...]. wie schön, dass du die im überlieferten "Original" so blutleeren Passagen mit Leben gefüllt hast, und auch das Ende, das ich hier las, ist ein viel wahrscheinlicheres!
>
> [I already knew that the known version of the fairy tale was surely a castrated one ;-) THIS HERE seems to me to be the true story, I mean, how it really happened [...]. how lovely that you have filled those bloodless, passed down, "original" passages with life, and also the ending here that I read is a much more likely one!]

Fans are acknowledging the validity in their practice of interpreting and rewriting tales in any way they deem necessary as long as they stay true to what they perceive as the overall content. They use the same creative authority as the Grimms, while simultaneously taking issue with many of the changes the Grimms made. As fan MonaGirl describes, she writes fan fiction "weil mir oft nicht gefällt, was die Autoren meiner Serien präsentieren. Ich schreibe dann gerne alles um oder erfinde neue Sachen dazu." [Because I often don't like what the authors of my series present. Rather, I like to rewrite everything or create new things for it] ("Warum schreibt ihr"). The tales are adapted to serve as representations of contemporary society according to the social activities and societal perceptions of those who tell them.

Community has long been placed at the apex of human connection and cohesion—where human thoughts and ideas unite (Avance 63). Fans use new social technologies such as the Internet to socialize as well as participate in creation and distribution of communal fan products. The Internet, at its best, provides the affordances for online communities like the "Grimms Märchen" fandom where fans can communicate, collaborate, and negotiate their fics. The tales and communication surrounding them may have moved to the medium of the Internet, but fan writers are participating in the folkloric tradition. Fan writers see their changes as ones which represent community and exchange: changes that are open to conversation and debate, even when that conversation happens asynchronously online. People were already telling and rewriting these stories. Fans have taken this existing narrative energy and moved it to a medium which provides the opportunity for more people to tell their stories. In this way, fan writers are participating in the age-old practice of telling and retelling tales.

While we might have the Grimms, Andersen, and Perrault to thank for classic, Western fairy tales, it is actually the host of storytellers, editors, translators, writers, adaptors, artists, scholars, teachers, and readers who have kept them alive in the various and diverse forms we know today (Haase, "Introduction" *The Reception* 20). Indeed, the endless modification and retelling of fairy tales as a part of cultural memory allows the many interpretations and answers fairy tales offer to everyone who encounters them. This, to a large degree, is why they are able to endure. Fairy tales, as demonstrated in their varied interpretations, contain the potential to play whatever roles we might need them to and answer any questions that we might ask. They have the ability to mirror whatever it is we wish to see and as such continually invite our reactions and reinterpretations. As fan Augurey writes: "Jeder hat schon mal irgendwo im Kino gesessen oder ein Buch gelesen und sich gedacht, 'was wäre wenn …' " [everyone has at one time sat in the movie theater somewhere or read a book and thought to themselves "what if …"] ("Anonym unterwegs"). It is this "what if?" that is the basis of all fan fiction and it is written by those who feel compelled to answer.

Fan fiction writers are taking part in the larger conversation which determines what cultural products mean for a society and how they can be interpreted—the act of taking this "what if?" and expanding and discussing it within their communities. They are not claiming to tell *the* story representative of the canon media, but rather *a* story. This story is seen as a possible version that is part of a much longer, conversational whole in which differing and even contradictory perspectives are welcomed. Fans insert their pleasures and demands back into mass cultural products and in this way are able to make the tales more inclusive of their community. It is important to include fan fiction in the study of folklore. The fairy tale as fan fiction is a continuation—yet another adaptation—of the "volatile and fluid" (Zipes, *Irresistible* 22) fairy-tale genre. The fairy tale can only continue to be revitalized by incorporating these voices.

CHAPTER 2

# A Quiet Space: Misogyny, Discrimination, and Online Communities

> It's up to us. One thing is certain [...]. The ability to access the Web will be either a great divider or a great equalizer; the path will either lead to jealousy and hatred or peace and understanding.
>
> —Tim Berners-Lee

Since the creation of the World Wide Web in 1989, the Internet has been described in polarizing ways. For some, the Internet promised to be a great equalizer, a place to bring together individuals regardless of physical location. Many looked to online interaction and hoped it would "accelerate the dynamics of social learning processes" where like-minded individuals could learn from one another over time (Miller, Kent D. 305). In a similarly utopic vein, the new world of cyberspace presented the idea of the absence of a physical body. The Internet was hypothesized as a place where people's minds, without the hindrance of physical limitations, could "meet" and discuss in a democratic forum. This optimistic view rendered physical location, and even our physical bodies, unimportant in online interactions. The Internet supposedly offered liberation from the limitations and prejudices of the world, and the text-only nature was seen to "facilitate greater inclusiveness across differences of gender, sexual orientation, and race" (Daniels 116) while creating a "collaborative democracy" (Enjolras and Steen-Johnson 108).

Yet the notion of the Internet as a kind of "disembodied utopia" has been widely criticized as being simply the wishful thinking of the advancement of technology ushering in a radically different form of interaction. It has since been dismissed as being theoretically "simply speculative" (Bromseth 271). Other critics have described the Internet as the antithesis of this utopic ideal. It has been pessimistically described as a place where anonymity promotes asocial behavior and as a platform which encourages people to be "more willing to speak out and to misbehave" (Megele and Buzzi 43). Some accounts even go so far as to claim that the Internet twists and transforms humanity into addicted and mindless consumers in the "online personality market" (Weissman 36). This online domain is said to be supposedly filled with liars and tricksters, complacent consumers, and harmful trolls[1] who wish to deceive. Accounts, both real and invented, of these examples as well as teens being addicted to social media and disconnected from the actual world run rampant (boyd 15).

Often the Internet is described as "utterly transforming society and the nature of being human" (Weissman 1). In 1994, the cover of *Time* magazine proclaimed the Internet to be a "strange new world" for humans to explore. The cover of the issue features a rocky, alienlike landscape with the text: "battles on the frontiers of cyberspace" ("The Strange New World"). The cover seems to reference the famous lines spoken by none other than William Shatner as Captain Kirk introducing each episode of *Star Trek* from 1966 to 1969: "Space … the final frontier" (Cubé). Rather than space as the "final frontier" it is "cyberspace" which is now the exciting new adventure. The Internet opens a world of possibilities which has (and will continue to) profoundly change the world we live in. As others have likewise claimed, digital technologies have not only revolutionized how we think, communicate, and interact, creating affordances for communication and growth previously unknown, it also reuses, recycles, and rethinks acts and processes that humans have undertaken for centuries (see Boellstorff; Phillips and Milner). The Internet is a mixture of both the exciting new possibilities and communicative processes that have long existed. We should be careful when discussing the Internet to neither glorify nor vilify the opportunities it presents. Rather it creates affordances for interaction to take place.

Tim Berners-Lee, the creator of the World Wide Web, wrote a powerful statement in 1999—just ten years after its invention, and nine years after writing the first web browser and web server. His was a prediction for how this invention might revolutionize daily life around the globe:

1 People who seek to create controversy through Internet comments, simply for the sake of creating controversy.

> It's up to us. One thing is certain. The Web will have a profound effect on the markets and the cultures around the world: intelligent agents will either stabilize or destabilize markets; the demise of distance will either homogenize or polarize cultures; the ability to access the Web will be either a great divider or a great equalizer; the path will either lead to jealousy and hatred or peace and understanding. (82)

And he certainly was not wrong. Looking at these diametrically opposed possibilities for the Internet, it is clear now that the Internet does both: it can stabilize and destabilize, homogenize and polarize, divide and equalize. It has led to both hatred and understanding.

Yet despite the trolls, the hackers, and the online haters who certainly *do* exist, in this chapter, I investigate "Grimms Märchen" as a relatively safe space where women especially may express their ideas online. Using data gathered in my study of the fandom, I observe that because the community is a private sphere which has been coded as feminine, it is therefore a safe space for women to converse online without fear of misogynistic attack. I first situate my study of misogyny within the fandom by discussing the role of the Internet in online communication, followed by a description of misogyny and discrimination in the actual world and online. I then share findings and statistics from my study which show that the fandom is a space that is largely free from misogynistic or discriminatory comments. Finally, I offer an explanation of these findings by describing the ways that the Internet does not belong to the public sphere. Using Zizi Papacharissi's definition of the *private* sphere as one which "interweaves multiple configurations of public and private to suggest spaces of cultural meaning for the individual" (138–139), I investigate exactly how and why a public space, such as the Internet, can constitute a private sphere and how spaces come to be coded feminine. Discussing the topic of the Internet with respect to the public and private sphere is especially important now with more discussion of the role of the Internet in free speech as well as discussions of what online platforms should and should not be allowed to do.

The Web has brought about Berners-Lee's predictions in various ways, and while new technologies may revolutionize *how* we communicate, they usually do not revolutionize *what* or *why* we communicate. As Berners-Lee both optimistically and pessimistically states: it comes down to us humans whether we use this new technology's capabilities for good or ill. In Western society, both the online and the actual world are increasingly enmeshed to such a degree that they cannot be entirely separated from one another. When fans discuss the role of the Internet in their lives, they stress that there are no longer boundaries between the online and the actual world:

> [Das Internet] ist definitiv ein Teil des Lebens heutzutage, und wird es auch immer mehr und mehr werden [...]. Es gehört zur Entwicklung des Menschen dazu, schätze ich.
>
> [[The Internet] is definitely a part of life nowadays, and will only become more and more so [...]. It belongs to the development of mankind, I would say.] (Altais)

With 89.4% of the European Union and 94.4% of Germany's population with Internet access ("Internet World Statistics") one can begin to understand comments such as these. Another fan writes in agreement, describing the many aspects of their life, registration for appointments and events, or gathering information, exists *only* in an online format. They write: "es ist korrekt, dass man ohne Internet [...] ein Sonderling ist." [it's correct that without the Internet one is [...] the odd one out] (Captain Trips).

## Public or Private? Determining the Role of the Internet

The public sphere has been a term which has dominated debate about the capabilities of digital media in scholarly and political discussions. Originally conceived as a place where people would be able to come together and overcome misunderstandings, the World Wide Web was described by Berners-Lee as a medium for the communication of people through shared knowledge (79). Communication online has only grown as more institutional practices in the actual world are inseparably entwined with the Internet. Discussions of the "public sphere" are often complicated by competing definitions of the word "public." The colloquial use of the term "public" is literal and refers to everything that appears in public and can be seen and heard by everybody (Arendt 50)—gathering places such as open squares, supermarkets, or even websites. The ideological definition of "public," referring to the public sphere, has been famously described by Jürgen Habermas as "a domain of our social life in which such a thing as public opinion can be formed. Access to the public sphere is open in principle to all citizens." This public sphere mediates between state and society and is a vehicle for public opinion to be formed. For this public sphere to function, citizens must rationally express and publicize their opinions freely for the public good or state action without coercion. Importantly, the public sphere deals with the political and focuses on the importance of reason and logic ("Public Sphere" 45).

Habermas's conception of the public sphere has met widespread feminist critique noting that this conception only includes heterosexual, educated, rich men and excludes not just women, but members of all historically excluded groups such as the L.G.B.T.Q.+ community, P.O.C., and religious minorities (Baetens et al. 191). This conception of the public sphere suffers from what has been often described as "gender blindness" (Meehan 414). If a man's role is in the public sphere of reason, then a woman's is in domestic spaces. Habermas's focus on the importance of reason and logic in the public sphere excludes emotions and relationships which have continually been gendered as more feminine (Brooks 17). Camille Bacon-Smith likewise discusses women's exclusion from the public sphere in Western society. Women who try to engage in the public sphere are met with great opposition. Their engagement is often dismissed as "unformed, unstructured, and unworthy of a public audience" unless women conform to the expectations of masculine culture (*Enterprising* 292). Though even then, women are often dismissed as being unfeminine and thus unworthy of participating in the public sphere. Women and historically excluded groups, then, are seen in many Western societies as inherently not belonging to the public sphere as well as public spaces where the wants and needs of straight white men are prioritized above others. This is especially true when common notions of the private are considered personal and domestic (and gendered feminine) and the public as political (and gendered masculine) (Brooks 25).

The public sphere, however, no longer exists as postulated by Habermas as he argues himself. Habermas argues that digital media has removed global borders which has only accelerated the deterioration of the public sphere (Habermas, "Warum nicht Lesen?" 103). With the Internet's move toward more inclusion and, as he claims, a leveling effect between participants where social hierarchies are no longer as important, has also come the weakening of the "filter function" of what people communicate online (Habermas, "Warum nicht Lesen?" 104). He argues that the Internet has merely been inflated to resemble a public sphere and at best, is but a fragmented public sphere with no checks and balances (Habermas, "Warum nicht Lesen?" 108). Some argue that modern technologies such as the Internet have played a significant role in the struggle to regain a semblance of the premodern public sphere as conceptualized by Habermas (Avance 64). Though certainly, as I will show, these technologies have not done so. The affordances which the Internet provides for communication and interaction do not constitute a public sphere (or even multiple public spheres or counterpublics which have been proposed by others [see, for example, Calhoun, Negt and Kluge, boyd, Enjolras and Steen-Johnson]) no matter how far reaching or visible that interaction might be, or even how political. There is the question of access not just to the Internet itself, but also to owning devices which can connect to the Internet such as cell phones, personal computers, and smart devices. Not only do individuals need to purchase access to the Internet, but also the devices.

Though the percentages of individuals who have Internet access is certainly on the rise (94% in Germany, 88% across the EU, 94% for North America) these figures assess neither the quality of access nor the knowledge and use of technologies required for Internet use. The availability and speed of access play a large role in how one can communicate with others online. These numbers likewise do not take into account that while Internet access and availability might be widespread in some areas such as North America and Europe, overall Internet access does exclude large percentages of the population such as throughout Asia with only 64% of the population with Internet access and across Africa with only 43%. And with the two locations making up the largest representation of Internet users consisting of just slightly more than 15% of the world population, overall representation should be seen as problematic with such an overrepresentation of North American and European voices online ("Internet World Statistics").

Questions of access and availability are certainly important to consider when discussing the Internet and online interaction, yet a fundamental reason why the Internet cannot be considered a part of the public sphere is the landscape of the Internet itself. The Internet exists as a series of websites and platforms that users can access for various reasons and to perform various tasks—whether this is to communicate with others, to passively watch videos or look at memes, or to use creative tools to produce new content. Websites and platforms are largely owned by corporations and operated by private individuals. Importantly as well, individual companies (such as Facebook, for example) often have more rights to content than the users who produce them (Garde-Hansen 138). Sites often have written into their terms and conditions that content created and produced by users can be distributed, reproduced, and displayed without written consent of the users themselves. Likewise, users communicate with others only in the very specific ways permitted by the sites. The layout of the site, whether direct messages or group chats are allowed—or any other structuring of the platform—is ultimately not a decision on the part of the user but has been pre-programmed and coded into the workings of the site itself. This communication takes place within corporate-designed systems which define how communication can take place on the platform (Garde-Hansen 137). Internet users do not simply communicate online, they are actively engaging in the technical structure of the websites created and developed in specifically designed ways.

With the Internet, technology determines the parameters of interaction. Platforms need to be created and coded, and the actual-world assumptions of developers are literally encoded within them. The technology is not necessarily determining the nature of interaction online, but it does determine the parameters within which that interaction can develop (Boellstorff 231). It determines who can access and join a site and which rules and regulations are enforced. As one fan points out,

> letztlich ist jede Webseite, jedes Forum mehr oder weniger eine Diktatur; auf manchen wird vernünftig die Ordnung aufrechterhalten, auf Anderen werden übelste Beleidigungen von denjenigen, die denken wie die Betreiber der Seite geduldet, und Andersdenkende für höflichen Widerspruch gesperrt.

> [ultimately every website, every forum is more or less a dictatorship; on some, order is sensibly upheld, on others the worst sort of abuses are tolerated as long as they have the same line of thinking as the operators of the site, and those who think differently are blocked for courteous dissent]. (Sionen Klingensang, "Das Internet")

The goals and concerns of the individuals and companies which own and run websites such as Facebook and YouTube among others do not necessarily align with promoting the common good or facilitating discussion which is ruled by rational reasoning. This capitalistic logic is one that does not fit with Habermas's conception of the public sphere as one with free access to all.

Likewise, platforms have algorithms which offer suggestions of what users should do or watch next, as well as to determine which ads to promote to specific users. Many questions and justifiable concerns arise when discussing algorithms and ad space specifically, as the questions of who can buy ad space and how those companies influence platform design and decisions are vitally important in the function of online platforms. Facebook and YouTube in particular have come under fire for their algorithms incentivizing users to share more extreme and even dangerous views on their platforms. Such dangerous views can range from conspiracy theories to COVID-19 denialism and anti-vaccination propaganda to even playing a crucial role in the events that led up to and including the January 6, 2021 insurrection at the U.S. Capitol (Thompson and Warzel).

The vital role that the Internet and the social media platform Twitter, in particular, played in the insurrection in the United States is undeniable as then-President Trump took to Twitter to inflame the passions of an angry mob by tweeting that then-Vice President Mike Pence "didn't have the courage to do what should have been done to protect our Country and our Constitution" and that the "USA demands the truth!" (Winsor et al.). As the breaching of the Capitol continued, a horrified public often quite literally learned about breaking news via tweet as trapped senators took to these online forums to inform others of what was taking place. Twitter later removed tweets and videos of Trump claiming that the U.S. election had been stolen along with other posts of misinformation, finally locking his account—which would eventually result in a total ban from the social media platform.

Twitter, and later Facebook, banning a head of state from their platforms sparked intense debates over the role of social media companies and freedom of speech. Immediately after the ban, there were claims that "free speech no longer exists in America" (quoted in Liptak). German Chancellor Angela Merkel likewise mentioned that the permanent suspension of Trump's account raised concerns about free speech, with her spokesman stating that "the right to freedom of opinion is of fundamental importance" citing that any curb to free expression should be decided by law and not private companies ("Angela Merkel"). Even Jack Dorsey, Twitter C.E.O., though defending the decision, said in a statement that permanent suspension of Trump's account could set a dangerous precedent and noted that it was a sign of the "failure" of the platform (Hamilton).

These events and criticisms highlight the extraordinary power that different platforms such as Twitter, Facebook, and other companies wield over online expression, and that online expression has very real actual-world significance. However, discussions of the Internet as a public sphere where users cannot be suspended or banned are still misplaced no matter how important these considerations may be. In the end, Twitter is a private company, and its C.E.O. is not a head of state who is beholden to the same considerations of freedom of speech as governments often are. Decisions from private C.E.O.s can also be prompted by fear of litigation rather than any intrinsic motivation of banning misleading information or removing hate speech. Litigation can be a powerful motivation to suspend and block certain users. Though, as law professor Gregory P. Magarian writes, social media companies hold a "concerning degree of power over public discourse" (Liptak). These considerations certainly do not free the companies from the responsibility of the content produced and shared on their platforms nor the function of the algorithms used which prioritize certain types of content over others. We should absolutely be worried about private power over speech and how private companies can be insulated from accountability and how quickly positions on speech can change as executives come and go. These concerns are complicated even further by the international nature of the Internet. If platforms are owned, operated, and used across national borders, who or which nation-states can and should decide what constitutes free speech and hate speech—especially when these definitions differ from one nation-state to the next?

My previous explanation of the construction of the Internet is not meant to define the Internet as a place devoid of civil discussion, outreach, or personal and community growth even if some of the most glaring examples listed previously might make it seem so. The same aspects that some individuals use to act badly on the Internet are also the same that enable others to open up and explore new ideas. My claim is that the Internet simply provides affordances for individuals to act and communicate with others and that those affordances are neither good nor bad. As media scholar danah boyd reminds us, "the mere existence of new technology neither creates nor magically solves cultural problems" (156). The Internet makes some of these cultural problems simply more visible. The fact that the Internet does not do away with inequalities is not a failure of the technology, but rather a mirror for the people that create and use it. And in the following section, I briefly contextualize a specific form of inequality, misogyny, in the actual world to highlight its form and effects online and within fan fiction.

## Misogyny in the Actual World

In her book *Haters: Harassment, Abuse, and Violence Online*, Bailey Poland defines sexism as "a combination of prejudice against persons based on their gender, combined with the privilege and power required to cause harm." Especially because white men hold and represent the majority of social privileges in the West such as political and financial power, the prejudices of this group are more likely to limit opportunities and cause other difficulties for women (2). Sexism, like all forms of discrimination, is inherently linked to privilege and power. This power is used to deny certain groups many of those same social, political, and financial privileges and to reinforce the superiority of the group in power. Though misogyny in patriarchal Western societies is certainly part of the cultural norm, it does not affect all women equally and sexism is highly racialized.

Women of color, even conforming to all aspects of Western patriarchal attitudes toward women, can experience both sexism and racism simultaneously. Here, women bear misogyny which is "defined by two [or more] layers of oppression" (Hamad 109). When discussing misogyny, we should investigate it intersectionally and consider the structures of power and inequality which can both benefit and disadvantage individuals (Cho et al. 795). As a cisgender, heterosexual, white woman, I, for example, experience misogyny in a fundamentally different way than a woman of color, a woman with a disability, or a woman who is a member of the L.G.B.T.Q.+ community.

Misogynistic attitudes can be broadly broken down into two categories: *hostile* and *benevolent sexism*. *Hostile sexism* is what many people initially think of when they hear the word "sexism." Hostile sexism consists of "overtly hostile feelings toward women, with negative assumptions toward, and stereotyping of nontraditional women in particular" (Nikolajeva 108). "Nontraditional" here can have a range of meanings, but can more generally be described as women who violate what are perceived as "traditional gender norms and stereotypes" in Western patriarchal society such as women in power, sexually active women, women of color, transwomen, queer and non-gender conforming individuals, among others. Hostile sexism looks to enforce "traditional," stereotypical gender roles of both men and women, justify the sexual exploitation of women, and maintain (usually white) male power and dominant social advantages. This can be achieved through derogatory characterizations of as well as actions toward women, and using feminine characteristics as marks and descriptors of inferiority.

*Benevolent sexism* can at times be more difficult to identify as on the surface it may seem positive. Like hostile sexism, benevolent sexism seeks to maintain male power and dominant social advantages albeit through disempowerment and patronization. Benevolent sexists often characterize women as "pure creatures who need protection from men." This reflects the idea that women should be adored by men, and that women are necessary to make men complete (and thus women must be "incomplete" if they are single). The rights and privileges men enjoy are characterized as well-deserved or even as "a responsibility that [men] must bear" (Nikolajeva

108). Benevolent sexism is often reinforced through the idolization of a particular stereotype of women, such as the agreeable and doting white housewife. I would likewise add to this definition that is often only white women who fit into the characterization of "pure creatures who need protection." Especially dating back to slavery and colonialist attitudes, Black women, for example, are often stereotyped as highly sexualized and incapable of being characterized as a "damsel in distress" (Hamad 77). This type of misogyny is "not only steeped in racism, it cannot be divorced from it" (Hamad 168). People can and often do hold hostile and benevolent sexist attitudes simultaneously. For example, if a woman dismisses comments or acts against benevolent sexist "suggestions" of how she should behave, the benevolent sexism can quickly turn hostile.

Men are certainly not the only ones who hold and reinforce misogynistic views. Women abusing other women is an observed issue both online and in the actual world. Often under the guise of feminism, distinctions of race, class, ability, and sexuality among others are used as weapons by (usually) white women to reinforce perceived social norms while simultaneously painting themselves as the victim (Poland 59). These actions reinforce the white woman's role as the "subordinate members of a dominant race" (Hamad 78), and emphasize the importance of investigating intersectionally the power dynamics which affect all aspects of a person's identity when discussing discrimination. These prejudices, perpetuated throughout much of Western culture, inhibit social opportunities for women and other historically excluded individuals, creating hard limits. Often, these limits are of an abstract nature, such as the level of social mobility these groups are allowed. These damaging sexist beliefs, however, menacingly encroach on physical spaces by threatening the safety of these groups. Both hostile and benevolent sexism profoundly shape a woman's ability (or inability) to feel secure and to have the sense of an undisputed right to occupy that space.

The limitation of movement is unfortunately not an infrequent response when women and historically excluded individuals report violent and threatening encounters in public (Ahmed 70). Women often hear "advice" that they should simply leave a dangerous situation (or never have been in one in the first place). This harmful suggestion simply enforces those spaces as belonging to privileged groups—usually white men—and maintains the idea that women are simply encroaching. The right to entitlement men experience is often deemed worthy of protection even at the expense of women's and historically excluded groups' rights to participation or even just existence (Vickery 42). Take, for example, the media sensation surrounding the sadly unsurprising response of Chanel Miller's rape by Brock Turner in 2015. Turner, a young white man, faced up to 14 years of imprisonment, but was sentenced to only six months in a county jail. Turner then served only three months for his "good behavior" (Dastagir). A widespread and publicized response to the case was that Turner's promising athletic career should not be ruined due to what was termed "a simple mistake." In this argument there is an absence of any consideration of lived realities Miller endured due to the rape and it likewise frames sexual violation as an accident that can just be shrugged off. Miller, a woman of color, was often attacked in the media as being at least partially at fault for her own rape since she was alone and had been drinking (Dastagir). This public victim-blaming reinforces the idea that women and historically excluded individuals are intruding on spaces occupied by privileged groups and must be expelled from them.

The limitation of speech can likewise be a form of distribution and reinforcement of power within a society. This becomes apparent when focus is placed on which groups are allowed to speak or which topics are allowed to be discussed (Bottigheimer 51). Study after study shows that in mixed-gender groups, men not only speak more, but interrupt more than women. In a study of mixed-gender group conversations, men were found to have interrupted more than 40 times on average whereas women interrupted only twice. Men are so used to being the primary voices heard in personal conversations, as well as in politics and the media, that any violation of "the norm" (i.e., white male voices dominating the conversation) is perceived as an oddity and even a threat that must be acted upon (Poland 14). Though I have begun by discussing the actual world, these forms of discrimination are just as integral to online worlds as in the actual world (Boellstorff 226). As danah boyd reminds us, the Internet simply "mirrors, magnifies, and makes more visible the good, bad, and ugly of everyday life" (24).

## Cybersexism

The origins of the Internet lie with the military and national defense during the Cold War. Perhaps owing more credence to the *Time's* formulation of the Internet as another "frontier" to explore, the earliest realization of the Internet was conceived during the Space Race with the U.S. Department of Defense's Advanced Research Projects Agency Network (A.R.P.A.N.E.T.) in 1958. In its earliest form, A.R.P.A.N.E.T. was a means for military and academic researchers to communicate for defense operations. Before being opened to the public domain by computer scientist Tim Berners-Lee with the development of HyperText Markup Language (HTML) in 1989, these communication networks were accessible only to limited individuals. Though even with the development of HTML, cost and technological prowess continued to be an access limitation (Blank, "Introduction: Toward" 2). With Internet origins rooted in defense and the academy, the development of the perceived "average Internet user" as a white, heterosexual, cisgender man comes as no big surprise (Poland 3). And certainly in a similar fashion which mirrors the actual world, women are often perceived as encroaching on online spaces.

Stories of doxing,[2] threats of sexual violence, and online stalking frequently hit the news. Take, for example, the #GamerGate scandal. Under the guise of video game reform, women video game developers were vilified, objectified, and violently harassed online (Nisbett 172). Headline-worthy stories such as #GamerGate hardly represent the sheer number of attacks and comments women receive online. While the term "troll" is used to refer to individuals who write generally inflammatory comments online of all types, studies have shown that Internet trolls are more likely to seek out groups and individuals who are historically excluded, or members of non-mainstream groups (Stromer-Galley and Wichowski 172). While cisgender, heterosexual white men are certainly also harassed and can be "trolled" online, it is usually their ideas that are attacked while women

2 Researching and publicly posting private and personally identifying information about an individual.

and historically excluded groups are often attacked on the basis of their personhood. That is, they are vilified simply for being themselves online.

The practice of lumping attacks on women online into the category of generic trolling, hides the very specific ways women are attacked online simply for being women (Vickery and Everbach 13). In my own experiences engaging in conversation in large online forums, I have likewise experienced this limiting of space. In instances of sharing or uploading content online, the comments garnered often have nothing to do with the content itself, rather I am simply informed to adhere to gendered norms. These comments ranged from being told to "get back to the kitchen," being dismissed as I was singled out, or instructed to "read a book" before I try to discuss the topic with men—even when the discussion is on a topic of my expertise. While I, too, have experienced more extreme comments, experiences like these openly reinforce idealized stereotypes of what women should be and do. Namely, this is the assumption that as a woman, I am not only uninformed, but should get back to my "rightful" place, serving in the home. Though these particular examples are innocuous compared to the sexually explicit death and rape threats that many women experience all too frequently, the exchanges nevertheless resulted in a restriction of space and engagement. Even on a superficial level with mild aggression, commenters are able to effectively immobilize the voices of women in these forums. The substance of the content I put forth was never engaged with. My ideas and arguments were not attacked, I was simply a target because I presented myself as a woman online—a woman who the commenters viewed as an intruder in their claimed space.

The advice given to women who experience gendered harassment online parrots the advice given to women who experience sexual harassment in the actual world: that online attacks should either just be ignored, that women should "just log off," or a statement that women should expect these types of comments when they engage online. The responsibility and burden has then been placed on the harassed. This results in those targeted never feeling a total belonging in these spaces at best, and can also result in a fear of these spaces or worse. This fear itself is a tool used by harassers to define spaces and determine who is allowed to occupy them. The resulting feelings of vulnerability and fear shape how women's bodies inhabit any space (Ahmed 70). Fear can lead to a refusal to inhabit public spaces in ways that anticipate injury. This refusal can appear in a very literal sense such as refusing to walk alone, a refusal to go to certain locations, or to walk at night, though it can also lead to refusal to engage in discussions both online and in the actual world. It is important to remember that the supposed solutions that women should remove themselves from public spaces and return to the home does not actually protect women since, according to the National Coalition Against Domestic Violence, one in three women have experienced domestic violence ("Statistics"). As this statistic shows, returning to domestic spaces that have been coded feminine does not always result in a lack of violence. The inequal power structures that subordinate women still remain intact.

The prominence of misogyny online has prompted the creation of the term "cybersexism" where sexists exert their prejudice, power, and privilege online. Cybersexists often rely heavily on anonymity, or perceived anonymity to conduct their harassment (Poland 22). The anonymity of the Internet has been said to lead to *deindividuation*, a "loss of a sense of self and social norms" (Reagle 94) which can result in asocial behavior in individuals. Experiencing deindividuation, they no longer associate their actions and behaviors with any real-world consequences or do not perceive that they need to follow any established social norms. When one can no longer see the person or people with whom one is interacting, it becomes easier to disregard the effects of one's words. Due to anonymity, an individual may be able to separate their online actions from their actual world self—the individual believes that they do not have to own their behavior (Stroud and Cox 295).

In a comment thread about the civility of the Internet as a whole, fans on *FanFiktion.de* nearly unanimously stated that the Internet is *not* a place for civil discussion. One user writes on the topic of anonymity:

> Das Internet ist ein weniger zivilisierter Ort als das "da Draußen". Die scheinbare Anonymität führt dazu, dass die Schreiber kein Blatt mehr vor den Mund nehmen und blind Information weitergeben, die sie irgendwo aufgegabelt haben. Prüfung von Quellen? Pfft!
>
> [The Internet is a less civilized place than the "outside" [the actual world]. The supposed anonymity leads writers to just lay it all out and blindly share information which they've dragged up from somewhere. Checking your sources? Pfft!] (Der Edgerton Bonus, "Internet")

Anonymity and deindividuation can go a long way to explain what appears to be the phenomenon of people behaving badly online. Yet new technologies are the most successful when they provide people with faster and easier ways of doing what they were already doing. Both cybersexists and sexists, when confronted, often argue that their comments were just a joke or "just entertainment," claiming that individuals who get offended by such comments and actions are just "people who are looking too hard" (Poland 8). As Whitney Phillips and Ryan Milner remind us, deindividuation has existed long before the Internet. Deindividuation is already well-established in social psychology with the study of what happens when individuals are subsumed by a crowd: specifically in mobs, protests, and so on (68–69). This is not to say that what one is able to accomplish with digital media is identical to a mob in the actual world; the difference is one of degree rather than kind. It is not technology that *creates* the desires to mock and troll individuals online. How we use the Internet is certainly up to us, and it is the human desire to use such technologies to ridicule others that should disturb us.

Yet despite the plentiful instances of cybersexism and harassment online, the Internet can also be used to give voice to people and groups who might otherwise be silenced in the actual world (Burdick et al. 93). Anonymity online does not *cause* negative effects such as narcissism and aggression, rather it creates affordances for this behavior to take place (Faucher 88). Indeed, studies have found that anonymity online can also have quite positive effects. In a study of online communities, Samer Faraj and Steven L. Johnson found that anonymity online affected the kind of ties that people formed online. Instead of forming attachments to specific individuals, anonymity not only fostered an attachment to the online community as a whole, but also supported the preservation and enforcement of community norms in a positive manner (1465). Physical invisibility online can also give people the courage to experiment with new ideas and behaviors with potentially lower risk than if they were to try them in the actual world among friends, family, and neighbors who are already familiar with their established identity (Megele and Buzzi 40).

Just as the Internet does not cause certain behaviors, more Internet access does not necessarily result in more engagement. Studies have found that while the Internet certainly makes discussion and engagement, and even civic involvement easier, it does not result in more people taking *more* collective action. The connection and communication possible online allows those who were already active to become more active, but those who were already less engaged in their communities, did not become more so (Bakardjieva 67). Similarly, the main reason fans cite for remaining on *FanFiktion.de* is that they had been searching for others with similar views and hobbies, and are happy to be together with other people who understand them. It is a place of connection with others for people who were actively seeking this connection. Lexila explains her involvement on *FanFiktion.de* as one which began as she was searching for others with similar interests. She writes:

> Gerade für mich als Hobbyautorin ist FF.de eine Möglichkeit, mit Gleichgesinnten in Kontakt zu treten, denn persönlich kenne ich niemanden, der ebenfalls [fan fic] schreibt und mit dem ich mich austauschen könnte.
>
> [For me as a hobby [female] author, FF.de is a possibility to come into contact with like-minded people because I personally don't know anyone who also writes [fan fic] who I could correspond with.] (Lexila)

Since the Internet mirrors the complexity of human emotions and interpersonal interactions, it is important to understand how Internet communication and community formation is both similar to the actual world, as well as the ways new technologies affect these interactions. To understand how the human and online elements of community formation are intertwined online, in what follows I detail my study of the fandom.

## Study of Fics and Comments within the "Grimms Märchen" Fandom

In my study of *FanFiktion.de* and the fandom, it quickly became clear that though cybersexism may run rampant online, it was almost entirely absent from the fandom itself. I certainly had anecdotal assumptions as to how interaction took place online as well as the frequency with which feminist themes came up for discussion. I compiled two data sets originally in the summer of 2020 to quantify findings about the authors and their fan fiction pieces, as well as comments within the fandom. With this data I was able to more accurately map communication and thematic trends to undertake a more focused analysis of why this fandom seemed to be relatively free of misogyny.

As can be seen from Figures 2 and 3, there is an overwhelming percentage of people who self-identify as women within the fandom. 88.5% of all authors and 96.6% of all commenters identifying gender are women.

I then broke these figures down to determine trends both in the comments and from the stories that were being posted. As can be seen in Figure 4, there is an overwhelming number of positive comments. Out of a total of 497 comments collected, 443 (89%) were considered to be positive and only four (0.8%) were determined to be negative.

Though the category *good* (289 comments)—denoting comments that were supportive and encouraging of the writing—is certainly the largest, it

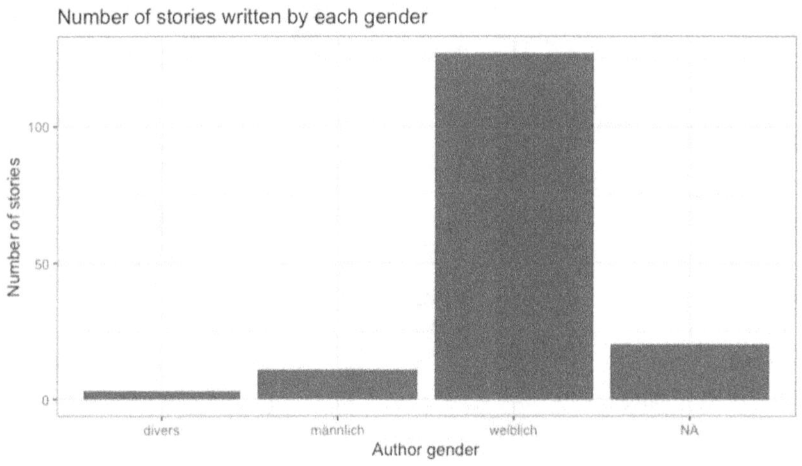


Figure 2. Graph: Number of stories written by gender.
Divers: *diverse* (nonbinary), männlich: *male*, weiblich: *female*.

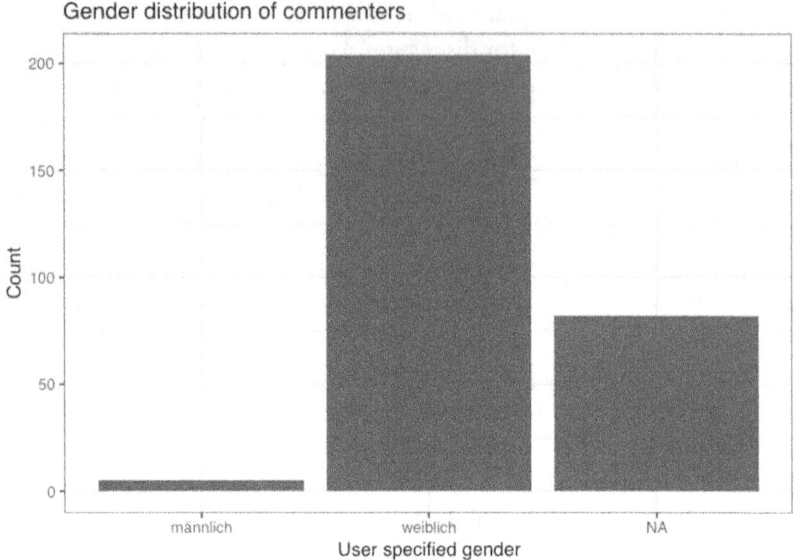


Figure 3. Graph: Gender distribution by commenters.

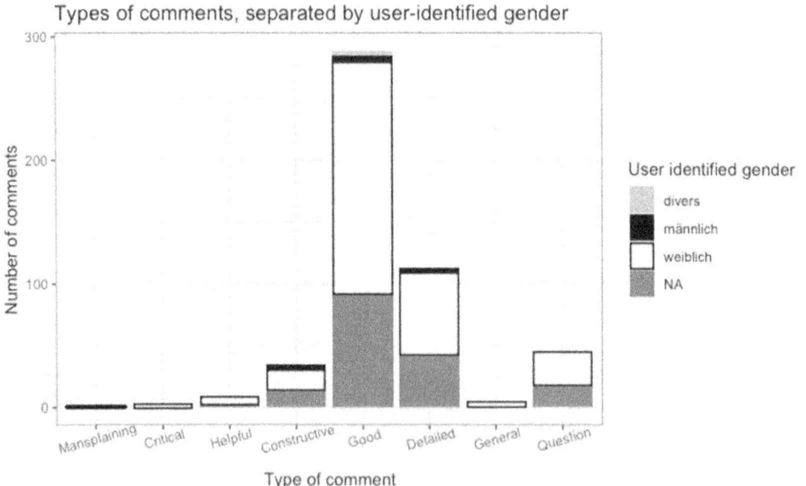


Figure 4. Graph: Types of comments by gender.

was not the only category that was used to determine the overall number of positive comments. The categories *helpful* (8 comments), *constructive* (34 comments), *detailed* (112 comments), were also considered to be positive feedback. Fans would detail what they liked about each fic, or perhaps what they found interesting. Some categories such as *general* (5 comments) or *question* (45 comments) were not considered to be positive or negative, but simply neutral, most often asking when the next chapter of the fic would be posted online—though these types of comments can certainly be implicitly positive and encouraging. The only comment types that were categorized as *negative* were *critical* (3 comments) and *mansplaining* (1 comment). These comments did not offer any constructive criticism or support, and stated only disapproval of the fic. Of significance in the data collected is the exceptionally small number of people who were writing negative comments.

In an investigation of data compiled about the fics themselves (Figure 5), 78 out of 161 fics (48%) were classified as having feminist-related themes—a substantial ratio. The categories of *bleak* (20 fics), *empowerment* (39 fics) and *leaning* (19 fics) were all classified as feminist-type writings. The *bleak* category focused on feminist issues seen through a pessimistic lens and included issues such as rape or oppression. *Empowerment* fics put women in liberating positions and broke from the traditional storytelling tropes of heteronormative relationships and marriage as the ultimate "happy ending." Finally, *leaning* fics contained several elements of feminism such as characters who broke gender roles, but were not as explicitly feminist as *bleak* and *empowerment* categories.

Also visible in Figure 5 are trends which were particularly interesting: men disproportionately wrote traditionally themed stories. 63% of all stories written by men were classified as *traditional*, meaning that they followed the canonical fairy tales' plot lines and character roles: a prince rescues a princess, they get married and live happily ever after. Men are writing only 6.3% of all stories within the fandom, but 23.3% of all traditional stories are written by men. These traditionally themed fics are not by any means bad or even discriminatory, but it is a strong trend within the fandom. I will postulate explanations for these findings in the remainder of this chapter. As discussed previously, all individuals online can have wildly different experiences: from cybersexism and discrimination to positive

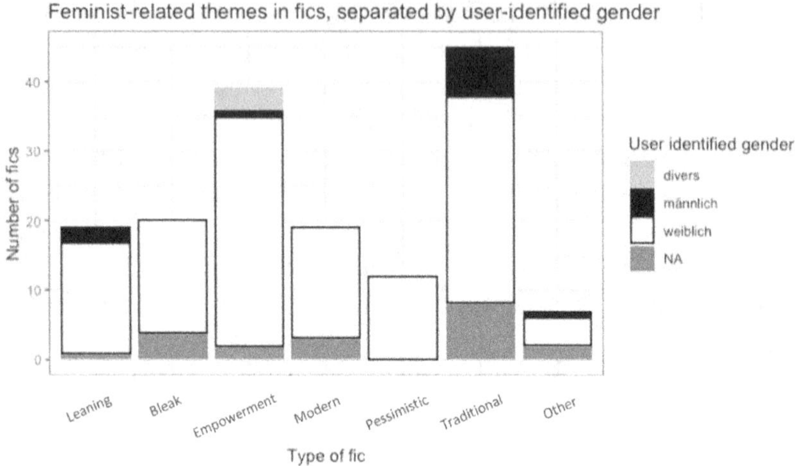


Figure 5. Graph: Themes in fics by gender.

community formation and understanding. The reason for this, I maintain, is that while the Internet itself might be a public space, it is by no means a public sphere. Far from the "collaborative democracy" (Enjolras and Steen-Johnson 108) that many people hoped the Internet would become, it is rather a series of private spheres, each with their own rules and norms.

## "So, jetzt fühl ich mich besser. Endlich mal ausgesprochen, was ich denke." [So, now I feel better. Finally got to say what I think.] (Valenfield): The Internet as Private Spheres

The "private" is often understood as confined to the domestic space of the home. And indeed, the earliest references to a type of "private space" refer to private property in the works of Plato and Aristotle (Papacharissi 27). Actions such as talking intimately, expressing emotions, child-rearing, and personal relationships—matters of the family unit—are traditionally considered to be private (Kumar, Krishan and Ekaterina Makrova

326) and ultimately, depoliticized. Increasingly, there is a profound blurring of boundaries between what is public and what is private. Not only do private matters come into the public sphere, but in political debates new laws and mandates are proposed on what has traditionally been considered private such as intimate relationships, reproductive rights, and modes of personal expression.

Hannah Arendt writes that the distinction between the public sphere and the private is one of the household and political realms which in ancient times were distinct and separate entities. Through time, and with the emergence of the nation-state in the modern age, these spheres are no longer distinct. She describes the difficulty in the modern age of understanding a division between the public and the private as life processes which were once considered private have now been channeled into the public realm. This has created a public organization of life processes themselves; that is, the necessities of life and personal survival have entered the public realm (Arendt 28–46). Certainly, it has become increasingly difficult, if not impossible, to argue that the private and public are separate.

The role of the Internet within the public sphere has been defined as "fragmented" or "incomplete" (Habermas, "Warum nicht Lesen" 108), yet one of the reasons why it has been difficult to categorize how the Internet fits into the public sphere is that the Internet is something else entirely. The conceptualization of the public sphere is incompatible with describing the complexities inherent to the Internet, how people use it, and the structure of the Internet and the various platforms themselves. Online media continue to change the conventional understandings of the public and private. The public and private are continually negotiated online with social media postings about personal matters being highly visible, the availability of personal information to others, as well as the rules and regulations of specific platforms which are online commercial entities themselves (Papacharissi 46). It is not that the Internet is neither public nor private as Habermas contends (Habermas, "Warum nicht Lesen" 107), but rather that it is both simultaneously.

Private spheres interweave "multiple configurations of public and private to suggest spaces of cultural meaning for the individual" (Papacharissi 137). That does not mean that conversations and involvement on the

Internet cannot be political, influential, or even highly visible. The distinction of the "private sphere" is also not visibility or lack of engagement with the political. What it refers to, rather, is the idea that the self remains the point of reference rather than a "public common good" as defined by Habermas as a crucial component of the public sphere. Though individuals may engage with the political, which has often been considered the "stuff" of the public sphere, what determines this as a series of *private* spheres is that individuals use these as spheres which have cultural, political, and social meaning for the individual and allow for connection with like-minded individuals.

In this definition, it is not that the Internet itself is a single private sphere, rather it is a plurality of private spheres. This helps explain why there are such disparate experiences across different platforms—because they are all separate private spheres. They each have their own rules and expectations. They can be collaborative or in direct opposition to other spheres. It is impossible to characterize all interaction on the Internet as a whole, because rules and regulations across various platforms are so different that it becomes quite difficult to compare them with one other. My usage of *private spheres* in this book is intentionally divorced from the types of gendered connotations typically associated with the private or the domestic. Each private sphere has its own rules, norms, and expectations according to its culture. Some private spheres may be considered more masculine, where women are criticized for even attempting to engage in discussion, and others are coded as feminine and therefore spheres where men do not feel they need to exert their authority.

While not all fandoms follow the same norms and can be coded differently, *FanFiktion.de* is a private sphere which has been coded feminine and the "Grimm's Märchen" fandom is a space where women are able to speak with relatively little misogynistic attack. Being coded as feminine associates fan fiction with the invisible feminine world which is also culturally associated with powerless people: women and children (Sadiqi and Ennaji 87–88). Groups deemed as "inferior" by those in power are commonly described with feminine characteristics (Eagleton 155). Associations between fandom and being emasculated are commonly made (Bronner 38), and generally speaking, fan fiction itself is coded feminine. Though demographics with online fan fiction are changing, in its pre-Internet existence fan fiction was authored almost exclusively by women (Bacon-Smith, *Enterprising Women* 4), and associations with fan fiction as effeminate and child-like, have persisted. Women have long been associated with the minor arts rather than the major—as merely "imitative rather than innovative" (Eagleton 161). A genre which is based entirely on creating texts based on the characters, plots, and worlds of previously published works fits neatly into these stereotypes and reductive generalizations. Fans describe the associations with immaturity and femininity, openly acknowledging their personal experiences with the stereotypes. One female-identifying fan writes:

> Das Problem mit Fanfiktions ist, dass sehr viele überhaupt nicht wissen, was es ist. Wenn sie es sich erklären lassen oder googeln, ist es etwas für junge Mädchen in der Pubertät oder gelangweilte Hausfrauen—zu beidem zähle ich nicht!
>
> [The problem with fanfictions is that many people have absolutely no idea what it is. When they get it explained to them or google it, it's something for young girls during puberty or bored housewives—and I'm not either of those!] (Katzelin)

Fan fiction has been described as largely female-dominant, functioning in a female sense of building, regulating and maintaining community (Hellekson 116). It follows then that within fan-fiction communities we can see a differing conception of community and space than those described previously which were centered around men's wants and needs in Western society. Describing community formation online, one fan states that "natürlich ist das Internet auch ein zivilisierter Ort, den auch hier [FanFiktion.de] gilt." [Of course the Internet can also be a civilized place because here [FanFiktion.de] counts too] (DerFeuerwolf). Since communities are distinguished by the style in which they are imagined (Anderson 6), fan-fiction websites such as *FanFiktion.de* are private spheres that function differently from others online. *FanFiktion.de* then offers women and historically excluded groups the opportunity to show what the conception of community means to them. This unique environment allows women to write about women's experiences in a "reality she constructs" where women have power to create and maintain communities (Bacon-Smith, *Science Fiction* 105). Thus it is a relatively safe space for women to post, comment, and share information about their concerns.

For a number of fans, *FanFiktion.de* is a place where they can go to talk with like-minded individuals, because their friends and families either do not understand what fan fiction is (or its importance to the fan authors) or they are not interested enough to read their fics or give feedback. This fannish, feminine conception of community is centered around the fannish gift economy: the exchange of immaterial gifts such as time investment and attention, with goals of community building and solidarity. In this space, fans talk about discomfort and harassment that they experience in the actual world, sharing their feelings, their personal experiences, and connecting with others. One fan describes:

> Meine Familie hat überhaupt keine Ahnung von [meinen Fandoms], welche die Bereiche sind, in denen ich lese und schreibe. Sie würden es nicht verstehen und erklären will ich es ihnen auch nicht, da es nur Zeitverschwendung wäre.
>
> [My family has no idea about [my fandoms], which are the areas I read and write in. They wouldn't understand them and I don't want to explain it because it would only be a waste of time.] (Sumpex)

This testimony illustrates a large part of the community formation within the private sphere of *FanFiktion.de*: that connection with others helps normalize experiences and creates a more inclusive community.

Comments from fans show time and again that fan fiction is continually dismissed as feminine or "girlish." The often implied and sometimes stated intent is to emphasize that fan fiction is not important enough for men and boys to waste their time reading or writing. One fan comments that her fan fiction is dismissed by her family: "Meine Mutter befand meine Tätigkeit für überflüssig, meinem Bruder war sie eigentlich ziemlich gleichgültig (Mädchenkram)." [My mother found my activity a waste and my brother was pretty indifferent (girl stuff)] (Panthera). My own experience of writing fan fiction or even collaborative original works with my (likewise women) friends was continually dismissed by others as "just silly things girls do," akin somehow to gossiping. This is not to say that men do not write fan fiction (as the data illustrates, they certainly do) but stereotypes abound of the boys and men who write fan fiction as antisocial and effeminate. A male-identifying fan explains that he keeps his online fannish activities hidden from classmates for fear of the stereotypes he would endure if they found out. He notes that in school, he has the reputation of being very athletic and has many friends; associations with fan fiction would bring about the stereotypes of being "kindisch" [childish], for "pubertäte Mädchen" [pubescent girls] and "Mädchenkram" [girl stuff] which he sees as harming the reputation he has cultivated at school ("Ist euch Fanfiktion peinlich?").

Yet even if different private spheres have the possibility of functioning as women define them, there is another aspect of community formation to consider when discussing flaming and harassing comments which occur online. Once communities become too large (around 500 deeply involved participants) they experience saturation which leads to lower involvement and structural stress (Gonçalves et al. 2). Community schisms occur in all communities (even in the actual world) once they reach an unsustainable size and a pressure point. These schisms often occur much more rapidly online, however, due to the intensity of Internet interaction. When a schism occurs within a community, it results in a breakdown of communication and a higher frequency of disinhibition of its members. The larger the community size, the more anonymity one might feel as well as the less of a connection to the community itself (Bacon-Smith, *Science Fiction* 83). In the fandom, the total number of unique authors was 106 with 291 unique commenters; thus with an overall fandom size of 385, it is well under the point of schism. These numbers support the findings discussed previously of the nearly absent negative commentary and the overwhelming number of positive and supportive comments within the fandom since the fandom has not reached the point of structural stress leading to communication disruption and disinhibition.

In addition to being a part of an online community of like-minded individuals, where fans do not need to spend time explaining or justifying their hobby, fans describe that they feel welcomed on *FanFiktion.de*, often due specifically to the fact that the fandoms are smaller and more intimate. Discussing which fan-fiction websites they frequent, fans write about their experiences, stating that "die Community und das Interagieren mit anderen Lesern und Autoren ist allerdings hier [*FanFiktion.de*] bedeutend besser [als auf anderen Webseiten]." [The community and the interaction with other readers and authors is admittedly significantly better here [Fanfiktion.

de] [than on other websites]] (Thoronris). Another fan describes their preference for the site as a feeling of comfort. The fan left another website because "dort fühlte ich mich nicht so wohl, sowie hier ^-^" [I didn't feel as comfortable there like I do here. ^-^] (Nymis). As another fan points out, on other fan-fiction websites, "der Ton ist dort ziemlich harsch." [the tone there is pretty harsh] (RavenclawGirl).

Though many fans participate on other fan-fiction websites, the overall feeling of togetherness and community seems to be what keeps fans participating on *FanFiktion.de* in particular. Many fans point out that while large (predominantly) English-language sites may be significantly bigger online communities, sometimes the overwhelming size can diminish what they enjoy so much about their fandoms: communication with others. Because the fandoms are so much larger, there is less of a sense of commitment to providing feedback on specific fics. Fan starkeeper explains that on *Archive of Our Own*, "die Leute sind (noch viel) passiver als hier" [the people are (still much more) passive than here] ("Auf welchen"). Attack09 writes that due to its smaller size, the "Reviewfreudigkeit" [enthusiasm for giving reviews] is significantly higher on *FanFiktion.de* ("Auf welchen").

When fans discuss the community and joy they feel on *FanFiktion.de*, they are also largely discussing their particular fandoms. Interaction on *FanFiktion.de* is still subject to breakdowns in communication as well as actual-world biases which fans lament exist elsewhere online. In large comment threads, for example, when the group of fans stretches across fandoms and the number of commenters goes above the schism point, we can see breakdowns in communication. On megathreads[3] in particular, one can see comments such as: "ich glaube, wir reden an einander vorbei" [I think we're talking past eachother] or "zumal ich denke, dass der Ursprung der Diskussion eben auf diesem Missverständnis beruht" [particularly, I think that the origin of this discussion touches on this misunderstanding] ("Gründe fürs wegklicken").

There are certainly many great interactions which take place within fandoms, allowing relatively safe spaces for women to discuss issues important to them, yet fandoms are not free of actual-world biases. The

3 Comment threads which consist of hundreds of pages of comments.

Internet has been shown by numerous studies to reproduce the same inequalities of class, gender, and race which already exist in the actual world (Baetens et al. 193). Some fandoms may be places where women can post feminist fics to great applause, though this supportive reaction also greatly depends on the fandom. While some fandoms are much more open and friendly to feminist ideas, others are more obvious about misogyny. The behaviors of individuals online ultimately mirrors that of the communities of which they are a part. The Internet certainly does not solve inequalities and injustices in the actual world, rather it mirrors it, and the same inequalities are apparent online.

Berners-Lee reminds us that when it comes to human behavior on the Internet: it's up to us. *FanFiktion.de* and its fandoms have become places where many individuals can come to converse with like-minded others. Anonymous participation online provides affordances for not only the good and the bad, but everything between; it just depends on the individuals participating. One fan succinctly writes: "Das Problem ist ja, dass es die ganzen Deppen die man im Internet so antrifft, auch in der Realität gibt." [The problem is, that all of these morons that you meet in the Internet also exist in reality] (Sionon Klingensang). While some digital media aspire to Habermas's public sphere, they are however, divorced from this ideal by the very nature of their construction.

With the affordances of the private spheres of the Internet, fan fiction has grown as a social and cultural practice. These private spheres are where the personal meets the political, and where individuals connect with others, yet with a continual reference to the self. Describing the importance of her fandom as well as the positive relationships she's formed with people online, one fan writes that she can now discuss more personal matters with her family. She writes: "ich hätte es nie gewagt, wenn ich hier nicht so ein positives Feedback bekommen hätte." [I would have never dared it if I hadn't gotten such positive feedback here] (wolfsfalle). Fans' metadiscussions of fan fiction show that the Internet is a part of their daily lives, and the relationships and friendships formed online are very real. Though certainly what one experiences online can differ depending on the individual private sphere one accesses.

Women are still raised in patriarchal societies which place strict expectations on gender norms as well as limitations based strictly on gender, yet as I have shown, not all private spheres online are dominated by men. Fan fiction shows a series of private spheres which can be formed by women's conceptions of community and space. These private spheres are ones where "die Männer sich eher fernhalten." [men steer rather clear of] (TamSang). Fan fiction is often considered the "literature of the subordinate" as it allows women to craft stories and worlds, and respond to media which is often characterized by an underrepresentation of women (Derecho 71). Fan fiction, and particularly the fandom on *FanFiktion.de*, remains a private sphere that is safe for women to communicate and share stories. It is because it has been coded as a feminine space that makes it a place where a large number of people identifying as women may shape and form the rules and norms.

CHAPTER 3

# The Event of Online Storytelling: Audience and Performance

> It is not the voice that commands the story ... it is the ear.
>
> —Italo Calvino

> We don't see things as they are, we see them as we are.
>
> —Anaïs Nin

Storytellers like to control their narratives, yet as Calvino states, it is not the speaker or writer who truly commands—it is the audience. Nin accentuates Calvino by stating that we do not understand a story through the storyteller's words, but rather through the lens of our own thoughts, experiences, and feelings. For each member of an audience, there is a potentially different interpretation of the story told. Moreover, the interpretation can change each time they experience the story, whether through oral performance, reading, or just remembering. While this process of understanding and interpreting a tale can certainly remain personal, with the listener or reader interpreting a tale for themselves silently, listeners and readers can take a more active role and influence the story itself.

Audience members have the power to shape and change the course of a tale. In oral storytelling, feedback from the audience is immediate, often altering the tale even as it unfolds. In understanding the storyteller's audience and how their contributions and interactive reception may change the shape of the story, it is possible to trace the development of a story. We can witness how the storyteller may change the story being told to fit both anticipated and unanticipated wants, needs, and interests of their audience. In the instance of adaptation to anticipated wants, the audience may add additional context, information, or a new perspective to the story. In adaptation to unanticipated desires of the audience, the teller may actively change the tale due to interest (or lack thereof) shown by the audience during certain parts. Likewise, the storyteller may fashion the tale to suit the prior knowledge of the audience. Widely known details may be shortened or even skipped over, while others may be elaborated if the audience has little prior experience with a particular concept.

In earlier oral fairy-tale cultures and eras such as during the Middle Ages, folktales and fairy tales served an emancipatory function as they expressed opinions, problems, and desires of the underprivileged. In modern times, the fairy tale has "more often than not been 'instrumentalized' to support bourgeois and/or conservative interests" (Bacchilega, *Postmodern* 7) and has moved away from the communal nature of this type of storytelling. One need only think of the Disney monopoly on modern fairy-tale versions which often push a conservative "someday my prince will come" narrative. Though Disney has begun an attempt to showcase stronger female characters, or ones who realize they do not need to be rescued by princes such as in *Frozen* (2013) or *Maleficent* (2014), these changes are likely triggered by market concerns: the monetization of the fairy tale. Even if the changes we see in films such as these are indeed beginning to show more active roles for women, they are created and disseminated by a large media conglomerate that does not represent their stories' beginnings in the realm of folklore. These companies hold proprietary rights over characters and specific plots and are not necessarily representative of the folkloric communities from which folktales and fairy tales originated.

Despite the sprawling fairy-tale industry, what we see with fan fiction is a breakaway from market demands and its instrumentalization and monetization of the folktale and fairy tale. While fan fiction bears certain similarities to oral storytelling with its frequent revisions based on commentary within the fan-fiction community, it is both uniquely innovative in the digital age, and a traditional form of storytelling: a hybrid form of storytelling which I have termed "intercreative storytelling." With the digital age have come inevitable changes to storytelling when computers and the Internet became components of the storytelling process. Throughout this chapter, I investigate how fan fiction writers aim to welcome multiple voices to reframe and retell fairytales through collaborative storytelling rather than restrict authorship to one individual. This form of storytelling is highly dependent on two characteristics of the genre: communal authorship and the reliance of fan fiction on a "fannish" gift economy—the giving, receiving, and reciprocating of usually immaterial gifts which result in the creation of social relationships on the basis of shared interest rather than monetization (Hellekson 114). Fan communities grow and thrive based on the fannish gift economy, and in what follows I investigate the importance of not just studying fans or fan fiction texts, but how fan fiction is always necessarily situated within a performative event of storytelling.

## Audience, Performance, and Technology

To most contemporary scholars, *audience* is what ultimately constitutes and defines an oral tale. John Miles Foley, for example, remarks that orality "requires an audience. It isn't complete without one" (*How to Read* 1). An oral rendition of a folktale, a story, or a poem is a performance. It is participatory, engaging, and, most importantly, an event of community and communion. Even if members of the audience cannot hear every word being told, the specific words themselves do not matter as much as the social connections built or reinforced during the experience. This is a time of connections, not only with the storyteller and their tale, but fellow audience members as well. The events of the story unfold at the same time for all, the tragic deaths, the merry meetings, and the unhappy partings. It is no longer just the storyteller's tale, it is a communal experience.

When a traditionally oral tale is written, authors and collectors often seek to mimic the presence of a storyteller on the page. In the Grimms' *Children's and Household Tales*, for example, we see a simulated storyteller addressing the reading audience, giving the illusion that the tale is told to the reader by a present storyteller, even at times simulating colloquial speech and grammatical patterns rather than the polished grammatical accuracy of an edited and published text. Likewise, in certain Grimm tales, we can see insertions of a simulated storyteller with asides such as: "In the time of Cock-a-doodle I went there, and saw Rome [...] There I saw a young ass with a silver nose which pursued two fleet hares, and a lime tree that was very large, on which hot cakes were growing [...] Have I not told enough lies?" (521). Here we can see direct references to a "storyteller," a supposedly identifiable "I." The asides attempt to replicate the immediacy of the oral storytelling process, such as the ability of the storyteller to ask their audience questions of clarification before moving on. For all these attempts, they still fall short since the reader is more limited in how they can interact with the author.

With published tales, the audience is still able to influence the progression of the tale, albeit in different fashions than an oral one. Audience members can influence the success of a work by contacting the writers directly if they are still living, through commentary from editors and publishers, publishing reviews or, perhaps most effectively, through economic means by deciding whether to purchase the book. These interactions can take a considerable amount of time to reach the storyteller rather than the immediacy of pleasure or displeasure with a live audience. Likewise, additions and revisions can be met with economic barriers if a work is published. With fan fiction, however, we see a blending of the audience interaction in oral tales and written texts—reaction may be immediate, changes may be made quickly without challenges of monetization, and communication between storyteller and audience is significantly more interactive.

Some fic versions replicate tactics taken in traditional, printed fairytale collections. In one fic based on "Dornröschen," or "Sleeping Beauty/ Little Briar Rose" (ATU 410), for example, the writer makes direct asides to the reader. She writes, after describing how the cursed princess fell into her death-like slumber:

> So vergingen 100 Jahre [...] Viele Prinzen hatten von der schlafenden Prinzessin gehört, alle hatten versucht zu ihr zu gelangen, aber keiner hatte es geschafft (ooooooooooooh eine Runde Mitleid). So wollte es aber der Zufall, (jaja gaaaaaanz zufällig) dass nach 100 Jahren ein gewisser Prinz Weiß zum Turm drang. Die Dornen wurden zu Rosen (ach wie romantisch) und er kam durch sie hindurch (war sowas von klar.)
>
> [So passed 100 years [...] many princes had heard of the slumbering princess, all had attempted to get to her, but no one had achieved it (ooooooooooooh a round

> of sympathy). So it happened by chance (yeahyeah juuuuuust by chance) that after 100 years a certain Prince White got through to the tower. The thorns became roses (oh how romantic) and he was able to get through them (which was obvious, of course).] (Limette02) (accessed 2020)

Just as with the previous example of the Grimms' tales, the writer places herself in the position of a symbolic oral storyteller, mimicking the interaction that might have taken place had this tale been told orally. Positioning a character to function as an identifiable storyteller who directly speaks to the audience is well known in written fiction, yet this type of mimicry is not common within the "Grimms Märchen" fandom. Rather than simulate a storyteller, fan writers often place themselves knowingly in the role, giving the audience a real storyteller, rather than a fictional one, with whom they may identify, and converse directly with their audience. Works of fan fiction do not just simulate speaking to the audience, fic writers invite conversations and commentary, and shape their tales according to the interactions of other fans with their fic.

Internet fan fiction bears deep similarities with the interactive and communal storytelling process of oral tradition, yet computer mediation has also significantly affected the mode of storytelling. Internet fan fiction cannot truly be said to be a part of either the fluidity and impermanence of orality or the printed permanence of literature, but rather is an example of "intercreative storytelling." I have borrowed and adapted the term *intercreativity* from Tim Berners-Lee. In the late 90s when he coined the term, the Web was still a largely passive form of media which Berners-Lee describes as "a glorified television channel" (80). Yet in his hope for the future of the Internet to become more creative and interactive, he describes "intercreativity" as "building things together on the Web" (82). Over two decades later, Berners-Lee's prediction has come to pass, and the highly interactive and transformative storytelling of fan fiction displays this intercreativity. In using the term "intercreative storytelling," I also take into account that while "written down" on websites, the fics are not permanent in the manner of published books and represent a text that is unstable. Websites are capable of being constantly and continually updated with little to no trace left behind for readers to follow changes being made. Indeed, as evidence of the fleeting impermanence of fics, some of the tales and comments quoted throughout this book now only exist in personal archives I collected for my research and analysis.

What Henry Jenkins terms "convergence culture" is helpful to our understanding of the development and often seemingly vast changes seen in storytelling with the introduction of new technology. Rather than describing new technology as replacing the old (though this does sometimes happen), Jenkins describes a system where different forms of media develop in response to one another, as well as to innovations in technology (*Convergence* 2). Books, magazines, and radio have not been rendered obsolete by movies, television, online streaming, and the Internet, but have adapted to exist alongside these innovations and technological developments. So too has writing and storytelling adapted as it has moved to an online medium: developing intercreative storytelling in response to innovation in technology. We can see some of these developments with an analysis of the role fan commentary plays in fan fiction writing.

Fan fiction versions of folktales are capable of rapid change once they are viewable by the public, unlike the canon editions they are based on. Because of this ability for rapid change, fan participation and multiple authorship has become an integral part of the fan fiction writing process and should be viewed as one of the defining aspects of the fan fiction genre. Like oral storytelling, fan fiction requires an interactive audience: it is not complete without one. While just as in live storytelling, some audience members are passive, fans are often quite active and can even be demanding of certain changes. Fan fiction is an extreme version of audience participation since each writer of each fan piece began as an audience member of a particular form of media (i.e., a reader or viewer of the canon). The writer of fan fiction then is an audience member who is reacting to the canon. In fan fiction, we have an audience member turned writer whose fic then in turn is commented on by other fans.

In a similar fashion to the immediate and direct reactions of audience members in an oral story, the comments from other users of *FanFiktion.de* often inspire the writer to revise or even rewrite their fic. In one interaction with a fellow fan, after receiving constructive criticism, author Atan responded, saying:

> Wurde geändert, danke für die Korrektur [...]. Daher: solltest du jemals Logiklücken, zeituntypisches Verhalten der Personen, weitere Rechtschreibfehler oder sonstige Kritik haben: Her damit!^^ [...] Bin dann gespannt, was du von der weiteren Entwicklung hältst [...] Vielen Dank für dein Review, auch dein Lob hat mich sehr gefreut.
>
> [Changed, thanks for the correction [...]. Therefore: should you ever find gaps in logic, people or conduct not typical of the era, further spelling mistakes or other criticism: send it this way! ^^ [...] Excited to see what you make of further developments [...] thank you very much for your review, also your praise pleased me very much.]

The writer is not only grateful for the feedback she has received, but asks for more corrections and suggestions. Likewise, she ends her response noting her anticipation of her fellow fans' critiques and comments on the progression of her fic. This comment shows expectations of reciprocity. Atan posts her fic for fans to read, and in return asks for their feedback. Thorne and Black comment that this interaction displays a "collaborative style of writing and the distributed nature of knowledge construction [...]. [F]an communities provide multiple opportunities for participants to collaboratively author fictions, share various forms of knowledge, and to perform as [...] experts and novices, on various topics" (271). This brief interaction shows community members sharing knowledge with one another and together these fans aim to change and edit fics to be the best (re)interpretations of and additions to the canon possible.

Just as with traditional fairy-tale telling cultures, fics are based on canon tales which are retold time and again. The stories themselves are constantly adapted to new themes, ideas and worldviews, and thus storytellers seek to have their stories retain relevancy to their audiences at a particular moment in time. To assure continued readability, the meanings of these stories must be kept alive by continued adaptation to changing views and circumstances. If this change does not happen, meaning gets lost (Assmann, Jan 74). If this meaning is lost, the stories simply cease to be passed on. Fan writers are thereby ensuring continuous readability by adapting the canon tales to changing circumstances. They update motifs to match contemporary beliefs; alter views and outcomes to match contemporary expectations; as well as to situate their fics with the needs of their audiences—just as oral storytellers have done and continue to do for theirs.

Fans generally reject the concept that stories inherently belong to one individual—that the author or authors of the canon have proprietary rights to the characters as well as the universe where the tales take place. Intellectual property such as published media is not considered by fans to be a "limited good" which is tightly controlled. They instead embrace a view of media as something which can and should be shared and accrues value in different contexts, or is otherwise enriched in various ways. This opens the media up to a wide range of alternative meanings (Jenkins, *Convergence* 256). This concept of shared ownership runs counter to the idea—and often copyright laws—of the author as the only one sanctioned to change the details of a tale.

While not true for oral storytelling cultures universally, this fan practice bears a resemblance to oral storytelling cultures—such as those studied by Milman Perry, Albert Bates Lord, John D. Niles, and John Miles Foley among others—where tales are seen as belonging to the community rather than an individual and every teller could be entitled to their own version. Yet when a tale is written down, it can be seen as a sort of liberation from many of the constraints of traditional storytelling and as an invitation for critical analysis. In their written forms, it is possible for traditional stories to take on a concrete shape, where storytellers and audiences can more easily adopt a critical approach. In writing, it is much more possible than in oral narration for the storyteller to gain the freedom to introduce something new or even unprecedented to the old and familiar material (Assmann, Jan 84). Since the audience and teller no longer need to rely on memory to circulate the tale, the brain is free to engage in new activities such as critical analysis.

Fan fiction, as a form of intercreative storytelling, adapts both the traditional, communal storytelling process, as well as makes critical and innovative changes only possible once a tale is written down. Like the singers and storytellers described by Lord and Foley, fan fiction writers are not seeking to tell entirely new stories—they are seeking to retell the old stories in the best possible way, in a way that will best fit with the ideas and expectations of their audiences. They do this to include their own new interpretations of the canon. Fans are not only retelling the same stories with added motifs and expressions but are critically engaging with them simultaneously.

## "Endlich können die mal sagen wie sie sich fühlen" [Finally they can say how they really feel] (Sturmklang): Fan Fiction as Communal Authorship

*FanFiktion.de* is set up to promote maximum interaction and collaboration between users. One form of this interaction is written reviews of individual fics. These reviews can be posted anonymously but contain a hyperlink to connect any user back to the commenter's personal profile if the user is registered on the site. There are also thousands of forum topics for users to interact with one another. Topics can range from personal thoughts and feelings to the discussion of different books and films to metadiscussions on writing fan fiction itself. Some examples of these forum topics include: "Welche Musik hört ihr zum Schreiben?" [What music do you listen to for writing?] "Inspirationsquellen," [sources of inspiration] "Vorausschauend und geplant oder einfach drauflos schreiben?" [looking ahead and planned or simply writing straight away?] and "Darstellung von Kindern in Geschichten" [depiction of children in stories] ("Forums").

While conversations between fans are still quite often asynchronous (e.g., when they leave comments or post on forums), the conversations nevertheless encourage fans to become more than just readers of stories, but also active participants. Some fan writers, for example, directly address their readers and ask them for suggestions. One fic writer makes a request of her fellow fans by writing: "Hast du zufällig irgendwelche speziellen Märchenwünsche? Im Moment überlege ich nämlich noch, was ich als nächstes schreibe." [Do you have by chance any special wishes for fairy tales? I'm currently still deciding what I should write next] (farfalla91, "Kommentar"). Here she looks for direct feedback and inspiration from fellow fans to craft her tales.

Once a fic is posted, other fans in the community continually comment with suggestions. Comments on user Wynssa Fel's fic entitled "Partycrashing für Fortgeschrittene," [Advanced party crashing], highlight the influence of the fan community on the development of fic pieces. Her tale is a handbook, written from the perspective of Cinderella (ATU 510A), for other princesses. One passage explains what a princess should do if she wants to be seen as traditionally (and stereotypically) sweet and pure in the eyes of a suitor. It reads,

> Bei der 1. Taktik geht es hauptsächlich darum den Beschützerinstinkt zu wecken. Drückt euch dazu vornehm aus, seid höflich, antwortet immer, lügt oder übertreibt auf gar keinen Fall! Sagt "bitte" und "danke," lächelt höflich, tanzt vorsichtig und macht, was er sagt. Wenn er langsamen Walzer tanzen will, dann macht das, und tanzt keinen schnellen Rumba!
>
> [The 1st tactic revolves primarily around appealing to the protector instinct. Express yourselves elegantly, be courteous, always answer, absolutely don't lie or exaggerate! Say "please" and "thank you," smile politely, dance carefully and do what he says. If he wants to dance a slow waltz, then do that, and don't dance a fast rumba!] (accessed 2015, since taken down by user)

A reader quickly commented that Wynssa Fel had chosen perhaps the wrong dance to use in contrast to a slow waltz. The commenter writes,

> Hey, sehr nette Geschichte (frag mich wie man nur auf sowas kommt *lach*) Da sind schon einige wahre Dinge dabei! Aber ich denke einen "schnellen Rumba" gibt es nicht? Soweit ich weiß ist Rumba ein langsamer Tanz. (Wenn dus besser weißt klär mich bitte umgehend auf =D ) Vielleicht solltest dus mit Foxtrott oder Cha-Cha-Cha austauschen. Liebe grüße.
>
> [Hey, really nice story (I ask myself how someone can think of something like that *laugh*) There are a few really true things there! But I think a "fast rumba" doesn't exist? As far as I know a rumba is a slow dance. (if you know better, then please correct me right away =D) Maybe you should replace it with Foxtrot or Cha-Cha-Cha Kind regards.].

Wynssa Fel writes back,

> Erst mal daaaankee schööön fürs Lesen und es freut mich, wenn es dir gefällt. : ) Ich hab leider keine Ahnung von Rumba, das war der erste Tanz, der mir eingefallen

> ist [...]. Danke dass du mir das gesagt hast. Nicht dass jeder denkt, ich hätte keine Ahnung^^
>
> [First of all thaaaank yooou for reading and I'm pleased that you liked it. : ) Unfortunately I have no idea about the rumba, it was the first dance that I thought of [...]. Thanks for telling me. Not so that everyone would think I have no idea^^] ("Kommentar")

She then went back to change the passage to read "dann macht das, und tanzt keinen schnellen Cha-cha-cha!" [then do that and don't dance a fast Cha-cha-cha!] In this brief interaction, community members share knowledge with one another and together the fans aim to change and edit their fics to be the best reinterpretations of the canon possible. It is a collaborative style of writing that allows members of the community to share their knowledge on a variety of topics.

The system of reader feedback is so widespread on the website that it has become an integral part to the fan fiction writing process and encourages other members to comment and make suggestions before the fic is ever finished. While this type of performativity with reader feedback, community interaction, and conversational components of the texts is not exclusive to fan fiction it does tend to be more pronounced within fan fiction communities. It is the "rawness and immediacy" (Busse 54) that makes these aspects of community exchange so visible. Wynssa Fels's fic can certainly be considered a text in its own right. It can be read, interpreted and analyzed just as other interpretations of fairy tales. Yet it is precisely the system of reader feedback, of the integral nature of the audience to the genre itself that requires us to investigate and analyze fan fiction not just as autonomous texts, but also as something which is left behind from a performative event. Scholars have likewise cautioned that the recording of oral storytelling—even if it is a video recording that can capture audience interaction, voice inflection, and physical movements—cannot be the same as the original event. It is but an "entity derived from the telling" (Schneider 21). Considering the nuances of the fan-fiction genre—such as the performativity that surrounds the texts—can help us keep in mind how this type of online storytelling functions. Intercreative storytelling also reminds us that we can lose an important layer of meaning if we focus only on words alone.

The following commentary from readers is an example of some of the interaction taking place around a work. In addition to fans sharing experience and knowledge in the creation of a fic, commentary can also serve as a form of norm maintenance. Several comments on one fic show that fellow fans determined the story was not up to the standards of the fandom. A particular fic contained multiple chapters of a continuous story each around 100 words long. Commenters write: "Öhm … / Interessante einleitung O.o / Vielleicht etwas kurz X3 / Nyaaaa … / ich denke, es wird noch mehr geben oder? / LG" [Um … / interesting introduction O.o / Maybe a bit short X3 / Oh wellll … / I think there's going to be more, right? / Kind regards] (Rissi-chan) as well as

> Hey … / also, die Geschichte ist echt toll, aber es ist sch … wer zu lesen. Bei deiner anderen Geschichte hast du keine Absätze gemacht, wolltest du das verbessern? / Kapitel sollten echt länger sein. / Ich hätte daraus ein One-Shot[1] oder wie das auch immer heißt gemacht. Dann lässt es sich nämlich einfacher lesen und man braucht dafür nicht so lange.
>
> [Hey … / so, the story is really great, but it's ha … rd to read. With your other stories you didn't do any paragraphs, did you want to fix that? / Chapters should really be longer. / I would have made a One-Shot or whatever it's called out of it. Then it's easier to read and one doesn't need as much time for it.] (Lea-Iruka)

The fans note the fact that the writer has not met the expectations of the site: the chapters are seen as far too short and in other stories by the same author, there are no distinct paragraphs which prevents ease of reading. The commenters themselves, as a part of the same fan fiction community as the writer, feel as though they have a right to shape and change the fics to fit within community norms. Fan fiction writers are creating their community and atmosphere collectively, and thus work to shape and change the fics appropriately. This sense of communal alteration of a tale is much more akin to oral narration where audience members can urge the storyteller to adapt their performance to their wants and needs. Thus, fan writers do not have an individual sense of fidelity to the canon or genre, rather a communal one where any member of the fandom can

1 Continuous story posted without any chapter breaks.

help enforce group norms. It is also understood within the fandom that if these fans leave constructive criticism helping the writer improve her story, that they will be accepting of constructive criticism in turn even if it comes from other users. The sense of reciprocity within the fandom is generally an indirect, communal expectation rather than an individual and direct one.

While certainly not all comments are given equal consideration in norm maintenance, others, such as the ones mentioned previously, show that many fans agree that this particular fic needs to be improved in order to live up to the expectations of the fandom. Just as in face-to-face interaction, the maintenance of community norms is crucial to the function of an online fandom. Having shared expectations not only helps with the community's survival, but it helps to make behavior and expectations more predictable, and likewise is a central component to the group's understanding of itself. Altering fics is understood as a process which can take place continually due to continued commentary.

Fic can be seen as a "work in progress" because of the potential evolution it can undergo in dialog with reader comments. Due to the continual commentary and revision, fics are an ever-expanding, ever-changing—even sometimes a contradictory—collaboration amongst fans (Busse 50). There are Betas who critique and help revise at the behest of fic writers, while other fans post stories chapter by chapter asking for reader commentary to continue the story arc, revising along the way using feedback from fellow fans. Fic writers do not write stories for silent, anonymous audiences. Rather, they make choices and effect changes which are part of authentic audience participation (Black 87). The writers are then not only interacting with others, but are simultaneously creating and further developing the fan community they belong to by setting norms and actively discussing what is and is not accepted within the community. Audience participation is expected and the process itself helps to define these norms. While many fics may indeed be excellent texts in their own right, this process of fan engagement can at times be more important than the actual product itself.

Of note as well in the previous fan interactions is the style in which the comment on Wynssa Fel's fic and Rissi-chan's are written. Though there are certainly many similarities between the suggestions and changes made by fans in the fandom and what takes place face-to-face, the existence of purely textual communication ultimately alters the interaction that takes place. With only textual communication, one can no longer hear voice inflections, see body movements or facial expressions: all of which aid in the interpretation of communication. To overcome some of these potential boundaries in conversation, users employ a hybridization of speech which mixes traditional literary writing with paralinguistic and physical cues to invite others to participate in conversation. With these cues, the online communities vary quite substantially from the traditional written register. When social settings such as storytelling move online, they must be adapted to the environment. For example, "O.o" (*confusion*), "X3" (*excited happiness*), "(:" (*smiling*) or writing out physical cues (which are almost always noted with asterisks before and following the word) such as "*freu*," (**excitement**) all seek to denote facial expressions or body movements which are not visible to the reader. This gives the comments a much more informal and conversational tone than if the cues were left out, which encourages readers to leave comments by humanizing the fic writers and making them seem more approachable.

The digital lean of online storytelling toward orality is not somehow a return of oral storytelling in an online format, but is rather an evolution, a new step in the "continuing and complexification and diversification" afforded by new media (Baetens et al. 131). While there are clearly influences of orality in the fan fiction community, the cues demonstrate a hybridization of written and spoken features. The use of these paralinguistic and physical cues begins to create a more inviting environment for comments. It is important to note however, that while facial expressions and other presumably unintentional cues such as body position or drifting eyes are difficult to control, written paralinguistic cues must be added intentionally. This allows community members more control over their expressions (or lack thereof). Indeed, studies have found that the physical absence of others in mediated forms lets users feel more in control of how they portray themselves (Lüders 456), allowing them to eliminate any unintended mannerisms and responses.

Yet while the fics are composed within the particular cultural context of their specific fandoms, they also are in constant interaction with the various outside communities of which the fans are a part. Some fans, for example, comment on the social consequences that fics touch on. This can be seen in the following comment from a series of stories entitled "Aus alt mah neu- Märchen mal anders" [Out of old somethin' new- Fairy tales done differently] by Maribelle 28. Her interpretation of "Schneeweißchen und Rosenrot" ["Snow-White and Rose-Red"] (ATU 426) depicts two sisters with little money who realize that their lives would be better if they were imprisoned because, as the sisters remark, "[d]ann haben wir Vollpension, einen Fernseher und W-Lan!" [then we'll have full board, a television, and WiFi!]

Sefira writes in response,

> Nun, ich finde du hast eine recht krasse Art die Märchen umzukrempeln. Du nimmst kein Blatt vor den Mund und stellst Hartz IV Empfänger in ein schlechtes Licht [...] sonst könnte man fälschlicherweise davon ausgehen, dass du etwas gegen sozial schwache Leute hast.
>
> [Now, I find that you have a really extreme way of changing around fairy tales. You don't mince matters and put welfare recipients in a bad light [...] otherwise one could falsely come to believe that you have something against socially underprivileged people.] (accessed 2020)

Sefira highlights the prejudice and discrimination inherent in Maribelle 28's depiction of welfare recipients where Maribelle 28 describes their lack of money as simply laziness. Here we can see norm maintenance not just with respect to the written word itself, such as with previous comments about the construction and readability of fics, but likewise norm maintenance with regards to social depictions. Sefira makes clear that within this space, welfare recipients should not be attacked.

Maribelle 28 replies to Sefira "ach so okay. also ich habe wirklich nichts gegen hartz 4 Empfänger nur es gibt halt wirklich leute, die so sind, das sind zwar wenige, aber es gibt sie." [oh, okay. well I really don't have anything against welfare recipients, it's just that there are really people who are like that, they are in the minority, but they exist] ("Kommentar"). She went back to change her story to reflect the criticism of her tale by adding a footnote, "Ich will hier keine Hartz 4 Empfänger beleidigen, es gibt aber auch Leute, die wirklich so sind." [I don't want to offend any welfare recipients, but there are also people who are really like this.] Though she has not altered the plot of her fic itself, she had added a footnote acknowledging Sefira's comment, seeking to conform to communal expectations.

*FanFiktion.de* is not merely a space for fans to post, read, and comment on particular fics. They are works in progress which not only invite responses but expect them. They likewise permit and encourage shared authorship, and create a sense of community between fans. This dialogic space displays a hybridization of oral and written modes of communication in online storytelling. Thus fan fiction displays both a replication as well as an extension of earlier storytelling-culture practices.

## The Fannish Gift Economy

As has been shown in the previous sections, discussion and comments have become inseparable from works of fan fiction. These are not just posts and comments, but a part of what has been termed a "fannish gift economy." This incorporates aspects of Marcel Mauss's and David Cheal's descriptions of the gift economy with the giving and receiving of obligatory gifts as "forms of contract" (Mauss 5). In the fannish gift economy, unlike in Mauss's and Cheal's investigations, fans are not risking social position and upholding social hierarchies—functions of gift giving in the traditional gift economy which can be obscured through appearances of love, friendship, and respect. The fannish gift economy does, however, consist of the obligatory giving and receiving of (often immaterial) gifts as a show of pleasure and appreciation within the fandom which supports and upholds the social structure of the fandom. Karen Hellekson notes that this fannish gift economy is made of three elements: to give, to receive, and to reciprocate. This gift exchange helps create and maintain social relationships within the fan community on the basis of shared interest (114). She goes on to note:

> Writer and reader create a shared dialogue that results in a feedback loop of gift exchange, whereby the gift of artwork or text is repetitively exchanged for the gift of

> [To leave no sort of reviews? I have to say, I would have [...] a guilty conscience because I'm a part of a community. That doesn't come into question for me.] ("Reviews schreiben")

Still others refer to the gift of reviews as "der [...] Lohn, den wir Autoren hier auf FF.de bekommen" [the [...] wage that we authors get here on FF.de] ("Das leidige Thema Reviews"). This creates the basis for both solidarity and social support, though it is also an "obligation that is callable at an unstipulated time" (Faraj and Johnson 1467) where fans are expected to give their time and energy in return for the fics they read.

The expectation, especially for reviews, can be seen in one fic entitled "Im Märchenwald ist die Hölle los," [In the Fairy-Tale Forest all Hell Breaks Loose]. The writer, Dea Tacita, leaves frequent Author's Notes (A.N.s) to stay in conversation with her audience. Many of her A.N.s directly address comments that have been left behind by other fans. She writes, for example,

> so, eine neue Szene, an dieser Stelle ein großes Lob an meine (einzige) Kommischreiberin Ghost cat, ich freu mich, dass es dir so gut gefällt^^.
>
> [so, a new scene, here big praise for my (only) comment writer Ghost cat, I'm pleased that you like it so much^^.]

This post states that the writer appreciates all comments she receives from fellow fans but shows that she expects a larger dialog surrounding her fic. By writing "(only) comment writer," she brings to her fellow fans' attention that she has only had one person leaving comments. She implies that a conversation between two is unacceptable, and her statement is one which suggests that more fans add comments. Dea Tacita's plea for more fans to enter the conversation works, and shortly after she received many more comments.

Similarly calling for fannish reciprocity for received gifts, one of the site moderators describes the expectations that come with using another fan as a Beta:

> Wenn du einen Alpha- oder Betaleser gefunden hast, die Chemie stimmt, es Spaß macht, sich über dein Projekt auszutauschen, dann macht es nur Sinn, ihn für seine Bemühungen auch zu "entlohnen".

> Erwähne deine Betaleser, verlinke ihn oder sie, wenn du deine Geschichte schließlich der Menschheit präsentierst [...] . Kleine Aufmerksamkeiten sind Gold wert. Eigentlich sollte es klar sein, dass du dich für die Arbeit bedankst [...]. Letzteres verlangt schließlich auch keiner. Betaleser machen es, weil sie es selbst wollen (in der Regel).
>
> [If you've found an Alpha- or Beta reader, the chemistry fits, it's fun to swap ideas about your project, then it only makes sense to "reward" him for his efforts.
>
> Mention your Beta reader, link him or her when you finally present your story to the world [...]. A little attentiveness is worth gold. It should really be clear that you thank them for their work [...]. Lastly, don't request/demand (verlangen) anyone. Beta readers do it because they want to (as a general rule).] (Riiru)

The moderator Riiru walks fans briefly through the expectations of the fannish gift economy by detailing exactly what fans should and should not do and expect, as well as the necessity of direct reciprocity in the case of using a Beta reader. Because of the large amount of work a Beta reader undertakes, payment in the form of gifts is both expected and necessary to maintain a good relationship within the community. What Riiru brings attention to is how important observation of the fannish gift economy is in fannish community building.

While direct reciprocity (such as what is detailed by Riiru previously) certainly exists within the fandom, indirect reciprocity is more typical in that each contribution an individual makes is seen as a contribution to the whole—distributed among community participants. Indirect reciprocity can develop for several reasons. One is that knowledge and expertise is uneven across the community. For example, while fan A may be able to serve as a Beta reader to an inexperienced fan B, fan B would unlikely be able to directly return the gift of expertise to fan A. While fan B can and should publicly thank and link fan A for their work as a Beta, they can also participate in indirect reciprocity by commenting on fics and supporting other fans. And since this interaction is largely visible to everyone within the fandom (with the exception of private, direct messages between community members), everyone has the chance to see the contribution and will be more likely and willing to help in turn (Faraj and Johnson 1468). New members to the fandom are likewise more likely to comment and support others if they see it widely taking place.

Some fan comments are easily identifiable as a part of the fannish gift economy. For example, DigiJasmin dedicates her entire fic to another fan as well as making sure to bring attention to everyone who helped craft the tale along the way: "Für Hexagana (mit gaaanz viel Liebe) / Danke an die Mitautoren: Liscz, myu-chan, fluffel41 und Kanaii" [For Hexagana (with muuuch love) / thank you to the coauthors: Liscz, myu-chan, fluffel41 and Kanaii] ("Wirsing"). On the surface, these gifts represent direct reciprocity: the posted fic is dedicated specifically to Hexagana. In addition, this fic writer recognizes each of the other fans who contributed to her fic. This was not a solitary effort, she shows in her A.N. The writer crafted her tale with the help of four other fans; and rather than sending the fic directly to Hexagana, it has been posted online as a part of the community, available for anyone to access. DigiJasmin announces before we can even read her fic that within the fannish gift economy she has both *given*, in that she dedicated her fic to a fellow fan and posted it for the community, and she has also *received* in that she worked together with others to write her tale.

The cycle of giving and receiving can be seen in examples of indirect reciprocity in the comment section. Another fan refers to DigiJasmin's fic as a gift, though it was not given to them specifically by the author. They write:

> Heyo / das war eins der schönsten Geburtstaggeschenke die ich je hatte *-* / um dich mal aus deiner FF zu zitieren: du bist (m)ein schatz, Danke!
>
> [Heyo / that was one of the best birthday presents I've ever received *- * / to quote you from your FF: you are my treasure, thank you!] (feuersalamander)

Like DigiJasmin and her dedication, this fic was received by a fan as a gift through indirect reciprocity. The fan then gives back directly to the writer by leaving a comment expressing how much joy reading the fic has brought to her. This cycle of both directly and indirectly giving and receiving gifts then continues and works to maintain social relationships and enforce community norms of both giving and receiving within the fan community.

Still other fans have interestingly sought to give gifts of symbolic "cookies" to their fellow readers and commenters. One fic writer ends her story with an A.N.:

> Jaja, ich weiß, ziemlich strange / aber ich hoffe ich bekomme trotzdem Reviews für die Story, ihr bekommt auch Kekse *kekshinstell* auf jeden Fall danke fürs lesen ;)
>
> [Yeahyeah, I know, pretty strange / but I hope that I get reviews for the story anyway, you guys also get cookies *placescookies* in any case thanks for reading ;)] (Captain Lifi)

There are no graphics here, hyperlinks, or any way for fans to actually receive physical cookies; rather we see her symbolic gift (with asterisks to denote physical cues that we as online readers cannot see) in the simple phrasing of "*placescookies.*" Any physical cookies would be beside the point: she wants to thank her fans for reading her fic and hopes that she will receive the gift of reviews. She symbolically replicates the gift-giving process that might have taken place had her story been told face-to-face.

In their responses, numerous fans not only note that they "take" these cookies, but leave other symbolic gifts in return: "Na^^ mal ein großes Lob an dich! Das hast du echt geil geschrieben! *schokolade raus hol und dir geb*" [Well^^ much praise for you! You wrote that really awesomely! *takes chocolate out and gives to you* So^^] (Nashima no ryuu). This symbolic gift exchange makes more visible what Hellekson describes in her discussion of fandom's gift economy. These "cookies" and "chocolate" serve no function other than building community between members. Another commenter writes:

> *keks nehm, genüsslich ess* mh danke für die Kekse und für diese story =) ich liebe nämlich märchen musst du wissen und da du meine storys gelesen hast glaube ich nicht dass ich groß erklären muss warum ich deine version vom märchen mag =)
>
> [*takes cookie, eats with pleasure* mh thanks for the cookies and for this story =) I actually love fairy tales, you should know, and since you've read my stories I think I don't have to explain much to you why I like your version of the fairy tale =)] (Hachiko)

Along with the obvious gift of "cookies," we can see another gift exchange taking place. It is clear in the comment that these two fans read and comment on one another's fics showing a continual loop of gifting and receiving through posting fics, reading, and then leaving comments.

Yet while some fan gifts may be overt, such as the dedication of a fic to certain individuals, or even the literal giving of imaginary and symbolic cookies to fellow fans, other gifts may not be as obvious to those outside of fan communities. Tisha Turk notes that fannish gifts do not only include more tangible gifts such as artwork or posting stories, but also the labor that surrounds the objects themselves. It is therefore not only the story or the comment acting as a gift, but the recognition of the amount of time it took for the fan to both engage and to create fan works (1.2). In fact, in service to the equality of fandom members, one of the greatest gifts that a fan can give is their time, and this can be readily seen in leaving reviews. Lengthy reviews within the fandom are not as common as brief comments, yet many of these reviews are, importantly, a recognition of the fic's worth and the fellow fan giving back by letting the writer know that their fic has been read and valued. Fans make these works for other fans to use as entertainment, otherwise there would be little point in posting fics online. Use is the "clearest sign of a gift accepted" (Turk 4.1). Some fans acknowledge the importance of showing that the gift was received just by letting the writer know that their fic was read and enjoyed.

Many comments are not critiques such as those mentioned in the process of norm maintenance previously, but are rather simply statements of "gift accepted." One fan writes:

> Vielleicht liegt es an der Tageszeit (Abend) aber ich bekam mehrere mir Lachanfälle. Ich warte gespannt auf die Fortsetzung! / Ein Grinsen grüßt.
>
> [Maybe it's because of the time of day (evening) but I had multiple fits of laughter. I wait anxiously for the continuation! / I send regards with a smile.] (Cosmodius)

In contrast to an oral tale told where the storyteller can see their audience and their expressions of pleasure or displeasure, fan community members must, entirely out of necessity, constantly be performing—that is: commenting and posting. It is the only way they can render themselves visible online. Thus the number of short, supportive comments demonstrate fans giving back by making themselves visible in order to let the writer know that their gift has been received by an audience.

Although within the fandom constructive criticism couched between statements of praise are the most common way to express the wish for change, there are rare occasions when truly critical comments can be found.

In the comment section of a fic based on "Little Red Riding Hood" (ATU 333) by KathaXD, DasKleineIchBinIch writes a rather scathing review:

> Ich bin ein ziemlich großer Märchen Fan und das ist eine Vergewaltigung an die Märchenwelt [. . .]. Meiner Meinung nach war das ein kläglicher Versuch, lustig zu sein.
>
> —der ebenso kläglich gescheitert ist [. . .]. —Aber sowas ist ja bekanntlich Geschmacksache.
>
> Und ich habe nur meine Meinung geäußert, was mein gutes Recht ist. / Also hoffe ich mal, dass du mich jetzt nicht anfallen wirst.
>
> [I'm a pretty big fairy-tale fan and that is a rape of the fairy-tale world [. . .]. In my opinion that was a pitiful attempt to be funny.
>
> —which just as pitifully failed [. . .]. —But such things are of course a matter of taste.
>
> And I have expressed my opinion, which is my fair right. / So then I hope that you won't attack me.]

Though in her full review DasKleineIchBinIch also details how displeased she is with what she considers to be an atrocious take on "Little Red Riding Hood," at the end of her comment DasKleineIchBinIch writes that while she has a right to express her opinion, fics are often largely a matter of taste. She also calls for a civil conversation with the fic writer, KathaXD. KathaXD's response highlights the recognition that all members of the community can have valid points even if they disagree. KathaXD writes in response:

> ich finde es nicht schlimm, dass dir meine Geschichte nicht gefallen hat, und danke dir, dass du es mir gesagt hast. Ich werde dich ebenfalls nicht anfallen. Es ist, wie du ja gesagt hast, Geschmackssache. Wie gesagt, danke für dein Review. Alles liebe.
>
> [I don't find it bad that you didn't like my story, and I thank you that you told me. I will likewise not attack you. It is, like you say, a matter of taste. Like I said, thanks for your review. All the best.] (KathaXD)

Even a negative review can be seen as a gift of sorts and underscores the expectations for social interaction, though this type of commentary was exceedingly rare (only 0.8% of all comments) within the fandom. DasKleineIchBinIch has let the fic writer know that she received and read the tale even if she did not like it. It is clear from KathaXD's response that she does acknowledge and appreciate the time taken by the commenter to leave a review.

While some fan gifts may be direct, such as dedications to specific fans or even comments back-and-forth, the fannish gift economy is considerably more intricate. While many comments may even appear to be directed at just one individual, they are not available only to that individual, rather the community as a whole and are intended to be read and considered by anyone who encounters them. These gifts are distributed across the community rather than concentrated in a single interaction. Any fan who comes to read fics or comments has access to all information provided by both the author and commenting fans and all interactions help to build community and solidify group norms.

There are many ways in which the Internet has affected the mode of storytelling and the evolution of folklore in small communities such as the "Grimms Märchen" fandom. Internet fan fiction is intercreative storytelling—a hybridization of oral and written modes of language in response to innovations in technology. The very nature of digital storytelling promotes rapid change; because the tales are intercreative, they are also fleeting. Communal narration and the sheer quantity of tales and comments posted online create an oversaturated market of knowledge. It is impossible in some fandoms on *FanFiktion.de* to read every fic posted. Yet this is not how fic reading works in practice and is therefore profoundly beside the point. Fic writers and readers choose to jump around within their fandoms, reading and writing fics of interest to them. Fics are not preserved in curated anthologies nor are they intended to be—they do not stand alone as authoritative works of literature, but rather exist alongside one another as all versions are seemingly invited and authorized. Fans frequently comment and suggest changes, while writers go back to edit and manipulate their stories time and again, maintaining their status as continual works in progress.

By giving and receiving gifts and participating in communal storytelling, fan culture both preserves its own autonomy (Hellekson 117) as well as solidifies the social ties and community-specific meanings of the fandom and the fics within it. These fans adapt their tales collectively to do so. Narratives are cultural tools we use to relate to and situate ourselves in the world around us, and they change over time due not just to cultural but also technological developments (Erstad and Wertsch 22). Importantly, two major characteristics of fan fiction are communal storytelling and the fannish gift economy which should both be taken into consideration in discussions and critiques of the fan fiction genre. The text of fan fiction never captures all of what is going on; it is the vital importance of interaction and community which complete the genre.

The Internet and digital storytelling have certainly offered new ways for folktales to evolve. Internet fan fiction allows new access to the amateur storyteller to write, share, and edit tales on a level which was previously impossible. Fan fiction writers take to digital media to spread their stories and debate them within their communities, using the intercreative nature of their tales as an opportunity to continually discuss, alter, and update their tales together. Sometimes fans even comment to beg each other for more:

> Hey / Diese Geschichte ist sooooooo lol! / Ich könnte beim Lesen nicht aufhören zu lachen / Kannst du bitte noch mehr solcher Geschichten machen??? BITTE BITTE BITTE BITTE BITTE / LG / PS: BITTE BITTE BITTE.
>
> [Hey / this story is sooooooo lol! / I couldn't stop laughing while reading / Can you please write more similar stories??? PLEASE PLEASE PLEASE PLEASE PLEASE / Kind regards / PS: PLEASE PLEASE PLEASE.] (Girlaftermidnight)

By looking into a fairy-tale fan community, we can trace the critical role of communal storytelling in modern fan fiction interpretations of traditional fairy-tale versions as well as the hybridization of oral and written modes of communication online. It is with this voice that people work at shaping anew, changing, and confronting traditional fairy-tale versions in ways that have adapted to methods of online storytelling, and actively engage with the master narratives set forth by collectors such as the Grimms.

CHAPTER 4

# Interpreting the Fairy-Tale Narrative

The fairy tale collection *Children's and Household Tales* by Jacob (1785–1863) and Wilhelm Grimm (1786–1859) has been widely acknowledged to have been edited and changed throughout the lifetimes of the collectors. Yet, the changes that occurred while the Grimms were alive hardly compare to the level of adaptation and reimagining the tales in their collection continue to experience long after the publication of their final 1857 collection. Indeed, Kay Turner and Pauline Greenhill describe the longevity and adaptability of the fairy-tale genre:

> The long-lived history of oral and literary fairy tales offers remarkable testimony to their enduring popularity. Certainly no other folk narrative genre has been as widely told and retold, interpreted and reinterpreted, or translated into other art and performance forms: ballet, folk dance, films, novels, short stories, games, cartoons, and graphic and other visual arts. (2)

While the Grimm anthology presents a polished, consistent narrative of how the Grimms believed the Germanic fairy tale should sound and how Germanic culture should be presented, fan fiction adapting these same tales in German-speaking countries today often confront the holes or inconsistencies in this narrative—showing that no single voice can represent a country and its culture. Modern fan fiction adaptations clearly express that the existence of multiple narratives are necessary to represent a culture.

Though fan fiction is being increasingly studied by scholars, close readings and literary analyses of particular fan texts—that is, fan texts read within context for their own sake rather than as a study of fan culture—remain the exception rather than the rule (Hellekson and Busse, "Fan Fiction" 24). With 88.5% of authors within the fandom self-identifying as women, it is important to investigate how women alter the canon tales. This private sphere is one which largely provides a safe space for women to examine the role the Grimm fairy tales can and should still play in their lives. While studying fans and fan cultures to determine general trends is certainly important, studying the changes and specific confrontations with the canon occurring in fan writing is necessary to show the worth and cultural importance of studying fan fiction as both creative works and important cultural products. Here, I investigate the fan community of "Grimms Märchen," which can be seen as a feminist space responding to patriarchal aspects of the canon texts.

Investigating these works of fan fiction can show, on the one hand, the continuing longevity of the fairy tale and the appropriateness of Internet fan fiction as a medium for fairy-tale adaptation and, on the other hand, the possibilities that fan fiction opens up for women to offer different and even contradictory interpretations of the Grimms' tales. More specifically, I discuss the changes in two works of fan fiction which represent the two largest forms of feminist rewritings within the fandom. The first fic was classified as *bleak* and is based on the Grimm tale "Sneewittchen" ["Snow White"] (ATU 709). It shows a pessimistic view of patriarchal society. Secondly, I focus on an *empowered* fic version of "Dornröschen" ["Little Briar Rose" or "Sleeping Beauty"] (ATU 410) which shows a rewriting in which the female character is empowered to make her own choices. These two rewritings show a clash between the values presented in the canon and more contemporary expectations for women, signaled by the depiction of the outdated expectations of a fairy-tale prince and the rejection of heteronormative marriage as a "happily ever after" ending tale. I intentionally quote the two fics at length to highlight the importance of fan fiction as cultural products which can indicate fears, wishes, and hopes within different communities.

Within an investigation into the adaptable, indeed the "volatile and fluid" (Zipes, *Irresistible Fairy Tale* 22) nature of the fairy-tale genre, I examine how these two fan-fiction versions reimagine classic Grimm tales by complicating gender roles in the traditional tales and creating a space in which women's concerns are brought to the fore. In analyzing the two fics, I have adapted three categories of change common in fan fiction from Henry Jenkins's seminal book on fan culture, *Textual Poachers* (162): (1) moral realignment: representing unjust violence and repositioning classically evil characters in a different light; (2) emotional intensification: delving into psychological aspects of the tales; and (3) refocalization: changing the focus in tales to either promote a new main character or represent characters as more self-sufficient than portrayed in classic German fairy tales.

In using Jenkins's categories of change, I aim to highlight the importance and relevance of both fan studies and fan fiction in the continued investigation and understanding of the fairy-tale genre. Fan fiction, itself a transformative process, invites, and even expects a multiplicity of voices in the interpretation of source texts. Investigating fan fiction that engages with fairy-tale source texts either directly or through employing fairy-tale themes and tropes is an important extension of fairy-tale scholarship. The fairy-tale genre has been repeatedly described as multifaceted and characterized by diversity; it is a genre that "resists a definitive reconstruction of 'original' meaning and even invites contradictory responses" (Haase, "Introduction" *The Reception* 16). Likewise, both fairy-tale and fan-fiction cultures have been described as offering "key critical alternatives to mass-mediated storytelling in their ability to undermine the coercive inevitability of any one ending" (Kustritz, "They All Lived" 6). With these elements already overlapping, bringing fan fiction and fan studies together with fairy-tale studies is the natural merger of two "volatile and fluid" genres in which the diversity and dissonance already inherently present in the fairy tale is actively exploited by fans. Thus, I investigate adaptations of "Snow White" and "Little Briar Rose" to highlight the importance of investigating the medium of fan fiction in exploring the longevity and adaptability of the fairy tale.

## "Ach was solls, die Zeiten haben sich wohl geändert. Jetzt muss man wahrscheinlich umdenken und sich der heutigen Zeit anpassen" [Oh what the hell, times have certainly changed. Now you probably have to rethink everything and adapt to today's times] (Cakolinchen): The Art of Fan Revision

Pauline Greenhill and Sidney Eve Matrix write that "the fairy tale genre has long been a shape shifter and medium breaker" (3), and this medium-breaking ability has enabled the fairy tale to quickly adapt to the Internet and thrive in a medium that is never considered by fans to be final or complete, one that never reaches a definite interpretation. The very existence of fan fiction—of texts that supplement or challenge the source text—suggests that completeness or an end state for tales is actually impossible (Coppa 231). Through the medium of fan fiction, the texts in the "Grimms Märchen" fandom offer their readers different glimpses into the fairy-tale world rather than aiming to provide a single, definitive interpretation; they also offer interpretations that are overwhelmingly written by fans who self-identify as women, representing an online space where women can take control of the fairy-tale genre. As Donald Haase notes, the fairy tales have never given the same answers to readers. What continues to keep fairy tales alive is the "potential to play whatever roles are given them, to have meaning conferred upon them, to give an answer to whoever asks the question" (Introduction 21).

Where the nineteenth-century fairy-tale collection *Children's and Household Tales* sought to create consistent representations of the traditional fairy tale, providing a narrative that could ostensibly connect bourgeois communities together and define a German national character,[1] the fandom on *FanFiktion.de* encourages and celebrates a multiplicity of voices. As demonstrated in Chapter 3, interaction on the website is not limited to registered users; anyone with Internet access and fluency in German can participate on the site ("Nutzungsbedingungen"). Fan-fiction writers can be said to be "transformative fans"—individuals who are critical of the media they consume. Because of the crucial nature of collaborative storytelling, feedback, and the fannish gift economy to the fan fiction genre, in discussions of the pieces later, I work to discuss them within this context.

As noted previously and discussed in more depth in Chapter 2, the *FanFiktion.de* fandom consists almost entirely of people who self-identified as women writers and could thus be said to be a space where women feel comfortable reimagining and rethinking the fairy-tale genre. Whereas women have traditionally been associated with the fairy tale—such as with

1 See, for example, works in English by Jack Zipes, Maria Tatar, and Marina Warner, who have detailed the changes made by the Grimms during the collection and editing processes to conform the tales to nineteenth-century bourgeois ideals and expectations.

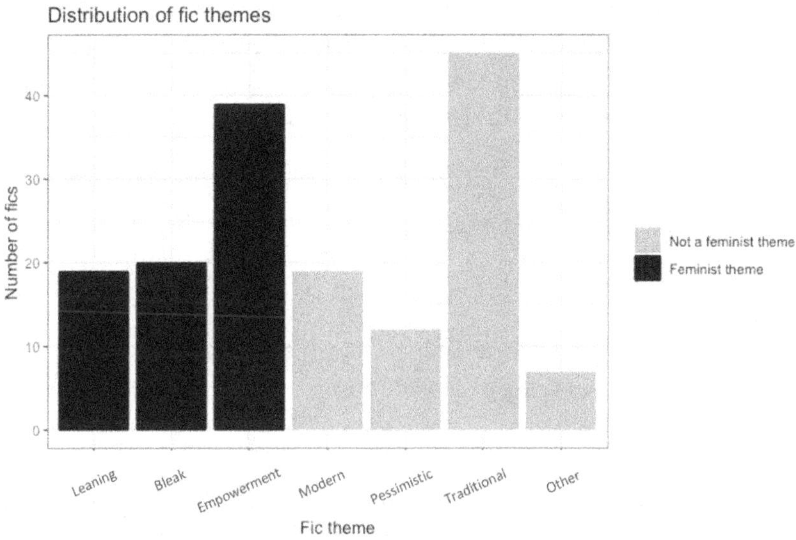


Figure 6. Graph: Distribution of fic themes.

the oral tradition of nursemaids and spinners—the canonical tales such as the Grimms', Charles Perrault's, and Hans Christian Andersen's are overwhelmingly male authored. And, in these pieces of fan fiction, women transform the canonical tales to be more answerable to their interests. Approximately half of the fics within the fandom directly or indirectly discuss questions of a woman's (in)ability to consent to male advances as can be seen in Figure 6.

On *FanFiktion.de*, the writers themselves identify their fandom as "Grimms Märchen," and it is because of this self-identification that I compare the fics that follow with the 1857[2] versions of the Grimm tales. Though many of the tales on the site clearly refer to versions by Perrault, Andersen, and Walt Disney, the fics have all been subsumed on the site under the larger title of "Grimms Märchen." For these fan writers, the Grimms have come to represent the *true* or even *original* interpretations of fairy tales—even if the version of the tales that the fics are based on does not stem from the

2 The most widely read edition of the Grimms' tales.

Grimm collection. Jack Zipes writes that the Grimms' tales and their interpretations have become "the cultural bread and butter" of most children in the West (*Fairy Tales* 66), and Heinz Rölleke has likewise noted that, since the middle of the nineteenth century, Germans have grown up learning to read with the Grimms' tales (12). This overgeneralization in the fandom attests to the massive success and influence that the Grimm editions have had on representations and expectations for the fairy-tale genre.

## "Sneewittchen" / ["Snow White"] and the Dangers of Patriarchal Expectations

My first comparison, "Schneewittchen" ["Snow White"] out of the series "Märchen—wie es wirklich war" [Fairy Tales—how it really was] by farfalla91 (accessed 2020), represents a subset of feminist rewritings within the fandom which I labeled in my study as *bleak*—or fics which highlight the toll that patriarchal societies exact from women. Fics in this category totaled 26% of fics which were labeled as having feminist themes. Farfalla91's fic shows many deviations from the 1857 Grimm edition of "Snow White"—emphasizing the roles and struggles of female, rather than male, characters and focusing on the notion of female solidarity. The Grimm version describes Snow White and the prince's wedding after the evil stepmother arrives:

> At first she would not go to the wedding at all, but she had no peace, and must go to see the young Queen. And when she went in she knew Snow White; and she stood still with rage and fear, and could not stir. But iron slippers had already been put upon the fire, and they were brought in with tongs, and set before her. Then she was forced to put on the red-hot shoes, and dance until she dropped down dead. (194)

The Grimm tale presents what has become a classic trope of maternal evil. The queen, introduced in this version as Snow White's stepmother, instantly cues the reader to see her as a depiction of rage and jealousy toward a young rival. Indeed, Maria Tatar writes that "folklorists would be hard pressed to name a single good stepmother, for in fairy tales the very title 'stepmother' pins the badge of iniquity on a figure. One can safely argue that the phrase *wicked stepmother*, which has a nearly formulaic ring to it, is pleonastic" (141). The stepmother in the Grimms' "Snow White" adheres to her formulaic role. The goal of destroying her more beautiful stepdaughter guides all her actions, including her final moment of jealousy and hatred that brings her to visit her stepdaughter's wedding uninvited. Sandra Gilbert and Susan Gubar note that "the central action of the tale—indeed, its only real action—arises from the relationship between these two women." "Snow White," they write, is a tale detailing the trials of the angel-woman, Snow White, and the monster-woman, the queen (26).

Farfalla91's version, however, describes a different story. Importantly, the tale depicts the queen as having a strong relationship with her own mother, and she uses the famed magic mirror to converse with her mother whenever she wishes. The queen is described as taking the gift of the mirror only "unter Tränen" [under tears] as she parted "von ihrer lieben Mutter" [from her loving mother]. After the queen marries the widower king, farfalla91's tale states,

> Die Königin hoffte, für dieses Kind eine ebenso gute Mutter zu sein, wie ihre eigene Mutter es für sie gewesen war.
>
> [The queen hoped to be as good a mother for this child as her own mother had been for her.]

Rather than presenting the queen as a "flesh-eating witch" figure who desires to eat her stepdaughter's lungs and liver, a maternal figure gone bad (Warner 310), farfalla91's version presents an image of true maternal care. This depiction of the stepmother imaginatively demonstrates how the roles of these female characters could be improved through cooperation and care rather than competition and jealousy.

In the fic, Snow White, who is presented as a spoiled princess, runs away from home of her own accord because she tires of the queen's emphasis on ruling the people of her kingdom benevolently rather than spending the wealth of the kingdom on clothing and jewels. The stepmother uses her magic mirror to watch over Snow White even when the princess is away. By assuring herself that no harm will come to Snow White while she is out in the world on her own, the queen waits for the time when Snow White has matured enough to be trusted with ruling over an entire kingdom. After living with the dwarves and learning what it is to work for oneself, Snow White has satisfactorily shown the queen that she has changed enough to take her place as ruler of the kingdom. This characterization of Snow White juxtaposes the fic version with the stereotyped Snow White in the canon as an innocent and pure young woman, by allowing her to have faults and learn from them. She is portrayed as multidimensional and thus, more human.

As the queen travels to the dwarves' home to bring Snow White back to the castle with her, the queen learns that Snow White has suddenly agreed to marry a prince she has only just met, and the queen attends the wedding despite not being invited. The adapted tale reads,

> Als sie nach der Zeremonie Schneewittchen gegenübertrat, um ihre Glückwünsche zu überbringen und diese ihre Stiefmutter erkannte, fing die junge Braut an zu weinen. Sie lief auf die Königin zu und umarmte sie.
>
> "Warum bist du gekommen?" fragte sie unter Tränen. "Du bist hier nicht sicher. Eigentlich ist hier niemand sicher."
>
> Erst jetzt bemerkte die Königin die Blutergüsse an Schneewittchens Armen, die nur dürftig vom Ärmel aus Spitze bedeckt wurden. Schneewittchen bemerkte den Blick und lachte freudlos. "Glaub mir, meine Arme sehen noch harmlos aus."
>
> [When the stepmother approached Snow White after the ceremony to wish her well, Snow White began to cry as she recognized her stepmother. She ran over to the queen and hugged her.
>
> "Why did you come?" she asked through tears. "You aren't safe here. No one is safe here."
>
> For the first time the queen noticed the bruises on Snow White's arms, which were only meagerly covered by the edges of her sleeves. "Believe me, my arms look completely innocuous (*harmlos*)."]

Later, the tale details that the prince has abused Snow White and that she fears for her stepmother's safety.

Feminist revisions of fairy tales tend to be "confrontational and provocative" (Zipes, "Struggle" 185), and here farfalla91's tale confronts the stereotypical expectation that happiness for women results in heteronormative marriage as well as the male exploitation of Snow White in the Grimm version. In the canon tale, Snow White, among many other women characters, is treated as a prize for the prince in the end. As Grimm tales often model rewarding passive and silent women (Jarvis 106), here the scene explores what the price of such passivity can be. Upon seeing the bruises, the stepmother vows to rescue her stepdaughter, but the prince learns of their plan. He speaks with the stepmother, and we learn of his sadistic intentions:

> Der Prinz lachte freundlich […] "Würdet Ihr mir die Ehre eines Tanzes erweisen?" […]
>
> "Nur zu gerne," antwortete sie deshalb und ergriff den dargebotenen Arm des Prinzen. Dieser führte sie zum Feuer, das in einem großen Kamin brannte.
>
> "Ich habe Euch ganz besondere Tanzschuhe vorbereiten lassen," plauderte er, während sie sich einen Weg durch die Menge bahnten.
>
> "Oh, ich tanze gerne in meinen eigenen Schuhen," antwortete die Königin, die sich fragte, was er wohl im Schilde führte.
>
> Auf ein Winken des Prinzen holte ein Diener mit einer Zange eiserne Schuhe aus dem Feuer, welche vor Hitze glühten.
>
> "Was glaubt Ihr, wie lange könnt Ihr darin tanzen, bevor Ihr tot umfallt?", überlegte der Prinz. "Eine Minute? Oder doch eine Stunde?" […]
>
> "Zwei Goldtaler, dass sie keinen einzigen Schritt machen kann!", brüllte jemand, und im nächsten Moment war die Luft angefüllt von Stimmengewirr. Wetten wurden angeboten und entgegengenommen, Vermutungen geäußert, wie sich solche Schuhe wohl anfühlen mochten, und vor allem gelacht. […]
>
> Zwei Wachen hielten nun die Königin fest, während der Prinz sich persönlich herunterbeugte und […] stopften ihre Füße mit Gewalt in die glühenden Schuhe. Halb wahnsinnig vor Schmerz stolperte sie hier hin und dort hin, bis der Prinz sie einfing.
>
> "Musik!", rief er, und als die Musikanten wieder aufspielten, wirbelte er die schreiende Frau durch den ganzen Ballsaal. Die Gäste applaudierten und johlten, als die Königin schließlich zu Boden ging. Einzig Schneewittchen stand in ihrem Brautkleid mitten unter den Gästen und weinte.
>
> [The prince laughed kindly […] "would you give me the honor of a dance?" […]
>
> "I would only be too glad," she replied and took the arm the prince had offered her. He led her to a fire which burned in a large fireplace.
>
> "I have some very special dance shoes prepared for you," he mentioned while they made their way through the crowd.

> "Oh, I like dancing in my own shoes," answered the queen and asked herself what he was up to.
>
> On a gesture from the prince, a servant fetched the iron shoes from the fire which were glowing from heat.
>
> "What do you think, how long can you dance in those before you fall over dead?" the prince pondered. "A minute? Or perhaps an hour?" [...]
>
> "Two gold coins that she can't even take one step!" someone howled and, in the next moment, the air was filled with the buzz of voices. Bets were offered and exchanged, and speculations were made of just how such shoes might feel and, first and foremost, was laughter. [...]
>
> Two guards now held the queen tightly while the prince personally bent down [...] and violently stuffed her feet in the glowing shoes. [...]
>
> Half-delirious from pain, she stumbled here and now there until the prince caught her.
>
> "Music!" he yelled and, as the musicians began to play once again, he whirled the screaming woman through the entire ballroom. The guests applauded and jeered as the queen suddenly fell to the ground. Alone, Snow White stood in her wedding dress among the guests and cried.]

This fic displays instances of emotional intensification and moral realignment. There is extreme emotional intensification with the character of Snow White in both her reaction when she sees her stepmother, as well as at the end of the tale when she is forced to witness her stepmother's death. Rather than simply state that the stepmother must dance to death in red-hot iron shoes as in the Grimm version, farfalla91's tale depicts the moral debasement of the prince and of the guests at the party who jest, jeer, and place bets on how long the stepmother will be able to stay alive. The fic details the final, terrible moments of the stepmother's life and how much she suffered. Many fan writers see their readings and interpretations as "teasing out the subtext" (Hellekson and Busse, "Fan Identity" 76)—that is, in this case farfalla91 teases out the exploitation of Snow White in the Grimm tale. Fans often read the source text against its historical and cultural context (76), and here the weight of living in a society that demands female obedience and passivity is brought to the fore.

There is also moral realignment in the important fact that it is the prince who is evil. Likewise, the stepmother has been cast in the role of a savior, though she is not successful. It is important to note that, in the Grimm tales, princes are often of noble character and save princesses from hopeless situations. In tales like "Cinderella" (ATU 510A), "Snow White," "Sleeping Beauty," and "Rapunzel" (ATU 310), the princess in some way or other feared for her life but is rescued in the end by a loving and well-intentioned prince. In classic Grimm tales such as "Snow White," the heroine must learn to be "passive, obedient, self-sacrificing, hardworking, patient, and straight-laced," and her happiness depends on how well she conforms to patriarchal rule (Zipes, *Fairy Tales* 69). Likewise, heroes are presented as dominant figures and work to protect the virtues of humbled "if not humiliated" female characters (Zipes, *Fairy Tales* 150). In the Grimms' tale, as Snow White learns these traits, she is rescued by a prince and rewarded for her adherence to white patriarchal norms—Snow White is beautiful, domestic, passive, and incomplete without her male rescuer.

Farfalla91's tale details a similar journey: one of a young woman learning to be passive and obedient, hardworking, and straight-laced. Like her fellow Grimm heroines, farfalla91's Snow White seeks salvation through heteronormative marriage. Yet, despite fully conforming to these expectations, she is not united at the end with a male savior. Perhaps in a perverted attempt to protect Snow White's virtues and to ensure that she remain passive, the prince succeeds in humiliating her into obedience at the end of the tale as she is forced to watch her attempted savior, this time a woman, die in agony.

The Grimm version of the tale presents a scene of seemingly justified violence at its conclusion. The greedy and, as is pointed out in the tale, "godless" stepmother is punished for her wicked life and the maltreatment of her stepdaughter. Snow White is rewarded for her good, obedient nature and kind heart by marrying a prince of wealth and high status—the supposed pinnacle of feminine desire in the canon. The reader is given the satisfaction of a conclusion where, in the end, all is as it should be as the evil queen has been punished and the kindhearted woman now rules beside her husband. In farfalla91's version however, the final scene is of senseless violence, one that does not provide the reader with a simple solution. The reader is left with a glimpse of a corrupt world in which the good are not only punished, but tortured, and the wicked are rewarded.

If there is any real love in the fic, it is between Snow White and her stepmother, yet we see that this love is no match for the overpowering cruelty of the prince. The prince is free to live and torture, and the tale ends with the ominous scene of Snow White, sobbing in the middle of a jeering crowd. Her father, similar to so many Grimm tales, is silently absent from the entire story. There is no simple resolution, and the reader is left to imagine the life Snow White will lead while married to an abusive and murderous man or perhaps hope for her eventual escape—though the prince's cruelty does not suggest such a task would be easily realized. This fan fiction presents a rejection of such clear-cut morals as provided in the Grimm version with the added affirmation that the world is often a senseless one in which the just are punished and the unjust rule—drawing attention this time to female suffering in a patriarchal world where women are expected to place their happiness in the hands of powerful men.

Stories such as "Snow White" are continually retold because they have some sort of resonance in the storyteller's life. Fairy tales lend themselves so easily to revision and reinterpretation because they consist of "chaotic symbolic codes" that have become highly ambiguous—and this ambiguity invites diverse responses (Haase, "Response" 235). A story that is continually retold does not necessarily need to be well constructed or even well told, but it likely does need a compelling plotline that leaves ample room for interpretation. And here fan fiction and the fairy tale come to a united front, as fan fiction can be understood only through an idea of supplementation and reinterpretation. Its very existence refuses an illusion of continuity of the source text—seeking to "fill in the gaps" by acting as if all readings of the source text were equally possible (Willis 166–168), indeed not just inviting but expecting continual reinterpretations and diverse responses.

Additionally, the medium of fan fiction allows versions of the Grimms' tales, such as farfalla91's, to potentially reach international audiences—which likewise encourages communal storytelling. While the changes farfalla91 has made may be interesting on their own, the responses to her tale show the importance of the fan-fiction community and its dependence on participation. Fan communities are often self-aware of the roles the texts play as transformative works (Hellekson and Busse, "Fan Identity" 76). In the comment section, other fans openly engage with the idea of changing and updating tales. While the average fic in the fandom garners between one and six fan comments, farfalla91's received nine, showing an above-average popularity for the fandom. One fan writes,

> Man merkt, dass du dir wirklich Gedanken um alle Details, die man verändern muss, gemacht hast und überhaupt … es macht alles so viel Sinn, dass man glauben möchte, dass sich die Märchen in Wirklichkeit genau so zugetragen haben und nur durch Gerüchte zu dem geworden sind, wie man sie heute kennt:)
>
> [One can see that you have really considered all of the details that need to be changed and really … everything makes so much sense that one could believe that the fairy tales actually happened this way in reality and it was only through rumor that they became what we know today:)] ("Reviews")

In farfalla91's response to this comment, she addresses the idea of bias in the source text and expresses interest in exploring other possibilities of the stories—ones that are multifaceted and with morals that are not so clear-cut. In this online format, we can likewise see aspects of folkloristic retellings. Fan fiction can function as the cultural equivalent of collective storytelling (Hellekson and Busse, "Fan Fiction" 21) because fans engage in metadiscussions of the changes that have been made—often suggesting further changes or alterations in the comment sections. Farfalla91 writes here (also referencing her fics based on "Little Red Riding Hood" [ATU 333], as well as "Hansel and Gretel" [ATU 327A]),

> Du hast mein Hauptanliegen erkannt: Eine Geschichte zu schreiben, aus der sich das bekannte Märchen hätte ableiten können, sei es, weil sie nur mündlich weitererzählt wird (da wird dann aus einem menschlichen "bösen Wolf" schon mal ein tierischer) oder weil nur eine Seite der Geschichte erzählt wird (sodass eine freundliche Kräuterfrau zur bösen Hexe wird).
>
> [You recognized my main point: To write a story that the known fairy tales could have originated from, be it because they were only orally passed down (here a human "evil wolf" becomes an actual animal) or because only one side of the story is told (so that a friendly herbalist becomes an evil witch).] ("Reviews")

The two fans directly address the changes and variation inherent in oral storytelling and suggest that eventually details change, and, out of complicated matters, simple explanations arise. The comments show a wish to (re)introduce differing or perhaps more complex aspects of the stories than the Grimm versions display, and the fans seem to recognize themselves as a part of that process—explicitly discussing the fairy-tale genre itself, as well as how and why one might renegotiate themes and plot. Farfalla91 is transparent in her changes, actively discussing the implications of her alterations with fellow fans. Other fans likewise express enjoyment that the characters in farfalla91's texts were no longer unidimensional portrayals of good and evil. They note that they came to feel sympathy for Rumpelstiltskin (ATU 500), as well as the witch in "Hansel and Gretel," or with a version of "Sleeping Beauty" that portrays the princess not just as sweet and innocent, but with malevolent characteristics as well ("Reviews").

Fan texts often work to expand the canon text in many directions by focusing on media that have "expandability built into their structure" (Stein 247). The conversation between farfalla91 and a fellow fan highlights the view of fan fiction expanding in potentially infinite directions within, of course, the constraints of the fandom. Farfalla91 does not claim to have written a definitive version, but simply one that *could* represent another side to the Grimm tale. Every fairy-tale retelling is a transformation as well as but a fragment (Greenhill and Brydon 136), and farfalla91 seems to recognize the fragmentary status of her tale. This recognition is one which mirrors other fics and commentary in the fandom as fans actively discuss their roles in the adaptation of the fairy tale. Writers in the fandom reframe, repurpose, and recreate characters, events, and settings to open up the source text to myriad interpretations. Importantly, these interpretations are overwhelmingly written by women who are often confronting the portrayal of female characters in the Grimm tales.

## Rewriting "Dornröschen" / [*"Little Briar Rose"*] to Showcase Women's Agency

My next comparison is between the Grimm 1857 version of "Dornröschen" ["Little Briar Rose"/ "Sleeping Beauty"] and Sturmklang's "Once upon a

Bloody Time: Hier ist die Dorne, aber wo bleibt das Röschen?" ["Here is the thorn, but where is the little rose?"] (accessed 2020). Sturmklang's fic represents an additional subset of feminist rewritings within the fandom which were labeled in my study as *empowering*—or fics which highlight women who are able to free themselves from patriarchal power in positive ways. This group totaled 50% of fics categorized as feminist retellings. In the Grimm version of "Little Briar Rose" when the prince is introduced, he is described as a fearless character determined to save a cursed princess:

> After long, long years a King's son came again to that country, and heard an old man talking about the briar hedge, and that a castle was said to stand behind it in which a wonderfully beautiful princess, named Briar Rose, had been asleep for a hundred years; and that the King and Queen and the whole court were asleep likewise. He had heard, too, from his grandfather, that many kings' sons had already come, and had tried to get through the thorny hedge, but they had remained sticking fast in it, and had died a pitiful death. Then the youth said, "I am not afraid, I will go and see the beautiful Briar Rose." (179)

He will stop at nothing to rescue her. In the face of nearly certain death, the prince is convinced that his strength and goodwill will prevail, and his quest will be successful even where others before him have failed. In some way, he sees himself as exceptional—the one who is finally worthy of rescuing the imprisoned and enchanted princess. The reader accepts at the beginning of the tale that the prince will be the remarkable one who makes it through the thorn hedge, as classic fairy tales do not tell the stories of the "many kings' sons" who failed but sing the praises of the few who succeed. From reading this description, it is also clear that the Grimm tale "Little Briar Rose" focuses primarily on the prince and his journey. The story, although named after Briar Rose, celebrates the prince who seeks out adventure and is rewarded with a passive, silent, and hardworking wife. Similar to the prince in "Snow White," the "Little Briar Rose" prince is presented as a male savior figure—the one who will be able to bring about Briar Rose's "happily ever after."

In Sturmklang's version, however, the prince is described rather differently—complicating the portrayal of masculinity as presented in the Grimm tale. The new story begins:

> Es war einmal … / … schon wieder so ein lächerlicher Prinz, der versuchte, eine Prinzessin zu retten und sie zu heiraten.
>
> [Once upon a time … / … there was once again such a ridiculous prince who tried to rescue a princess and marry her.]

Already it gives the reader the image of an unnecessary quest, and the tone of the tale suggests that the prince will most likely fail to win over the princess. Sturmklang's tale begins with the traditional fairy-tale opening of "es war einmal," [once upon a time], but uses double ellipses and a line break, an exaggerated hesitation, to show that she intends to parody the image of the exceptional prince being rewarded with a princess for his efforts. The fairy tale has served as a primary site not only for asserting but also for subverting ideologies of gender (Haase, "Preface" vii). In its opening lines, this version presents a clash of values with the Grimm tale and promises such subversion of traditional fairy tale expectations. Sturmklang's tale portrays the old trope of a gallant prince rescuing a helpless princess as a tired one, not relatable to modern life. The princess does not need saving, the tale suggests already in its opening sentence. Marriage does not need to be her "happily ever after." Here, the tale engages in an overt discussion of gender role expectations in canonical fairy tales.

In the Grimm version when the prince finally sees the innocent and pure Briar Rose, we read the description of a passive princess who silently awaits her rescuer as she is frozen in time:

> There [Briar Rose] lay, so beautiful that he could not turn his eyes away; and he stooped down and gave her a kiss. But as soon as he kissed her, Briar Rose opened her eyes and awoke, and looked at him quite sweetly. / Then they went down together, and the King awoke, and the Queen, and the whole court, and they looked at each other in great astonishment …. And then the marriage of the King's son with Briar Rose was celebrated with all splendor, and they lived contented to the end of their days. (180)

The prince has succeeded in his endeavors. Here we see again that the tale focuses primarily on the journey of the prince: Briar Rose is described only through his gaze and his assessment of her as a fitting bride. His persistence has been rewarded, and Briar Rose has been freed from an evil curse. They live happily ever after—and he has not only been her savior, but the entire court's, as well. Yet, while the tale presents the success of the brave and fearless prince, it is one that has been described as presenting a "marvelous model of prudence for young women" (Zipes, *Fairy Tales* 52). Indeed, Kimberly J. Lau describes the more sinister implications of Dornröschen/Sleeping Beauty as a model aimed toward socializing girls. Like the Grimms' "Snow White," "Sleeping Beauty" emphasizes expectations for women under white patriarchal norms:

> Sleeping Beauty (ATU 410) is the quintessential Grimms girl. Deep in slumber, she is nothing but a pretty face, a supple body there for the gazing, there for the taking. She is passive, yielding, available, and—of course—silent, enchantingly incapable of speaking her mind, much less voicing any resistance to the hero's advances. (121)

In the Grimm version of the tale, Briar Rose directly speaks on one occasion only, when she discovers the cursed spindle—the object that will doom her to a deathlike slumber and silence. The only time Briar Rose makes a decision of her own, to touch the spindle, the decision brings about the downfall of the entire court.

In Sturmklang's version, their meeting ends quite differently. Much like the Grimm tale, the prince believes himself to be heroically rescuing an innocent and helpless princess. Once he finally sees her, however, she is not sleeping as he expects but walking freely around the castle. In Sturmklang's version, the story of Briar Rose is reimagined to center on its titular character and highlight her agency. This version of the scene consists almost entirely of Briar Rose's direct speech, and it is the prince whose speech is restricted. In the text, the prince speaks on but a mere four occasions and only in short questions directed toward Briar Rose, asking her for clarification. When she realizes the prince was expecting her to be peacefully asleep, Briar Rose exclaims,

> "Ich hatte es satt, dieses ganze langweilige Leben! Ständig sind irgendwelche Narren um mich herumscharwenzelt und diese Feen—schrecklich! Ständig betüttelten sie mich, wollten mich in irgendwelche furchtbaren, pinken Kleider quetschen und nie hatte ich mal eine ruhige Minute. Meine einzige Freundin wurde dann, ironischerweise, die dunkle Fee. Ich hab mich bei ihr entschuldigt, weil man sie bei den Einladungen übergangen hatte. Sie hat mir dann geholfen. Sie hat alle in Schlaf

> versetzt und die Dornenhecke entstehen lassen und ich kann endlich alles tun und lassen, was ich will—und ich hab meine Ruhe!" Sie klang sehr zufrieden.
>
> ["I got so sick of this whole boring life! Constantly some idiots bowing and scraping around me and these fairies—horrible! Constantly coddling me and wanting to squeeze me into some sort of terrible, pink clothes and I never had a quiet moment. My only friend became, ironically, the dark fairy. I apologized to her for not being sent an invitation to the party. Then she helped me. She made everyone go to sleep, made the wall of thorns grow and I can finally do what I want—and I have my peace!" She sounded very pleased.]

Exasperated, Briar Rose details the gender norms that were thrust upon her by patriarchal rule. Rather than relishing the wealth, jewels, and expensive clothing fitting of her status as royalty, Briar Rose describes herself as limited by them. This fic is an example of refocalization. What was the tale of a heroic man rescuing a princess and marrying her so that she could be happy has become one in which the princess has grown tired of conforming to white patriarchal expectations. The fairy is likewise not a bad or evil fairy, but simply a "dark" fairy who was upset due to a miscommunication. Whereas the canon tale was focused on the journey and trials of the prince, Sturmklang's version focuses on the difficult life of the princess, which, before the thorn hedge grew to protect her—through the help of her new, female, friend—was defined by outdated notions of white femininity. She no longer wishes to be the stereotypical princess in pink, surrounded by good fairies granting her the attributes of the supposedly perfect white woman: beauty, grace, an even temper, musicality, ability to dance perfectly, and a beautiful voice (Zipes, *Fairy Tales* 39). She longs for her own life, free of the immense demands and expectations placed on a royal woman. Rather than having her life dictated by others, she wishes to finally live a life of her own. For her to achieve this, there is no room for a prince who is still taken with the ideals of stories written in the 1850s, as the prince in Sturmklang's tale appears to be.

Sturmklang's fic articulates a particular worldview—one that rejects the gender roles of the canon—and, by performing it openly on the site, her fic invites new perspectives and allows for a transformation of existing perceptions. Fan fiction is always both original and derivative. That is, Sturmklang's text exists alongside the Grimms' version; as the fic remains in constant conversation with the Grimms, it can actively analyze the source or canon text. Together, she and fellow fans discuss her changes and what it means to shift the emphasis away from the prince and onto the princess, shaping the tales within their community through participation rather than passive observance.

Sturmklang's fic was very popular on the site, receiving 15 user comments, and the agreement and enthusiasm over what she has written are obvious, as fans directly engage with her challenge to stereotypical character and gender roles. One fan writes in the reviews,

> Wie sich die "Prinzessinnen" einfach selbstständig machen, das ist einfach super! Diese Bissige Art, die man von ihnen sonst nicht wirklich gewohnt ist, einfach zum totlachen XDD vor allem diese (Achtung Sarkasmus) überaus schlauen Prinzchen, einfach toll;)
>
> [How the "princesses" have made themselves independent is great! This snappy manner, which one is not normally used to, is hilarious XDD especially these (warning sarcasm) exceedingly smart little princes, simply terrific;)] ("Reviews")

The fans continue to remark on the agency of the princess in the tale. One fan writes simply and energetically: "FRAUENPOWER!!!^^ Einfach toll!" [WOMEN'S POWER!!!^^ / Simply wonderful!] Another comments, "Woah! / Ich finds toll, wie du den 3 Prinzessinnen hilfst den Prinzen mal ihre Meinung zu sagen!" [Woah! / I find it wonderful how you helped the 3 princesses to finally speak their minds to the princes!] ("Reviews"). No longer does the princess sit in a tower while waiting to be rescued; it is the prince who is described as lacking agency—driven merely by the tradition of the canon tale with no real will of his own. Indeed, in this tale, it is the prince, not Briar Rose, who is commanded to fall asleep. In the concluding lines of the fic, Sturmklang parodies both the fate of Briar Rose in the Grimm tale as well as the traditional German-language fairy tale ending of "und wenn sie nicht gestorben sind, dann leben sie noch heute" [and if they have not died, they are still alive today]. In the concluding lines we read of the prince's fate:

> Die Augen fielen ihm zu und das letzte, was er sah, bevor er—für wahrscheinlich immer!—einschlief [...], war das grinsende Gesicht von Dornröschen.

> Und wenn er nicht gestorben ist, dann schläft er auch noch heute!
>
> [His eyes closed and the last thing he saw before he fell asleep—perhaps forever!—[…] was the grinning face of Briar Rose.
>
> And if he hasn't died, he's still asleep today!]

These two writers' adaptations reframe, repurpose, and recreate characters, events, and settings within a fan-fiction community that prides itself on an abundance of fairy-tale reconceptualizations. The fics within the fandom display this process in a medium that lends itself well to the continual change and reinterpretation of fairy tales. These fairy-tale fan fictions showcase the enduring popularity and elasticity of the genre.

Fannish writing thrives online because of a sense of productive freedom born of the transformations of published materials that fan writers are a part of. The two tales that I discussed present creative outlets by emphasizing pastiche, appropriation, and intertextuality within the constraints of working with and on published materials (Stein and Busse 193–195). In this way, the two fan writers do not seem to be outright rejecting the Grimms' tales—indeed, their fan texts could not exist without them and depend on their continued existence. The fandom likewise represents varied feminist responses to the portrayals of white patriarchy in the Grimms' tales. Though the Grimms' fairy tales are filled with female characters, their representation is often one of passivity and obedience. Here the two fan texts highlight the dangers of a patriarchal objectification ("Snow White"), as well as the reclaiming of female voice and agency ("Here is the thorn").

It is with fan fiction that a multitude of stories that previously would have remained within small circles of family and friends are able to potentially reach international online audiences. Individually, the two fics presented here show the fascinating longevity and flexibility of the fairy tale beyond the realm of literature in print and mass culture. Taken collectively, the fics within the fandom are symptomatic of the struggles and priorities of the communities to which the writers belong. When looking at how the fics themselves respond to one other, as well as how the fans receive and change them, we can arrive at a better understanding of the ever-changing nature of the fairy tale and of a feminist space where women can reclaim and reconsider the roles canonical fairy tales play in their lives.

CHAPTER 5

# Fairy-Tale Fan Fiction and Questions of Women's Consent

Despite collection, editorial, and publication activities which have long been dominated by men, fairy tales are strongly tied to women. Women are often represented as oral sources, and numerous figures as well as main characters in fairy tales are women and girls—think for instance of Little Red Riding Hood (ATU 333), Sleeping Beauty (ATU 410), Cinderella (ATU 510A), and Rapunzel (ATU 310). In Western canonical versions, women are often the inspirations for storyteller images which adorn the frontispiece or populate the imaginations of their listeners and readers, or else they are the silent, suffering heroines in the tales themselves (Bottigheimer, "Fertility" 49). As Shawn Jarvis notes, "it is actually specious to suggest that there has been a 'male domination of the genre.' What there has been is a male domination of the *canonical* genre" (120). Often the silent, beautiful prize for valiant adventurers and princes, female characters in traditional stories transcribed and edited by men are reduced to the role of waiting patiently to be rescued or else surviving difficult trials to be taught "proper" white feminine behavior. As Perrault reminds us at the end of "The Sleeping Beauty in the Wood:": "For girls to wait awhile, so they may wed / a loving husband, handsome, rich, and kind: / that's natural enough, I'd say; / but just the same, to stay in bed / a hundred years asleep—you'll never find such patience in a girl today" (96). Yet with modern fairy-tale revisions, women have "more consistently and en masse worked to re-flesh the fairy tale" (Bacchilega, *Postmodern* 48).

In this chapter I explore the metanarrative engagement between the "Grimms Märchen" fandom and the fairy-tale genre as a space for feminist critique. I look specifically at how feminist reimaginings foreground the often-problematic treatment of feminine consent (or lack thereof) to male advances in traditional fairy-tale versions of "Rotkäppchen" ["Little Red Riding Hood"] and "Dornröschen" ["Sleeping Beauty"/ "Little Briar Rose"]. While there are fic versions of 35 different tales within the fandom, revisions of these two are by far the most prevalent. There are 31 different versions of "Little Red Riding Hood"—nearly 20% of all narratives in the fandom. This is a high proportion considering that the majority of tales within the fandom (even including famous tales such as "Rapunzel" and "Hansel and Gretel" [ATU 327A]) have five or fewer fics. It is certainly of note that a tale which has repeatedly been described not only as a narrative about rape but also one where the victim must bear responsibility for her own sexual violation (Zipes, *Stick* 28) would be the most prevalent fic within the fandom. Likewise the titular character in "Little Briar Rose," the second most prevalent fic with 18 different versions has often been described as the "quintessential Grimms girl" (Lau 121) who foregrounds the passivity often demanded of white women in patriarchal societies.

Fic reimaginings are often not as concerned with the plot of the canon tales, but rather what the tales mean for the present. Here one can see a refocus in the tales not just on feminist retellings, but specifically on women's consent and the (in)ability of women's voices to be heard and legitimated both within the canon tales and in the broader societies of which fandom members are a part. Indeed, many of these fics function as a fictional corollary to real-life discussions of assault and violation, detailing how women and girls have to live among predators in patriarchal societies. I highlight specifically this refocus of canon tales as these fics have been posted after the beginning of the globally influential "#metoo" movement aiming to give voice and credibility to victims of sexual assault and harassment. It is of no wonder, then, that the two most prevalent canon tales for fics in the fandom are ones which portray sexual assault and delegitimation of a woman's right to choose.

## "Dornröschen" / ["Little Briar Rose"] and Male Responses to Women Speaking

It is impossible to determine all texts or different media that influence a particular fairy-tale retelling, since even when authors explicitly mention their pre-texts, this does not preclude other influences (Joosen 10). Yet the fics discussed throughout this chapter share a defining relationship with the canon versions as shaped by the Grimms and Perrault and offer critiques and new perspectives of the canon. While they certainly have become the foundational versions in Western society, the Grimm and Perrault versions obscure the rich tradition of storytelling in which tales are retold and changed continually. Though as fic writers are participating in the fairy-tale tradition of retelling tales, they show a reclaiming of the fairy-tale tradition. Fan fiction "extends and replicates the practices of collective authorship common to many earlier fairy-tale cultures" (Kustritz 249). Investigating these works within the field of folklore shows the validity of Internet fan fiction as a medium for fairy-tale adaptation. The possibilities that fan fiction opens up for women allows them to offer tales of resistance to the Western patriarchal norms so inherent in the canon versions.

The fic versions of "Little Red Riding Hood" and "Little Briar Rose" discussed in this chapter are not portrayed as definitive versions of the Grimm tales. Rather they are presented as one part of a much larger conversation held by the fan community where myriad perspectives are not just expected but welcomed. It is likewise a fan community that appears to recognize its part in the fairy-tale tradition, reclaiming the tales from the dominance of the traditional fairy-tale versions. As one fan writes in an author's note preceding their fic:

> Das Erzählen von Märchen ist ein gewichtiger Teil der Alltagskultur. Das ist heut nicht anders wie vor Hunderten von Jahren.
>
> [The telling of fairy tales is an important part of everyday culture. It's not any different today than it was hundreds of years ago.] (Pterano Dante)

The fics work to stimulate emotions and perceptions and use these to connect members of the community to a broader social context (Greenhill and Brydon 136). Throughout this chapter I demonstrate the heavy emphasis the tales place on the experiences and voices of women characters. Every version offers but a snapshot, a view of the story that refers back to its predecessors, though a strict fidelity is "profoundly beside the point" (Greenhill and Matrix 1). In fan fiction, the ever-adapting fairy tale is developed in a medium which flourishes on adaptation, revision, and reinterpretation. Donald Haase notes that the "diversity of critical fairy-tale interpretations encourages sober consideration of the genre's remarkable potential for meaning" ("Response" 236), and for this reason I discuss several changes that take place in "Little Red Riding Hood" and "Little Briar Rose" fics in relation to the canon versions.

Little Briar Rose has been described as the quintessential Grimm woman who exists only to be observed and judged by men, unable to speak her mind or offer any resistance to male advances (Lau 121). While in the canon versions of "Little Briar Rose"/"Sleeping Beauty," the majority of the tale is focused on the distress of the princess and her rescue by a king or prince, the *empowering* fic "Dornröschen," (accessed 2020) written by nonbinary community member Tintenstreuner, focuses nearly exclusively on what takes place within the castle after the prince, named Ludwig, wakes the princess: showing a different interpretation of the passive, docile, and beautiful Briar Rose.

When he finds the cursed, sleeping princess, we read:

> Ganz verzückt kniete Ludwig neben dem Bett nieder. Selbstverständlich musste man eine Prinzessin küssen, wenn man sie von bösen Zaubern befreien wollte! Überhaupt schadete es nie, schöne Frauen auch zu küssen, selbst wenn sie noch gar nicht verhext schienen.
>
> [Completely enraptured, Ludwig knelt before the bed. Obviously, one had to kiss a princess if one wants to free her from an evil spell! Anyway, it never hurt to kiss beautiful women even if they didn't appear to be cursed.]

Here the fic parodies the trope of men rescuing women through their affection and likewise brings to the fore the assumption in traditional fairy-tale versions that male characters are entitled to kiss beautiful women. Ludwig then bends down to kiss Briar Rose and wakes her from her curse:

> Ludwig war ganz außer sich vor Stolz. Er hatte es fertiggebracht, eine schöne Prinzessin zu erlösen, und mit ihr ein ganzes Königreich! Dafür gebührte ihm ja wohl mindestens die Hand der Erretteten […].
>
> "Habt Ihr mich gerade geküsst?" […]
>
> Nun, es war ihr selbstverständlich gestattet, ihm ihre Dankbarkeit und Bewunderung auszudrücken.
>
> [Ludwig was beside himself with pride. He had managed to free a beautiful princess and with her, the entire kingdom! For that he was due, of course, at least the hand of the rescued princess […].
>
> "Did you just kiss me?" […]
>
> Now, she was of course permitted to express her gratitude and admiration to him.]

In the canon versions, Briar Rose's passivity, certainly a product of her silence, is one of her most becoming features. In her deathlike slumber, she arouses "an irresistible longing" in the man who comes across her (Lau 122). In Tintenstreuner's fic, the prince likewise feels an irresistible longing toward the beautiful princess. Yet here, rather than express her gratitude as Ludwig desires and expects, Briar Rose continues speaking:

> "Würdet Ihr mich auch jederzeit *ohne meine Erlaubnis* küssen?"
>
> Ludwig blinzelte. Wie bitte? Sie wollte, dass er ihre Erlaubnis einholte?
>
> "Wie stellt Ihr Euch das vor, Prinzessin? Ihr werdet zum Lohn für meine Heldentat meine Frau, wieso sollte ich Euch da um Erlaubnis …"
>
> "Ganz sicher nicht."
>
> "Was?"
>
> "Ich werde *nicht* Eure Frau." […]
>
> "Aber ich habe Euch gerettet!"
>
> Die Prinzessin seufzte. "Habt dafür vielen Dank. Ihr werdet reich belohnt werden. Und nun geht".

> ["Would you just kiss me anytime *without my permission*?"
>
> Ludwig squinted. Come again? She wanted him to get her permission?
>
> "How do you imagine that, princess? As a reward for my heroic deed, you're going to be my wife, why should I ask for your permi—"
>
> "Absolutely not."
>
> "What?"
>
> "I will *not* be your wife." [...]
>
> "But I rescued you!"
>
> The princess sighed. "You have my thanks. You will be richly rewarded. And now go."]

The prince in Tintenstreuner's fic first shows confusion at her response to his discussion of marriage, but then after her repeated dismissal of his affections as the fic continues, he begins to display irritation at Briar Rose's objections. As Ruth Bottigheimer succinctly states, "a scholarly treatise is not needed to document centuries of male impatience with and irritation at women talking" (*Grimms* 51), and Tintenstreuner's fic deals almost exclusively with this topic. Ludwig cannot comprehend why Briar Rose would want to negotiate his reward and not silently agree to be his bride as she does in traditional fairy-tale versions. His confusion appears to be caused by years of male privilege which the canon tales have helped enforce, and this has led to his expectation of easily obtaining his desires. The fic highlights the absurdity of winning a woman as if she were a prize.

Fandom has long been described as a site of "ideological and cultural resistance to the heteronormative and patriarchal values" which often shape mass media (Jenkins and Shresthova 1.9), and Tintenstreuner's fic challenges the "someday my prince will come" formula which dominates mass media even today (Pershing and Gablehouse 156). Briar Rose, the "model female" in canon versions (Zipes, *Fairy Tales* 40), has the task of showing reserve and patience. She exists only for marriage as she patiently waits while the prince seeks adventure to rescue her. If the princess does speak (albeit only minimally) or reveal any character traits, it is but to "demonstrate how submissive she can be" (Zipes, *Fairy Tales* 40). Conversely, Briar Rose in Tintenstreuner's fic dominates the conversation—a role she is not permitted in the canon. She explains her view of the prince's wish to marry her:

> Es scheint mir, als habet Ihr nicht das geringste persönliche Interesse an mir [...]. Das habt Ihr entschieden, bevor Ihr mich kanntet, und nur, weil Ihr einen Lohn erwartet, der in mir bestehen soll.
>
> [It appears to me as though you don't have the least bit of personal interest in me [...]. You decided that before you knew me and only because you were expecting a reward, which comprises of me.]

After further negotiation between the two, as Briar Rose repeatedly refuses Ludwig's advances, the fic ends:

> Nun war Ludwig tüchtig gekränkt.
>
> "Ihr mögt mich also nicht!" maulte er beleidigt, "Ihr wisst mich gar nicht zu schätzen! Pah!" Er erhob sich aufgebracht und rauschte zur Tür. "Dann habt Ihr mich auch gar nicht verdient!" warf er blasiert hinter sich, bevor er die Treppe zurück nach unten rauschte [...]. Konnte keine Liebe für ihn—Ihn!—empfinden, weil—*weil sie ihn nicht kannte*, pah! Törichtes Frauenzimmer!
>
> [Now Ludwig was thoroughly annoyed.
>
> "So you don't like me!" he moaned, offended, "you don't know how to appreciate me! Bah!" He angrily lifted himself up and rushed to the door. "Then you haven't even earned me!" he threw presumptuously behind himself before he rushed down the stairs [...]. Couldn't feel any love for him—Him!—*because she didn't even know him*, bah! Foolish wench!]

Here we see the prince's attempt at flipping the narrative back on the princess, highlighting the double standard often surrounding expectations of women. While Ludwig expects Briar Rose to be overjoyed that she is desired by him after only seeing her outward appearance and knowing nothing of her, once rejected, Ludwig attempts to blame the princess for dismissing him before even getting to know him. His final thoughts are to spurn Briar Rose's ideas as simply "foolish" in comparison to his own desires.

Tintenstreuner's fic utilizes one of, if perhaps *the* most, passive women in traditional fairy-tale versions to directly discuss questions of women's consent. Briar Rose attempts to logically explain to the prince why she does not wish to marry him and be won as a prize. Unfortunately, as we read in the end of the fic, she is not able to convince the prince of the validity of her feelings. The prince ignores her thoughtful explanation and dismisses it as foolish words. If Western canonical versions tell us anything about the behavior and manners of women, it is that good white girls are silent: having typified feminine virtue in the cultural matrix (Goldstein 61). While Tintenstreuner's fic ends with the realization that strong women expressing their thoughts and desires are often easily dismissed, it does foreground the necessity for women to stand up for themselves and not simply bow to male desires. The prince may dismiss Briar Rose as nothing but a "törichtes Frauenzimmer" [foolish wench], but the fic still leaves the reader with a woman who stood her ground and did not bend to the prince's will no matter how much he tried to assert his supposed authority over her.

## Rewriting "Rotkäppchen" / ["Little Red Riding Hood"] to Highlight the Brutality of Objectification and Victim Blaming

It perhaps comes as no surprise that fics of "Little Red Riding Hood" are the most numerous in the fandom on *FanFiktion.de*. The famous tale has been described as likely suffering "more interpretive trials and tribulations than any other fairy tale" (Tatar 39). Academics across disciplines have interpreted the tale through many theoretical lenses, though for many the tale is about puberty, sex, and sexuality (Kohm and Greenhill 260). After all, the wolf (the canon versions suggest) knows no better since he is just a wild beast, but Red Riding Hood, as both Perrault's and the Grimms' versions let us know, "should have been better brought up" (Warner, *Beast* 243). Because of this assumption, Little Red Riding Hood is burdened with responsibility for the incident from the very start of the tale.

Particular fairy tales encapsulate and embody discourses which have become culturally relevant. When tales are retold, faithfulness to the source text becomes less important than how it is interpreted in the present and represents current hopes, concerns, and fears (Kohm and Greenhill 261). Through analyzing the versions of "Little Red Riding Hood" throughout the fandom, it became clear that for the fandom, Red Riding Hood is a key figure in articulating a growing cultural discourse about sexual violation and what role women's consent and responsibility plays. Nearly all "Little Red Riding Hood" fics dealt with sexuality as a major theme, though every Red Riding Hood fic that was classified as *bleak* was about rape or attempted rape. While canonical versions symbolically seek to represent some "unquestionable natural state of being," many modern versions seek to expose the "generic and gendered 'lie' or artifice" (Bacchilega, *Postmodern* 35). Like other modern retellings, within the fandom, various versions of this tale show that there are alternative ways of viewing desire, seduction, consent, and violation than the canon versions demonstrate. Yet unlike many modern fairy-tale versions where the fairy-tale characters are more often represented as "more complex and ambivalent" than the Grimm and Perrault tales (Kohm and Greenhill 258), fics within the fandom often retain unidimensional characters to highlight the evil nature of the (attempted) rapist and the innocence of his victim. In these fics, the aggressor is always depicted as a man. Many of the most popular fairy tales can be described in terms of a "beauty contest" in which women are seen and ranked by men in the tales as to who is the most beautiful or the most perfect prize. Little Red Riding Hood is certainly no exception to this rule. She is continually described as sweet and lovely; she is a girl one only needs to see to fall in love with (Grimm 96). And certainly, traditional fairy-tale versions state continuously that "beautiful girls are never ignored" (Joosen 65).

This objectification of women, the practice of seeing them only through the "male gaze" which determines their worth and relevance based on their appearance—as objects of heterosexual male control and pleasure (Vickery and Everbach 7)—defines to a large degree the canon versions. Yet older oral sources detail that Little Red Riding Hood was not always portrayed in this light. In eighteenth-century French versions, Little Red Riding Hood takes control of her sexuality and performs a slow striptease for the wolf before slipping into bed with him (Tatar 23). She shows a natural and relaxed attitude toward her own body and sex, becoming the seductress in the face of her attempted seducer. In positive portrayals of the tale within the fandom, as well as in other modern adaptations which appear outside the world of fan fiction, Little Red Riding Hood often reclaims her sexuality, becoming a seductress for her own pleasure with no ill consequences at the conclusion. Some fics linger on the description of the wolf as Little Red Riding Hood stares and assesses his worth through his appearance. It is she who decides that he is worthy of her attention. These fics flip the narrative of the male gaze and present a version which is decidedly marked by a "female gaze."

Revisions of "Little Red Riding Hood" often ask what the relationship of wolves to young women is. Are the wolves predatory creatures? Misunderstood victims? Or perhaps even protectors? (see Zipes, *Irresistible* 143). Interesting as well are fan interpretations wherein the male wolf becomes female. In these instances, the female wolf is never an enemy and always a friend or protector of Little Red Riding Hood and her grandmother. The aspect of fear which marks the traditional fairy-tale versions utterly disappears as soon as the wolf becomes female. In another fic with a positive depiction of the wolf, he is a charming werewolf with whom Little Red Riding Hood has fallen in love. Together they have a daughter who, like her father, is a werewolf, something that suggests both feminine characteristics, as well as a fierce, untamed nature. Here women can even be born of wolves, inheriting their wild and intrepid characters.

While there are certainly positive portrayals of the "Little Red Riding Hood" narrative where women face no danger and are in control of their own sexuality, or women are portrayed as wild and free with their own wolfish side, certainly the overwhelming majority of "Little Red Riding Hood" reimaginings within this fandom were classified as *bleak* and have disastrous outcomes for the red-hooded girl. Fic writers themselves indicate the suitability of the fairy tale for the sinister, noting that "märchen sind ja sowieso schon kleine horrorgeschichten" [fairy tales are already little horror stories] (Wolfspirat). In this respect the fic versions follow a trend within modern fairy-tale adaptations. The bleak turn taken by modern fairy-tale versions has come out especially in visions of women creators (Warner, *Once Upon a Time* 176). Indeed, many adaptations highlight and embody a struggle over attitudes and depictions of sex roles as well as toward male and female power (Haase, "Feminist" 9) which we can see in the following examples.

The following fic, abyzz's "Der Wolf" [The Wolf] (accessed 2020), reimagines the titular character as a human man rather than an animal. While canon versions contain morals suggesting that the wolf should be interpreted as a man—those "most dangerous wolves of all" as Perrault's tale cautions us (103)—on trend with many filmic versions, most fics in the fandom portray the wolf as a human man. As Little Red Riding Hood makes her way to her grandmother's house, this time in a modern setting filled with enormous, looming buildings described as "meterhohe Schluchten" [meter-high ravines] and quiet, but dangerous-looking grey streets under pouring rain. The fic opens presenting a world just waiting to swallow a girl like Little Red Riding Hood. Unlike the girl in the Perrault and Grimm versions of the tale, one who is either too naïve to survive or so oblivious and unreliable that she must be saved from herself (Bacchilega, *Postmodern* 58), in this fic, Little Red Riding Hood already senses that she is being followed, and suspects that her follower means her harm. Abyzz writes: "Unheil. Sie spürt es. / Irgendwo ist ein Wolf." [Evil. She feels it. / Somewhere there's a wolf.] As Little Red Riding Hood walks down the street, it is not just one man, but evidently all men who are potential dangers. She sees men lining the streets, smoking along the sidewalks, waiting. Though we are left unsure as to what they might be waiting for, the description suggests that it is likely nothing good:

> Gierig saugen [die Männer] an den Stängeln und blasen mehr und mehr Grau in die Welt hinaus.
>
> [Greedily [the men] suck on the stems[1] and blow more and more grey out into the world.]

Abyzz's word choice also draws attention to the overt sexualization of this young girl by the men around her. The verbs "saugen" [suck] and "blasen" [blow] here denote that the threat surrounding Little Red Riding Hood

1 "Stängel" [stems] is slang for cigarettes. To retain the sexual imagery of the original German, I have chosen not to reword the sentence to incorporate the American English slang of "smokes" for cigarettes.

is specifically sexual. Eventually the “wolf,” a large, unnamed man, steps in front of the girl, blocking her path. He bends down and forces her to look him in the face. Abyzz continually reminds the reader of Little Red Riding Hood’s danger and references the man’s predatory nature. She describes him with a clear warning: “Es sieht aus, als würde er sich hinkauern, ein Raubtier auf der Jagd nach Frischfleisch.” [It appears as if he would hunker down, a predator on the hunt for fresh meat.]

“Little Red Riding Hood” is categorized as a warning tale, one which provides a negative model detailing how girls and young women should behave (Zipes, *Fairy Tales* 39). In traditional fairy-tale versions, Little Red Riding Hood is eaten by the wolf because she gives expression to her fancy by straying from the path. The tales present this action as the girl receiving her due punishment for not behaving as girls ostensibly should. Yet what we see in many fic versions and certainly in abyzz’s text, is that the girl has not strayed from the path. Rather, she tries desperately to avoid the wolf. In this and other *bleak* Red Riding Hood fics, the Red Riding Hood character is presented as an innocent and persecuted heroine. She is shown to be an undeserving victim of hostile antagonists such as “the wolf.” (Jones 20). This fic does not show us a girl who is misbehaving, rather we see a man forcing her to interact with him.

Little Red Riding Hood never arrives at her grandmother’s house and the fic comes to a conclusion:

> Seine Hand ist auf der Schulter des Mädchens und an ganz anderen Stellen und er flüstert
>
> “Lass mich dich nach Hause bringen. Ich pass auf dich auf [...].” Seine Hand ist an dem Rücken des kleinen, zierlichen Wesens [...]. Unter seinen Füßen macht der Erdboden ein saugendes Geräusch.
>
> Sie werden verschluckt.
>
> Vom Regen.
>
> Vom Schrei.
>
> Vom Geruch nach Kuchen und Wein.
>
> Und von Unheil.
>
> [His hand is on the girl’s shoulder and on entirely other places and he whispers

> "Let me bring you home. I'll watch out for you [...]." His hand is on the back of the small, fragile creature [...]. Under his feet the earth makes a sucking noise.
>
> They are swallowed.
>
> By rain.
>
> By screams.
>
> By the smell of cake and wine.
>
> And by evil.]

The moral of both canon tales is a warning to girls to beware and not stray from the path lest they be swallowed by hungry wolves. The wolf in the canon is presented as the "natural instrument of lawful punishment" (Bacchilega, *Postmodern* 58). Abyzz's fic redefines this canon expectation, as it is not just the wolf who swallows Little Red Riding Hood, but the world itself. Unlike the Grimm version, there is no hunter who comes to save Little Red Riding Hood; she is simply swallowed whole. While this ending does duplicate the Perrault version of the tale, abyzz's fic specifically focuses on the innocence of the young girl, her fear, and the fact that she has done nothing wrong. The world is simply a place where young girls must fear men and where often, like the anonymous men lining the street, no one will come to their aid.

Fans tend to engage with canon texts not in a detached way, but in a very emotionally involved and invested one (Gray 10). The focus of fics tends not to be on plot, as it is expected that the plot in the canon tale is well known by fellow fans. Rather, fics—especially those authored by women—focus on interpersonal relationships between characters and psychological development (Bacon-Smith, *Science Fiction* 257). While there are certainly similarities between fic adaptations of the tales and other modern (especially postmodern) versions, what sets these fics apart from many other modern retellings are their replications of earlier fairy-tale cultures with collective authorship within the community.

One fan in the comment section discusses the pedophilia seemingly inherent in the canon "Little Red Riding Hood" tale as well as the fear many women and girls feel when walking alone:

> Ich weiß, dass das mir als kleines Mädchen so ging—ich weiß gar nicht mehr, warum, aber ich sah in jedem Fremden einen potenziellen Entführer und selbst den fünfminütigen Schulweg bewältigte ich alleine nur ängstlich und zitternd […]. Aber ich mag es immer sehr gerne, wenn Märchen auf die Moderne übertragen werden und irgendwie ist Rotkäppchen fast prädestiniert für dieses Kinderschänder-Thema. […] Wenn ich mal eine Tochter haben sollte, werde ich ihr wahrscheinlich keine roten Pullis kaufen.
>
> [I know that it was like that for me as a small girl—I don't know why anymore, but in every stranger, I saw a potential kidnapper and I could only even manage the five-minute way to and from school with fear and shaking […]. But I always really like it when fairy tales are brought into modernity and somehow Little Red Riding Hood seems almost predestined for this child-molester theme […]. If I should ever have a daughter, I will probably never buy her red pullovers.] (Himmelgrau)

Himmelgrau's full comment is quite lengthy. She takes considerable time with both descriptive and analytic commentary, focusing on what she thinks and feels while reading the fic. Importantly what she focuses on, especially at the end of her comment, is that even if one is not in a fairy tale being chased by a wolf, the world is often a place where girls continually feel as though they are in potential danger. A world where, as abyzz's fic describes in the end, they might be swallowed whole. As can be seen through this fic as well as others within the fandom, the fics as well as the comment sections provide a forum for fandom members to directly discuss their fears and lived experiences with others.

Another *bleak* "Little Red Riding Hood" fic, yumichan18's "Rotkäppchen—oder 'Eine schreckliche Realität' " [Little Red Riding Hood—or "a horrible reality"] (accessed 2020), describes a similar situation to abyzz's, though now Little Red Riding Hood is not a young girl but a young woman named Melanie. While abyzz's fic decidedly leaves much of the imagery of what happens in the end to the reader's imagination, yumichan18 takes a much more direct approach, detailing exactly the dangers encountered by Melanie, and specifically the dangers of men who feel entitled to women's bodies. Like abyzz's fic, and similar to many "Little Red Riding Hood" fics, yumichan18 places the "Little Red Riding Hood" tale in a modern setting. Rather than a forest, Melanie needs to traverse a rough neighborhood far away from any subway station to reach her beloved grandmother. As soon as she steps off her train, Melanie has a feeling that she is being followed. Though Melanie cannot see him, the reader is given foreshadowing to the main events of the fic:

> Der Mann folgte ihr schon seit dem Bahnhof, hatte sie regelrecht erwartet und das Grinsen in sein Gesicht wurde mit jedem Schritt, den sie tat, breiter. Heute würde er sie kriegen. Viel zu lange hatte er sie nur aus der Stille beobachtet. Heute wurde es Zeit, dass sie sich begegneten.
>
> [The man had followed her already since the train station, had outright expected her and the grin on his face became wider with every step she took. Today he would catch her. For far too long he had watched her just from the shadows. Today would be time for them to meet.]

On her way to her grandmother's apartment as it begins to grow dark, Melanie is met by two men. First, she encounters a man who (as the narrator informs the reader, but Melanie is ignorant of) offers her well-meaning advice to beware in this area of the city. He offers to accompany her for part of her journey. She rejects his offer as she does not wish to be followed. The second man who gives Melanie the same offer, however, is the "wolf." Though the reader has been given additional information to determine their intentions, Melanie cannot tell the difference between the advances: between the traditional fairy-tale version of the "hunter" who saves Little Red Riding Hood and the "wolf." Here we see that the difference between the two is not as obvious as traditional fairy-tale versions seek to portray it, and to Melanie, every man who approaches her is a potential attacker. While her character has been consistently described throughout the fic as a caring and kind person who is seeking to comfort her sick grandmother, when she encounters the two men she reacts with biting and defensive comments, seeking to be quickly rid of them so that she may continue on her journey.

As Melanie walks quickly past the "wolf," we read "'Sie hat Feuer. Umso besser.' Dachte sich der Kerl nur zufrieden." ['She has fire. Even better.' The guy thought to himself, satisfied.] In the canon, young girls and women are expected to display humility and modesty and to be self-effacing and self-denying (Zipes, *Fairy Tales* 150). Here the man targets Melanie specifically because he views her as not displaying these traits. He has decided that Melanie should belong to him and thus will do anything in his power to obtain her as a prize. In the canon a woman becoming man's possession—a prize for his good deeds—is presented as the fulfillment of her dreams; enacting the "someday my prince will come" fantasy. In yumichan18's fic, this same trope is used to draw attention to the fact that the man is making this choice against Melanie's will. As they briefly speak, we read the man's thoughts: "Er musste sie haben. Er musste sie bändigen. Sie würde ihm gehören. Ihm allein!" [He had to have her. He had to subdue her. She would belong to him. Him alone!] He feels entitled to her and is determined to possess her.

Although Melanie walks past the man, he continues to follow her to her grandmother's apartment and blocks her way to the entry, forcing her to talk to him. Afraid, Melanie decides to return to a well-lit gas station she passed on her journey, convincing herself that lights and other people will protect her. Unbeknownst to her, the man has stolen the key to her grandmother's apartment from her pocket while he was speaking to her and enters the apartment while Melanie leaves. She returns later, finding the front door ajar. Once inside, she immediately begins to feel afraid, and is suddenly overpowered by the "wolf" who throws her to the bed. Melanie attempts to free herself from his grip, and when she realizes she cannot, she speaks to the man to gain more time to break free.

> "Warum?" tropfte ihre Stimme fast tonlos von ihren Lippen [...].
>
> "Weil du hier durch die Gegend rennst als könnte dich nichts und niemand aufhalten. Als wärst du stärker als der Rest der Welt. Als wäre dein hübsches Gesicht dein Freifahrtsschein für alles! WEIL. DU. MICH. PROVOZIERST!" Schrie seine schrille Stimme ihr immer noch gnadenlos ins Gesicht.
>
> ["Why?" her voice dripped almost without tone from her lips [...].
>
> "Because you run around this area as if nothing and no one could stop you. As if you were stronger than the rest of the world. As if your pretty face were your free pass for everything. BECAUSE. YOU. PROVOKE. ME!" screamed his shrill voice still without pity into her face.]

This dialog highlights and reveals the control of women's bodies exemplified in traditional fairy-tale versions and certainly still widely justified in patriarchal societies. The fic lists many of the most common tropes used by those who wish to control women by placing the blame on the victims themselves and emphasizing that her manner of dress as well as the way she carries herself was inviting male attention. One of the key interpretations of the canon "Little Red Riding Hood" is that women are responsible for their own rape (Zipes, *Stick* 35). By placing the tale in a modern setting, yumichan18's fic details that regrettably, attitudes toward women's responsibility and accountability for their own sexual violation have remained largely unaltered to the present day. Unfortunately, as Jack Zipes reminds us, "the [modern day] mass media's dissemination of images [...] continues to suggest that women lure and seduce men and ultimately are responsible if anything happens to them" (*Stick* 39).

Yumichan18's fic continues as the man begins choking her. As she frantically tries to breathe, we read: "Melanie schrie, auch wenn dieser Schrei tonlos blieb." [Melanie screamed, even if this scream remained without sound.] In canon versions, women have been either told or shown that their art, or their way of presenting themselves and being seen by others, is an art of silence (Gilbert and Gubar 43). Melanie is forced into silence as her attacker strangles her into obedience, physically preventing her from uttering a sound. This fic highlights the theme of the *femme fatale* often present in traditional fairy-tale versions informed by "men's anguish in the face of female indifference" as these versions often show "the tenderness of masculine desire and the cruelty of the female response, rather than women's vulnerability to male violence" (Warner, *Beast* 295).

Fan fiction does not seek to somehow erase or override the canon. On the contrary, the appropriation essential to fan fiction involves not just reworking aspects of the canon to accommodate shifting perspectives and interests, but also accepting certain core premises in the canon (Jenkins, "Afterword" 362). Thus yumichan18's fic incorporates many tropes of the Western fairy-tale canon which portray white women as being virtuously silent, judged only by their marriageability and passivity. Their level of desirability is ultimately judged by men so that they may be possessed by them. These same tropes are used specifically in yumichan18's fic so that they can be subverted. As the fic continues, Melanie's attacker makes a deep cut across her face, in his view somehow perversely freeing her from the difficulties her beauty has caused her: "Schön, nicht wahr? [...] So nimmt dich keiner mehr! [...] Du gehörst mir!" [Beautiful, isn't it? [...]

No one else will take you like this! [...] You belong to me!] As her attacker cuts Melanie's face, the scene likewise brings into explicit view what many canon tales seek to convey to girls: your looks are your only asset (Joosen 66). Whatever Melanie might be or do is of no consequence. As a white woman, she exists as a pretty face for men to enjoy. Often in canon versions, this patriarchal view is communicated implicitly. We see through different actions or character descriptions that outward beauty and appeal to men is of utmost importance. Pretty white girls get rescued, and unfortunately both ugly white girls and women of color are often put into the same category and are written as evil or lazy, not "womanly" enough and thus not desirable for marriage. In this fic, however, the attacker states this view blatantly, highlighting the dangers of such patriarchal views. Yumichan18's fic details a grave statement on traditional fairy-tale depictions of the creation of the ideal woman.

The first man who offered her help does end up rescuing Melanie from her attempted rapist after hearing gunshots ringing from the apartment. The fic ends with a sobering interpretation of the messages of traditional tales:

> Das alles war kein Traum, kein Märchen. Es ist Realität. Ihre Realität [...]. Und Melanie wird lange brauchen um das zu verarbeiten. Das alles, was an einem Abend geschehen ist. Ein Abend, der ihr ganzes Leben verändert hat [...]. Das Leben wird weiter gehen, auch wenn sie immer wieder an diesen Ort zurückkehren wird.
>
> [That was all no dream, no fairy tale. It is reality. Her reality [...]. And Melanie will need a long time to work through it. Everything that happened one evening. An evening which changed her entire life [...]. Life will go on, even when she returns to this place again and again.]

Here the fic quite clearly states that this is a reality many women must endure, and it is one which will haunt so many for their entire lives. While she may have been ultimately rescued by the "hunter" figure, the fic does not lead us to believe that had she listened to his advice initially, the conclusion of the story would have been avoided. Had the "wolf" not succeeded on this day, he would have simply waited for another opportunity. Life may go on, we read, but Melanie will forever be trapped by this moment, returning to the memories of these horrors again and again. The fic leaves the reader with no solution or happy ending, only a vivid description of what can happen to women in patriarchal societies and in patriarchal narratives such as the traditional fairy-tale versions where men are written as being entitled to women's bodies and women are written as prizes or punishable conquests. These revisions are meant to be "confrontational and provocative," (Zipes, "Struggle" 185) and to be seen as social commentary on the treatment of women.

Communities learn how to tell their own stories by absorbing and rewriting stories and histories which appear as relevant to them, and the canon versions still maintain an impressive dominance in Western Societies today. Yet the fic writers see the canon tales on which their tales are based as incomplete, somehow frustrating in their incompleteness, and thus the fans adapt and change the tales to fit with contemporary ideas and expectations. It seems clear through the examples in this chapter that many members of the fandom community do not agree with the idea of women without agency waiting to be rescued, nor do they appear to accept the unidimensional portrayals of morals as depicted in the canon tales. Likewise, the community appears to reject the idea of each tale having a "happy ending," as the worlds in their tales are much more complex than those of the canon—and the changing realities can be seen in them.

Of note is that both of the most popular tales to be reimagined within the fandom deal explicitly with questions of a woman's autonomy. "Little Red Riding Hood" with questions of assault, rape, and whether a woman should bear responsibility as the victim, and "Little Briar Rose" with a woman's ability to choose her own partner as well as being able to consent (or not) to a man's physical advances. The fandom serves as a site of resistance to the patriarchal norms espoused not just in the canon versions, but still in Western society today with patriarchal views of a woman's responsibility in the case of her own violation and her right to bodily autonomy. The fics within the fandom use this space to subvert traditional tales and bring attention to the unjust expectations and suffering of women in patriarchal societies.

The fairy tale has consistently been described as an ever-evolving genre. It is a genre which moves and adapts fluidly and easily to different media. These fairy tales are intertextual, multivocal, and transmedial cultural practices which put into action a complex sense of what fairy tales can do, an awareness that the fairy tale genre is not singular or simple (Bacchilega, *Fairy Tales* 27). It is important to include fan fiction in the study of folklore and the fairy tale as fan fiction is a continuation, another adaptation of the volatile fairy tale genre, notably with an emphasis on reclaiming the tradition of fairy-tale cultures of communal authorship and participation. This communal spirit of adaptation and revision brings awareness to the provisional and fragmentary nature of individual retellings as well as the fans' collective role in the fairy-tale tradition.

Much of what is at stake in fairy-tale fan fiction be summed up by this brief exchange between two fans on the site. One fan writes with playful sarcasm: "Manchmal frage ich mich was bei dir in deiner Kindheit schief gelaufen ist, dass du die Märchen so arg veralberst:D." [Sometimes I ask myself what went wrong in your childhood that you mess around with fairy tales so severely:D.] And the simple reply: "ich weiss es ja selber nicht. Dabei liebe ich Märchen" [I don't know it myself. I love fairy tales] (KaLiBeYT13). What this brief interaction shows is that fics are certainly not a rejection of the canon, but rather a labor of love. These are amateur writers in the truest sense of the word: someone who engages in an activity purely for pleasure and due to admiration. The fics are not just subverting, but also reaffirming that the tales have a place in their communities and an impact on their lives. Fans are participating and discussing the changes and adaptations together to establish meaning within their communities and determine the role this narrative should play in their lives: negotiating, subverting and often resisting the harmful and dangerous depictions of women and girls forced to live under patriarchal norms. They are part of the living performance of the folklore tradition—"for better and worse and for everything in between" (Phillips and Milner 25).

CHAPTER 6

# Storytelling and Its Reconstruction of Identity through Identity Play

Storytelling helps define and situate us within our societies. People tell many stories throughout their lives, but ultimately stories can help people define themselves as well as establish connections with other members of their communities. Stories are invariably colored by present experiences, new discoveries, or different societal beliefs and priorities. Indeed, narrative is widely recognized as playing a large role in human consciousness in general and promoting identity formation (Wertsch 56). One of the ways people narrate their identities is through folk stories. As folklorist Juwen Zhang notes "folklore is all about identity and thus defines identity" (449). Both personal and group identity can be investigated and defined by observing folklore-in-practice.

As we have seen in previous chapters, folktales and fairy tales continue to be a vital part of everyday life. Some of these expressive stories and behaviors are shifting in different ways as people work to formulate and construct meaning in their everyday lives alongside advances in technology. Though some, such as the fan fiction discussed throughout this book has moved to a new format online, folklore is nevertheless linked to questions and discussions of selfhood, community, and equality. Stories told online—just like the stories told face-to-face—are placed within the frameworks of our personal lives and solidify our place within the communities of which we find ourselves a part. In their online writings, fans examine and make changes by borrowing and inflecting mass cultural products, emphasizing topics and concerns they have identified as either mis- or underrepresented within mass media and culture. When new plots and interpretations within folktales and fairy tales begin to take hold, it is often evidence that something culturally significant has shifted. Fan writers play with the canon to determine the role these traditional tales still serve in their understanding of themselves and their own cultural identities. They play with narrative to play with identity.

Play and playfulness with narrative and transformative possibilities have been noted as key features of online cultures (Bromseth and Sundén 274), and I have shown aspects of this sense of play in previous chapters through investigations of communal storytelling, how fans critique and interact with the canon, as well as the importance of the fannish gift economy. Online play, while it can be innocent or even insignificant, can also be utterly serious. Thinking of online identity construction through notions of play and performance is synonymous with the many ways in which the self is created, recreated, and evoked in online worlds. Investigating identity as a type of performance, or being created through play, allows us to explore it not as fixed, unified or final, but as something that is ever part of a creation process. Humans are inevitably members of groups and communities which form our sense of a "we" identity and pattern the social frameworks through which we see the world. Folklore—ever multiple, evolving, and jointly constructed—can importantly tell us what different communities know or at least what they *think* they know about the world around them, revealing different hopes of who or what a society may become, fears of what might take place, as well as prejudices and intolerance.

In this chapter, I investigate how fans use folklore as part of the formation of their personal identities through identity play, as well as the part fan fiction writers play in (re)determining the role that traditional tales play in broader culture. They consciously and unconsciously negotiate their identities in relation to others within the fandom with respect to larger social narratives. Ultimately, a sense of identity is constructed both by a sense of who we are, as well as by the boundaries of who we are not; inclusion and exclusion are different sides of the same coin. As we explore the tales told within communities as part of their folklore, we should likewise consider who is telling stories; who is listening; who the main actors, protagonists, and villains are; and importantly who is refusing to engage, being ignored, or being excluded.

I begin by discussing the role of narrative in personal and communal identity play. As examples of both the inclusion and exclusion inevitable in personal and communal identity construction, I use examples within discussion forums on *FanFiktion.de*—open to all users of the site—which explicitly engage with representations of sexuality (specifically with discussions of FemSlash) as well as race and ethnicity. These comment threads show in-depth discussions on these topics in both positive, supportive ways and in discriminatory and bigoted ones. To investigate these views in practice, I likewise explore representations in fics within the "Grimms Märchen" fandom of race and sexuality in particular. Folklore, as everyday expression by everyday people, of course cannot just be emancipatory or liberatory because it is still deeply encoded in specific communities and, to one degree or another, relies on and reinforces social norms. After all, folklore as a kind of "artifact of identity" (Del Negro and Berger, "Identity" 129), is a way that individuals and groups help construct images not just of themselves, but also how they distinguish themselves from those perceived as "Others."

## The Role of Identity Play in Framing Personal and Communal Identity

Discussing why they write fan fiction, fans on *FanFiktion.de* often described it as a hobby, something fun, or "um mich selbst besser auszudrücken" [to better express myself] ("Warum schreibt ihr"). While fans certainly did discuss the honing of their craft—describing things more accurately and in detail or practicing proper grammatical functions—it is also clear through various responses that "expressing oneself" means something much more intimate than learning the mechanics of new narrative forms. Fandom provides a space where fans can articulate their specific wants, needs, and concerns. As one fan writes, "Schreiben kann […] ein Seelenstriptease sein." [Writing can be […] a striptease of the soul] ("Warum schreibt ihr"). Though it may be a humorous construction, thinking of narrative as a type of "striptease of the soul" does evoke the type of identity play that can take place through narration. This "play" is a series of continued investigations and expressions of the self. As Judith Butler writes of the self: "I am not formed once and definitively, but continuously and repeatedly" (6). Identity formation is never completed, but rather a constant evolution. Just as fan fiction can be described as continual "works in progress," (Busse and Hellekson, "Introduction: Work in Progress" 6) so too is identity a continual work in progress through the act of identity play.

Fan writer Lady Sonea describes writing as a "persönliche und geistige Weiterentwicklung" [personal and spiritual furthering of development] which can be a way to work through one's own feelings and experiences. It can have "eine therapeutische Wirkung" [a therapeutic effect]. She describes in more detail how the writing of fan fiction has helped her continue to grow and develop as a person:

> Indem ich mich mit den Figuren einer Geschichte auseinandersetze, setze ich mich auch mit mir selbst auseinander. Indem ich mich in sie hineinversetze und versuche, sie zu verstehen, lerne mich besser in andere Menschen hineinzuversetzen und Verständnis für sie aufzubringen. Indem ich recherchiere, bilde ich mich weiter. Indem ich eine Handlung entwickele und Handlungsfäden miteinander verknüpfe, fördere ich mein logisches und strategisches Denkvermögen. Und so weiter und so fort.
>
> [Because I grapple with the characters in a story, I also grapple with myself. Because I empathize with them and try to understand them, I learn to better to empathize with other people and have understanding for them. Because I research, I educate myself further. Because I develop a plot and narrative threads, I foster my logical and strategic intellectual power. And so on and so forth.] ("Fanfiction schreiben")

Lady Sonea describes in some detail the different aspects of identity play she engages in through narrative. Identity play takes place on the threshold between fantasy and reality and necessarily requires a psychological space where individuals can safely explore different concepts of the self without fear of judgment (Stanko et al. 2). As can be seen through Lady Sonea's description, she is engaging in identity play through her fics themselves, shaping and molding not just characters, plots, and motifs, but also investigating and discovering things about herself in the process.

In a similar description, Erzaehlerstimme illustrates the role that writing plays in her life. She notes that even the act of writing creates a space where she feels she can finally express concepts and ideas that she had previously felt uncomfortable sharing with others:

> Ich habe unheimlich viele Sachen in meinem Kopf, die raus müssen. Wenn ich schon mit niemandem darüber reden kann, dann schreibe ich sie eben auf und verarbeite sie so. Manchmal ist es wie eine Selbsttherapie und die habe ich manchmal nötig, wenn mich bestimmte Gedanken nicht loslassen, die ich mit niemandem besprechen möchte.
>
> [I have an incredible amount of stuff in my head that needs to come out. If I can't discuss it with anyone then I just write them down and work through them that way. Sometimes it's like a self-therapy and that's sometimes necessary for me when certain thoughts that I can't discuss with anyone won't leave me.] ("Warum schreibt ihr")

Stories allow people to express what can often be very private concepts and ideas differently than—and sometimes even impossible in—direct conversation. Since the point or moral of stories can often be implied rather than stated directly, they offer a way for people to tell, discuss, and even disagree without antagonizing each other directly (Prins 83). This creates a series of personal and even intimate entanglements that fans work through in their writing. This intimacy and emotional vulnerability is a hallmark of fan fiction writing. Certainly, the identity play discussed by fans previously can be seen by investigating fics within the fandom as well. The changes and interpretations fans show in their stories show a sort of doubling of their interpretation process of the canon. The fan interprets the canon, and their fic in turn projects their interpretation of themselves and their social world. These fan-fic narratives impact not just their sense of identity, but the fairy-tale genre itself as we see clashes in values between fics and the canon tales, struggles over the construction of gender roles and expectations, and complications of unidimensional narratives and happy endings. The joy and plight of different characters, or the changes in plot development can become a means for fans to convey their own personal struggles and concerns while working through them.

Though narration has long been seen as a means of fostering identity creation, communication online provides affordances different from those available before digital technologies. Certainly, authors have long written and published anonymously or pseudonymously for various reasons, yet both the abundance of narrative visibility through being posted in public forums as well as social interaction online allows some users to explore identity in ways that more limited offline social networks are unable to sustain (Avance 67). As discussed in more in detail in Chapter 3, for example, online forums can give users more control over their reactions and responses than face-to-face settings. Stanko et al. discuss three types of identity play narratives that can take place in online worlds: the possible self, the improbable self, and the impossible self. The "possible self" fosters identity play through speculative ideas of who one might, would like, should, or even fears becoming in the future. "Impossible" and "improbable selves" can likewise foster learning and growth through the exploration of selves that, while perhaps interesting or enticing to consider, are unlikely to be taken on or incorporated permanently (3). "Impossible" and "improbable" selves are used, rather, as a type of thought experiment such as the one mentioned by Lady Sonea when she considers the thoughts and perspectives of characters largely different from her own personality. Though these characters may not be adopted into the fic writer's sense of self, working through their thoughts, rationale, and ambitions is still a learning experience and help them to better understand people different from themselves. These thought exercises through identity play can all be equally important in the formation and discovery of one's conception of self.

Online interaction which is often either anonymous or pseudonymous can make the Internet an ideal location for identity play. Some users take the work of their narrative and identity play to different levels, trying out different versions of themselves online before incorporating those aspects of their identity to be visible in the actual world. One fan writes that they feel their personality is different online than in the actual world. They explain further that their identity play online is that of the "ideal self:" "Ich versuche allerdings, mein Ich von hier mit in die Realität zu nehmen, da es mir doch ziemlich sympathisch ist" [I try however, to bring my Self from here back into reality because it's very likable/sympathetic] ("Anonym unterwegs"). Here is a place where users can discover their passions and interests, confront personal issues, and respond to or work through them with acts of creativity. Fans can take on and work through different identities as a means of figuring out who they are as well as who they are not.

Because of the narrative and identity play taking place, these writings and the subsequent interaction online should be seen as a site of self-discovery and self-making. Folktales and fairy tales, as "ideologically variable desire machines" (Bacchilega, *Postmodern Fairy Tales* 7), highlight what we wish or fear to become, and are a superb vehicle for this type of identity play. Almost no one feels any qualms about narrating, discussing, or interpreting fairy tales. They have been interpreted time and again as problematizing identities and differences, reinforcing social norms, or as narrative escapes. Fans use their fics as a creative means of relating experiences that respond to ambiguity and anxiety.

The construction of our individual identities is indeed important, though along with the development of the "I," humans are also inevitably part of a "we" that links identity to being part of a group and extends beyond the boundaries of one's personal life and experiences (Assmann, Aleida 38). While the stories that we share with others can be fundamental in our own personal discovery and development, the society, communities, and groups which we see ourselves a part of also largely influence our sense of self. Many of these influences occur without our explicit knowledge. Discussing these forces, Judith Butler writes:

> I do not arrive in the world separate from a set of norms that are lying in wait for me, already orchestrating my gender, race, and status, working on me, even as a pure potential, prior to my first wail. So norms, conventions, institutional forms of power, are already acting prior to any action I may undertake, prior to there being an "I" who thinks of itself from time to time as the seat or source of its own action. (6)

This is of course not to say that we are incapable of our own action, but that while a person may take individual action, there are simultaneously multiple influences guiding the outcomes and decisions in the process. Societal attitudes on gender, race, status and so forth and the power dynamics that come with them can both help and hinder actions taken, and these attitudes will likewise inevitably determine community members' thoughts and beliefs. The task, then, is to consider that all individuals are both acting and being acted upon simultaneously (Butler 6). Interpretations of identity are situated within a social world, and it is within the context of this social world that the meanings of the stories people tell come to life.

Part of the social world that fans within the fandom are responding to, as mentioned in previous chapters, is the position of women in subordinate roles within a patriarchal society. Values of domesticity and patriarchal authority—where strong-acting and speaking women are often characterized as wicked and innocent and persecuted heroines are humbled and domesticated—are espoused in the canon tales by both the Grimms and Perrault. As Steven Swann Jones writes, the victimization of innocent and persecuted heroines—usually from parents, siblings, in-laws, or husbands—forces us to investigate *how* female development in fairy tales is depicted (24). Often, though not always, taking the form of domestic abuse, the persecution suffered by these heroines can be seen as representations of the types of problems young women can encounter and societal views of those same issues (39).

In response to these motifs, many modern adaptations depict men who exercise their authority and power over women as a danger. Within the fandom, fics can be seen to cultivate a particular group identity of women-identifying writers who highlight and oppose the suppression of women's voices in patriarchal cultural norms. In one such fic, Cela's "Der Wolf und Rotkäppchen" [The Wolf and Red Riding Hood], the plot follows very closely the Grimm version of "Little Red Riding Hood" (ATU 333), though it does portray Red Riding Hood as "rein" [pure] and "unschuldig" [innocent]—emphasizing her role as the innocent and persecuted heroine.

After the wolf has attacked her grandmother, Little Red Riding Hood arrives at the house. The wolf tries to attack her and, as in the Grimm version, a hunter comes and shoots the wolf. While the wolf is certainly the villain seeking to prey on an innocent girl, in Cela's version briefly before the wolf is shot, we read that the hunter is described as the wolf's "Rivale" [rival] as the hunter too has been following the girl. As the fic ends, the hunter walks over to Little Red Riding Hood and begins to lead her out of the house:

> Lange hatte er gewartet, Vertrauen aufgebaut und beobachtet. Er konnte es nicht zulassen, dass dieses Tier ihm alles kaputt gemacht hätte. Denn er war der Jäger. Und was ist schon der Unterschied zwischen Jäger und Wolf?

> [Long had he waited, built up trust, and watched. He couldn't allow that this animal would destroy everything for him. Because he was the hunter. And what's really the difference between hunter and wolf?]

Cela's fic is reacting against the canon tale and reinforces a sense of group identity within the fandom as a community that seeks to redefine gender norms and expectations. The fic supports this identity through its questioning of stereotypical portrayals in canon tales of men who use their strength to act as a helpful rescuer to women in danger. Depictions of identity are related to societal views and perceptions as they are receptive to individuals' positions in society, made and remade in complex and unequal social orders, and related to questions of power (French 340). Portrayals in the canon, such as the patriarchal depictions of either the damsel in distress, or the idea that the woman who strays from her path deserves to be punished and humbled, all contribute to one's self-identity and how members of the fandom see themselves since the canon tales are an active part of their folklore. The fics with their reinterpretations of the canon tales inevitably concern themselves with questions of what these depictions mean today and whether they are still influential.

Different stories which are popular within different communities can give us important information about the community that produced them (Bottigheimer, *Grimms' Bad Girls* 167). The type of artistic articulation inherent in fan fiction writing, a self-conscious working through and combining motifs and techniques from other sources, works to highlight self-reflexivity and re-visitation of history, subjectivity, and language as well as storytelling itself (Bacchilega, "Postmodernism" 75). The fairy tale lends itself well to this project of making and unmaking. There is a wide applicability of their symbolic associations as can be evidenced by the vast and diverse contexts in which they have been received and reinterpreted. From smaller and more personal circles such as those told and interpreted by parents, children, and family members, to wider interpretations with scholars and psychoanalysts, to political propaganda with the National Rifle Association (N.R.A.) using rewritten fairy tales to support gun rights (Barnett) and of course famously, the Nazi Party. The cultural selectivity of icons and images, such as reusing and repurposing specific fairy tales and folktales time and again, highlights the power of narrative as a strategy to create an identity—of how the "I" identity fits into the "we."

Most of the examples mentioned previously have been comments from fans about general personal development and identity construction. Online, fans discuss some aspects of this identity creation process explicitly: concepts of gender roles and expectations in Western patriarchal society as well as sexuality, race, and ethnicity. While there are certain aspects of identity that some had hoped would become insignificant online since people would ostensibly no longer engage in conversations with preconceived notions about one another based simply on appearance, these aspects of identity nevertheless remain largely intact (Kendall 319). While technology might be changing, the folktales and fairy tales that continue to be told and distributed online are still profoundly human and linked to identity in the actual world. When people's lives in the actual world are shaped by misogyny, homophobia, xenophobia, racism, and other forms of bigotry and hate, whether as perpetrators or victims, it inevitably becomes visible online. Undeniably, what we say and do online pulls from what we already know or rather *think* we know both about ourselves as well as the world around us; both positive and negative. With the discussion of "we" who belong in communal identity construction is also an inherent conception of "they" who do not. In what follows, I investigate two topics where fans actively discuss the inclusion or exclusion of individuals based on their sexual, racial, and ethnic identity.

## "Ich rede jetzt von den Medien" / ["I'm talking now about the media"] ("Warum wird FemSlash"): Identity Construction and Women's Sexuality

Within various forum threads on *FanFiktion.de*, members of the L.G.B.T.Q.+ community write that they come to places like *FanFiktion.de* "um Menschen [zu finden], denen es genauso geht wie mir" [in order [to find] people, who have experiences like me] and that they are pleased to find a place online where they are able to speak and discuss their experiences with others to better understand and accept themselves ("Transgender/Bigender/Androgyn"). The actual world can be a place rife with inhibitions, barriers, and obstacles that individuals must compete with and overcome in everyday interactions. It is perhaps the anonymous and pseudonymous ways that interactions take place online that can facilitate unprecedented levels of affection, intimacy, and informality. This can bring into focus just how disruptive those obstacles and barriers in the actual world can be for different members of society for varied reasons (Plant 143). Here I investigate how fans discuss specific obstacles and barriers they experience in the actual world through their discussions of a specific fan fiction genre: FemSlash.

In threads on *FanFiktion.de*, fans describe that they write and prefer to read FemSlash—fics featuring queer women's relationships—"weil [sie] Representation schmerzlich vermisse[n]" [because [they] bitterly miss [having] representation]. Dawnbreaker writes that she began writing FemSlash

> weil mir lesbische Figuren in Spielen und Filmen fehl(t)en. Tauchen sie auf, sind es fast immer Witzfiguren und das macht mich wütend. Klischees eben vom männerhassenden Mannweib. Schlimm so etwas [...]. Ich empfinde dies als sehr erniedrigend, genauso wie die Darstellung von Schwulen [...]. Ich möchte dagegenhalten mit meinen Geschichten.
>
> [because I lack(ed) lesbian characters in games and films. Should they appear, they are almost always clown figures and that makes me furious. Clichés of man-hating butches. Horrible, those depictions [...]. I find this to be very degrading, just like the depictions of gays [...]. I would like to go against that with my stories.] ("Warum wird FemSlash")

Other fans' comments similarly indicate that their affinity to FemSlash is not just that they wish to see more representation of the L.G.B.T.Q.+ community within popular media, but that often the characters portrayed in popular media are done so stereotypically and offensively. The lack of representation as well as misrepresentation in the media can be strong driving forces for the creation of fan fiction. Multiple reports across decades have shown that exposure to harmful stereotypes in the media such as the ones described previously can lead to serious real-life consequences. The images and characterizations portrayed on screen both reflect as well as reinforce preexisting social beliefs (Poland 7). If narrative is strongly tied to identity construction, then certainly negative, stereotypical representation in media can produce and reinforce negative or stereotypical associations within not just the individual, but in society-at-large as well. These fans explain that their motivation to write fan fiction is their own attempt to make the canon more inclusive and more accurately representative of the L.G.B.T.Q.+ community.

As a specific example of a fic written to increase inclusivity, we can look to Perscitia's "Die Gänsemagd in Sonnenau" [The Goose-Girl in Sonnenau] (accessed 2021), where the main character is able to learn self-love and acceptance once she finds true love, not in her "Prince Charming," as she assumes, but rather in another woman, Sophie. Sophie helps main character Elizabeth realize that she is unhappy attempting to conform to societal expectations of heterosexual love and marriage as a woman's happy ending. Throughout the fic, Sophie continually encourages Elizabeth to reflect on her choice to try and remain with the prince by repeatedly asking her "bist du glücklich?" [are you happy?] She reminds Elizabeth that true love should not cause one to live in self-doubt and unhappiness. As the story comes to a close, Elizabeth has finally realized that she can only be happy once she leaves her life of forced conformity—with marriage to a prince and the expectation of merely producing heirs to the throne—and joins Sophie. Sophie gives Elizabeth one more chance to go back to her prince, before leaving together. Sophie speaks:

> "Noch kannst du dich entscheiden, noch kannst du zurück."
>
> [Elizabeth] schüttelte den Kopf.
>
> "Nein," sagte sie bestimmt. "Das kann ich nicht […]. Ich hoffe, es macht dir nichts aus, wenn ich ein Weilchen hierbleibe," lächelte sie und ging auf Sophie zu. Sophie legte ihr die Arme um die Taille und strahlte sie an […]. Elizabeth grinste und fuhr der anderen liebevoll durchs Haar … und als sie ihre Lippen auf Sophies drückte, wusste sie, dass sie endlich dort war, wo sie hingehörte, in ihrem Sonnenau.
>
> ["You can still decide, you can still go back."
>
> [Elizabeth] shook her head.

> "No," she said assuredly. "I can't […]. I hope it's not inconvenient for you if I stay here a while," she smiled and went over to Sophie. Sophie laid her arms around her waist and beamed at her […]. Elizabeth grinned and pushed [her hand], full of love, through Sophie's hair … and as she pressed her lips to Sophie's, she knew that she was finally there where she belonged, in her Sonnenau.]

Perscitia's fic shows that multiple happy endings to fairy tales are possible, and that this was one that was personally fitting for Elizabeth and Sophie. While a "Prince Charming" might be an ideal ending for some, for others it can feel like being trapped. Finally in the end, only after she is honest with herself about her feelings for Sophie, can Elizabeth be content and live her "happily ever after."

Though Perscitia's fic is certainly of interest on its own, it was a contribution to a project started by another fan. In an Author's Note (A.N.) at the beginning of the fic, Perscitia writes: "Wilkommen! Danke, dass ihr euch für diesen Beitrag zum Projekt 'Märchen Female-Slash' von Hikari D Tenshi interessiert." [Welcome! Thank you, that you guys are interested in this contribution to the project "Fairy Tale Female-Slash" from Hikari D Tenshi.] The project is one started by fan Hikari D Tenshi in order to bring more attention to FemSlash and, specifically, to promote the writing of FemSlash fairy tales in particular.

Hikari D Tenshi describes her project:

> Da ich gerade am Schreiben einer Story für das Projekt "Mami, warum küsst der Prinz da einen Jungen?" bin und ich es schade finde, dass da nur Male Slash erlaubt ist hatte ich die Idee für dieses Projekt. Vielleicht haben auch noch andere Lust ein Märchen dieser Art [FemSlash] zu schreiben.
>
> [Because I'm currently writing a story for the project "Mommy, why is the prince kissing a boy?" and I find it a shame that only Male Slash is allowed there, I had the idea for this project. Perhaps others have a desire to write fairy tales in this way [FemSlash].] ([Projekt])

Hikari D Tenshi's project is well received by all 12 individuals who joined the thread, though it is of note that the number of participants and replies remain small. There are many reasons why this may be, given the large number of discussion threads on *FanFiktion.de*, and that there might be multiple points where similar topics are posted or crossposted (posted in more than one place) online. Hikari D Tenshi's project, however, highlights something of importance: that FemSlash is a relatively uncommon occurrence. This is recognized by fans as well given the presence of threads such as "Warum wird FemSlash seltener geschrieben als MaleSlash?" [Why is FemSlash less common than MaleSlash?]. The seemingly general term for homosexual relationships—"Slash"—also nearly always refers just to male/male relationships; the term FemSlash has been created for female/female relationships. Notably, at the time of this writing there is also a lack of terminology to mark stories that feature nonbinary characters. The term "Slash" itself derives from m/m pairings in *Star Trek* fan fiction ("Slash")—though that is certainly not to say that MaleSlash is as wildly popular as fan fiction seems to get the reputation of having (Busse 49). Scholarship on FemSlash specifically remains incredibly sparse and the existence of women writing about queer women in fan fiction is generally ignored (Narai 1.1).

Rates will certainly differ from fandom to fandom given the canon the fandom is based on, though within the "Grimms Märchen" fandom, out of 161 fics only 13 could be identified as "Slash" in general—only 8%—and of those 13, 4 were "FemSlash" (slightly less than a third.) To ask the same question that fans asked each other: Why *is* FemSlash less common than MaleSlash? Of participants in the threads discussing FemSlash, several attempted explanations arise which give insights into the influence of Western European societal expectations of fans on *FanFiktion.de*. And we should keep in mind that fan fiction is still largely written by women. Listed in no particular order, though assuredly interrelated, fans explain that (1) FemSlash has a harder time staying within the rating rules of fan fiction websites due to (ostensibly) inherently more overt sexualization than MaleSlash, (2) the MaleSlash genre is largely a heterosexual female fantasy that has nothing to do with L.G.B.T.Q.+ communities and therefore, fans write, focuses on men as the object of its heterosexual female readership's desire and, (3) the amount of FemSlash depends on the fandom and the canon material and therefore the specific audiences of those canons.

Point #1 suggests that sexual experiences between women are somehow more explicit than those between men. Comments from fans reveal a fair amount of veiled (and sometimes quite explicit) homophobia. Comments appeared multiple times stating that FemSlash "scheint noch schwieriger als bei maleslash zu sein, dass man innerhalb der Regeln bleibt" [appears to be more difficult than maleslash to remain within the rules] ("Warum wird FemSlash") of the rating system to limit explicit descriptions of sex. This perspective is largely unexplained by fans, rather it is an assumption which most within the comment thread treat as self-evident. Comments such as noting that FemSlash is "etwas anderes ... Besonderes" [something different ... special] ("Warum wird FemSlash") likewise suggests an exoticization of the pairing. These descriptions of FemSlash are significantly different from the ones noted previously from L.G.B.T.Q.+ fans who state that they write FemSlash for the sake of having more (and more accurate) representation. Many comments in the thread stemming from people self-identifying as straight seem to try and define FemSlash as risqué, dirty, and decidedly "other." There appear to be different standards within the thread for Male- and FemSlash, and the bar for FemSlash in this thread seems to be on the floor. One fan writes:

> wenn deine Figur sich nicht jede zweite Minute in den Schritt greift und darüber redet wie dämlich Frauen sind, machst du alles richtig.
>
> [if your character doesn't grab herself in the crotch every two minutes and talk about how stupid women are, you're doing everything right.] ("Warum wird FemSlash")

Apparently, as long as queer women characters do not behave like asocial sexual deviants, they are viewed here as "appropriate" portrayals. Fans within the thread often rely upon and reinforce stereotypes of queer women as being unable to control themselves around other women.

Thinking through the ideas of identity play with comments such as these can help us understand where these homophobic comments might be coming from. These reactions to FemSlash are examples of "impossible" or "improbable selves" for many of the straight women commenting in the thread. Though there are L.G.B.T.Q.+ fans on *FanFiktion.de*, one can certainly see sharp lines nevertheless being drawn by other fans around who is considered a part of the community and who is not. With FemSlash in particular, especially within these threads, homosexuality is both "othered," and exoticized. While people may at times be more comfortable expressing extreme views online than they would in the actual world, such expressions of bigotry often reflect the true beliefs they hold. Those perspectives and opinions, extreme or not, are also not confined to or created solely in online spaces. It is important when discussing queer/feminist politics to discuss how people online are neither disconnected from discourses of gender and sexuality nor from the material specificity of the actual world (Bromseth and Sundén 275). Societal influences and experiences absolutely transfer to online interactions since people are both acting and being acted upon simultaneously. Here we can likewise see that the existence of MaleSlash and FemSlash does not necessarily equate with overall acceptance of the genre or L.G.B.T.Q.+ community members.

Heteronormative expectations for relationships become more obvious in users' attempts to defend their statements against FemSlash which end up revealing deep-seated, though perhaps subconscious, homophobia. It is certainly telling that for many fans, these are the depictions they believe to be true of homosexual relationships in general, and queer women specifically. In one example, a fan attempts to justify their homophobic stance on FemSlash:

> also, ich persönlich habe weder etwas gegen Schwule noch was gegen Lesben. Aber ich muss gestehen, dass es mir unangenehm wird, wenn ich weiß, dass ein Mädchen in meinem Umfeld lesbisch ist.
>
> [so, I personally don't have anything against either gays or anything against lesbians. But I have to say that it's uncomfortable for me when I know that a girl in my vicinity is lesbian.] "Schwul/lesbisch/bi")

The comment is couched in a failed attempt to free the fan from attacks that they are intolerant. They attempt to justify their following comment, yet it is obvious from their description of being uncomfortable in the presence of queer women that they believe on some level the stereotype of hypersexualization—of queer women somehow being unable to control themselves around other women.

The overt sexualization of women is often linked with heterosexual male desire and the male gaze since representations of women, especially two women in an intimate context, are displayed in various popular media simply as sexualized objects to be inspected for the viewer's pleasure and oriented toward men (Bauer 55) rather than representing any sort of accurate portrayal of women's sexuality. Homophobic women are likewise often afraid of queer women due to a preconceived notion—adopted from experiences with men—that if someone is attracted to them, they will be aggressively pursued whether their advances are invited or not. Unfortunately, many homophobic comments and types of homophobic behavior are shown and reinforced in forms of popular media, especially with depictions of sexual relationships (or even just encounters) between women being hypersexualized, exoticized, and treated as casual flings. If they are not, queer women in popular media are, as Dawnbreaker mentions, treated as comical figures who just act as foils to other characters. Fans who reject this oversexualization of straight women with their dismissals of FemSlash, by stating that it is difficult for FemSlash to stay within the rules of graphic sexual content on *FanFiktion.de*, could be rejecting situations which they have been conditioned to understand as objectification in much of popular media, though they are nevertheless engaging in homophobic discourse to do so—dismissing actual experiences of queer women.

The refusal to critically examine what is portrayed in popular media or acknowledge the effects these stereotypes play is known as the "third-person effect." And it is precisely those who assume that stereotypes in media do not affect them who are the ones most likely to absorb these harmful and discriminatory messages (Poland 8). The misguided belief that the messages and images do not affect individuals can lead to a passive acceptance of bigoted and discriminatory portrayals. Fan fiction can certainly push against these harmful stereotypes in the media and craft new narratives which are more representative and inclusive. Nevertheless, fandoms cannot entirely escape the pressures of social norms and how these norms may form individual perceptions.

Point #2, that the MaleSlash genre is largely a heterosexual female fantasy, is certainly interconnected with Point #1. The stereotypical depictions of queer women in many comments, such as those discussed previously, reinforce dominant heteronormative expectations of Western European society, even if they do so with positive depictions of male homosexual relationships. Comments make clear that while the category of "Slash" can allow a place for L.G.B.T.Q.+ fans to write and share stories, fandoms in general are not always places supportive of the L.G.B.T.Q.+ community.

Fics and comments which are not supportive reveal wider societal views and expectations of L.G.B.T.Q.+ relationships. Highlighting the misrepresentation of homosexual relationships within the "MaleSlash" category, Dawnbreaker describes a conversation that took place with a friend:

> Interessanterweise liest ein schwuler Freund von mir kaum Maleslash Geschichten, wenn diese von Frauen geschrieben werden. Er meint, sie würden ihre Moralvorstellungen auf Männerpaare übertragen und das schreckt ihn total ab. Letztendlich sind es dann Frauenfantasien, aber nicht seine.
>
> [Interestingly, a gay friend of mine reads barely any Maleslash stories if they are written by women. He says that they're written with their [women's] ideas towards morality just transferred to male couples and that completely puts him off. In the end they're just women's fantasies, but not his.] ("Warum wird FemSlash")

Dawnbreaker's conversation with her friend, and similar comments in response to her post, show how depictions of homosexual relationships within fandom can still reinforce heteronormative expectations. Some of these fics are not truly representative of the L.G.B.T.Q.+ community and depict attitudes, norms, and behaviors of heterosexual relationships with simply one character "gender bended," or depicted as another gender. While comments from fans at the beginning of this section showed that some fans enjoy writing and reading FemSlash because they crave more and appropriate representation, here we can see from Dawnbreaker's description that fan fiction is also not free of inaccurate and harmful stereotypes.

With a general sense of "if one man is attractive, then two are doubly so" as an explanation for the preference of MaleSlash, many fans note that they find male-presenting characters simply more desirable. Self-identifying heterosexual women describe within the threads that they are more interested in MaleSlash because they are attracted to men and therefore are more interested in reading stories with a male love interest; this is described as more important to them than identifying with a female protagonist. Of course, while there are also those who feel that it is important to identify with the protagonist based on gender, some straight women writing and reading MaleSlash write that they feel that gender is secondary to identifying with other personality traits of the main character and therefore create male characters who follow heterosexual women's conceptions of relationships. In a similar vein, some fans note that they believe a relationship between two male characters removes the power imbalance inherent in many heterosexual pairings and they perceive these same-sex depictions as allowing them to write relationships in a more balanced and "ideal" way ("Warum wird FemSlash"). Though this is certainly an attempt to reformulate power dynamics, it is also an inaccurate portrayal of male same-sex relationships as highlighted by the comments from Dawnbreaker—sharing gender alone does not erase power dynamics within relationships. This portrayal still describes male same-sex relationships through a heteronormative lens rather than a homonormative one (Van Eeden-Moorefield 565). This depiction of MaleSlash highlights both the appropriation and misunderstanding of male same-sex relationships by some women writers of MaleSlash fics.

Finally, point #3: The amount and acceptance of FemSlash leans heavily on the fandom and the canon material. BreitzbachBea writes "hätten wir hier eine größere Gemeinde an LGBTQA+ Frauen, hätten wir vielleicht auch mehr FemSlash" [if we had here a larger community of LGBTQA+ women, we would perhaps have more FemSlash]. Though another fan responds to her comment that: "Och, ich glaube schon, dass es hier genügend LGBTQA Schreiber/innen gibt [...] es hängt auch viel vom Fandom ab" [Oh, I really believe that there are enough LGBTQA writers [...] it depends a lot on the fandom] ("Warum wird FemSlash"). Fans note that depending on the canon media, there are frequently fewer women characters (or main characters) to include in their fics, so male characters might lend themselves better to relationships in fic for those particular canons. Canon media which already contain L.G.B.T.Q.+ characters, for example, could lend themselves to many more Male- and FemSlash interpretations. Likewise, while some fandoms will be more accepting of Male- and FemSlash fics, certain fandoms are known to be more bigoted, racist, and misogynistic than others depending on the canon. For example, in a survey of people who visited Comic Con—a yearly convention dedicated to awareness and appreciation of pop culture art forms—numerous women cited anime fandoms in particular for being more obvious about misogyny both in content of the canon and the fandom due to some anime canon media that overly sexualize or objectify women characters (Nisbett 179). If a fandom revolves around a book, film, or show that supports misogynistic portrayals of women, the fandom is also more likely to have more misogynistic fan fiction, fan art, or other fan interpretations.

While there are many examples of intolerance, there are likewise many fans coming together and supporting one another, showcasing multiple ideas and opinions on the website. While there are certainly trends within specific fandoms that are crucial to discuss, no one functions entirely within fan culture and there are no claims to fan culture as being somehow self-sustaining (Jenkins, *Textual Poachers* 3). People are members of multiple communities and groups simultaneously and will gain understanding, experience, and be influenced from many different directions. Communities and groups, in the actual world as well as online, often contain seeming contradictions. Not all associations are good ones, and not all communities are effective for all users at all times (Avance 67). Despite the bigoted beliefs that some fans have on *FanFiktion.de* one fan writes:

> Mir fällt allgemein auf, dass hier in der Community mehr verstanden wird, als in anderen Foren. Ich denke mal, das schwierigste ist, zu lernen, mit sich selbst ins Reine zu kommen.
>
> [I've noticed in general that here in the community more is understood than in other forums. I think that the hardest part is to learn to come to terms with oneself.] ("Transgender/Bigender/Androgyn")

That *FanFiktion.de* and various fandoms can be both inclusive as well as exclusionary is not something that is contradictory, but rather something that is inherent in all communities.

## "Nein, ich meine wo du *wirklich* herkommst." / ["No, I mean where you *really* come from."] ("Eure Erfahrungen"): Identity Construction and Race/Ethnicity

In conversations about race and ethnicity, fans were much more likely to discuss their experiences in the actual world than those online. One thread on *FanFiktion.de* deals exclusively with racism ("Eure Erfahrungen mit Rassismus, Sexismus, Antisemitismus, etc." [Your experiences with racism, sexism, antisemitism, etc.)]. This thread was started on June 17, 2020, nearly a month after demonstrations erupted in the United States over the filmed murder of George Floyd, a Black man, by a Minneapolis police officer. Demonstrations soon began to take place outside the United States as people demanded justice for yet another brutal murder of a person of color by police and calling for an end to systemic racism. The Original Poster (O.P.) of the thread, Lamy Lestrange, even cites the event as one of the reasons for starting the discussion. She writes,

> zur Zeit wird oft über sowas [Rassismus] gesprochen, auch mit der Sache mit dem Mord an George Floyd, etc.
>
> [currently there's a lot of discussion about such things [racism] also with the situation about the murder of George Floyd, etc.]

In this thread, fans spoke of their experiences in the actual world. Lord Anubis, a fan who describes themself as "zur Hälfte chinesisch (und sehe aber eigentlich nur asiatisch aus, meine deutsche Seite sieht man jetzt eher nicht)" [half Chinese (and actually look just Asian, one can't see my German side as well)], explains that they have experienced jokes at their expense due exclusively to their appearance. They write that these discriminatory comments have only increased due to the spread of COVID-19 and the tendency for both people and the media to place the blame on China for the spread of the pandemic. They note, however, that even before COVID-19 they heard comments on their appearance.

> Aber natürlich ist das auch nicht nur in Deutschland so, in China werde ich dauernd mit Englisch angesprochen, als ob man mir nicht zutrauen würde dass ich Chinesisch sprechen kann. Manchmal habe ich so richtig das Gefühl nirgendwo wirklich dazu zugehören oder zu Hause zu sein [...]. Weil überall wird mir gesagt, dass ich doch eigentlich genau auf die andere Seite gehöre.
>
> [But of course it's not just like that in Germany, in China I'm always spoken to in English like one wouldn't dare think I could speak Chinese. Sometimes I really have the feeling that I don't belong anywhere or have a home [...]. Because everywhere people tell me that I belong exactly on the other side.] ("Eure Erfahrungen")

Lord Anubis brings up an issue common not only to people who are a part of multiple cultures (such as themselves who live in Germany but have family that they visit in China), but also people who do not fit stereotypical expectations of, in Lord Anubis's case, what a "German" looks like. Lord Anubis is both "too Chinese" to be considered German as well as "too Western" to be considered Chinese.

Even when fans discuss their personal experiences in the actual world, one can see how these attitudes and beliefs from the actual world transfer to how they respond and react online. The O.P. of the racism/sexism thread begins by sharing her personal experience with racism by writing that since her father and grandparents come from North Africa, she has been harassed because of her appearance by fellow students at her school. She notes that due to her hair and skin color, she has been accused of having "einen behaarten Körper" [a hairy body] and as being a "behaartes Türkenschwein," [a hairy Turkish pig], revealing flippant racist and xenophobic remarks that seem to indiscriminately "other" everyone with brown skin as "Turkish." Similarly to Lord Anubis, she explains that her language abilities are placed into question. She states she has been asked even by professionals such as doctors if she can speak any German.

It is obviously racist to call a non-white person by the names Lamy Lestrange lists, though the questioning of her language abilities by doctors is also racist. Pauline Greenhill writes that racism is discourse about difference and specifically about "differences that make a difference" (227). For Lamy Lestrange, her skin color has clearly been seen as a difference in how doctors interact with her and likely, in how they treat her medically. Race might be a cultural construction which is based on appearance and sociocultural status among other factors (Greenhill 227), but the cultural aspect does not make it less real or harmful for people who are othered like Lord Anubis and Lamy Lestrange.

The responses to Lamy Lestrange are telling. There are certainly people like Lord Anubis responding and sharing their own experiences with racism. Yet there are others who jump in and try to "help" Lamy Lestrange by noting that perhaps, due to her comment that she is harassed for having seemingly excessive body hair, that there is something medically wrong with her hormones causing her to have more hair than she should.

In comments, someone writes that she should go to the doctor to be tested for some sort of hormone imbalance. Lamy Lestrange initially replies to the comment about hormonal imbalance as portraying unjust views of how women should appear, noting the obsession in much of Western culture for women to continually shave and appear hairless. Though when the commenter replies again, once more bringing to attention their suggestion about seeing a doctor, stating that they are just trying to offer her advice, Lamy Lestrange replies:

> Ich weiß (bzw hoffe) dass du das nicht böse gemeint hast aber erstens hab ich nicht gefragt was ich tun soll, sondern ob ihr schon Erfahrungen mit Rassismus gemacht habt, zweitens hab ich eine ganz normale Körperbehaarung, die aufgrund meiner Gene einfach nur dunkler und auffälliger sind! / Drittens ist sowas genau das was ich meine, immer bekommt man solche blöden Kommentare, die verletzend sind auch wenn du das wahrscheinlich für eine angemessene Reaktion hältst. Ich habe NICHT gefragt warum ich das habe und was ich tun soll!
>
> [I know (or rather hope) that you didn't mean that badly but first, I didn't ask what I should do, rather if you guys have already had experience with racism, second, I have a totally normal amount of body hair which is, due to my genes, simply darker and more noticeable! / Third, that's exactly what I meant, one always gets such stupid comments which are hurtful even though you probably view it as an appropriate reaction. I did NOT ask why I have it and what I should do!]

Comments like those from the fan who claimed they just wanted to "help" show either an ignorance or denial of the different power dynamics of some groups over others. Clearly for Lamy Lestrange, her skin and hair color are differences that make a difference in how others treat her. The fan who continually offers their unsolicited advice is still making a racist comment even if it was unintentional. Lack of intent does not free one from how the consequences their comments or actions are received. Similar to the media discussion about L.G.B.T.Q.+ representation, we likewise see here examples of the "third-person effect." Fans in this comment thread who claim to be unbiased and unaffected by negative portrayals in the media are precisely the ones who seem to lack the most awareness of offensive remarks they make. As the thread continues, there seems to be a fundamental misunderstanding of what exactly constitutes as racism when certain fans comment that at times they are looked at strangely or receive comments for having red hair, appearing Swedish, or for different amounts of makeup they apply. Finally, the thread begins to devolve into various members saying that questions posed specifically to individuals who do not appear European or who have seemingly strange names are meant well and therefore cannot possibly be racist. The questions that Lord Anubis (and certainly many others) pointed out as being hurtful such as "where do you come from?" (and the even worse variant: "where do you *really* come from?" when individuals reply by stating their local home town) are excused. Multiple fans describe their negative experiences with the question "where do you come from?" -AngelOfMusic- writes:

> Dann sollen die Leute lieber gleich fragen, ob man überhaupt deutsch ist oder nicht. Für mich ist das einfach versteckter Rassismus—nur weil man nicht das typisch deutsche Aussehen hat.
>
> [The people should rather just ask if one is even German or not. For me it's simply hidden racism—just because one doesn't have the typical German appearance.]

In reinforcing various stereotypes, some users show the enactment of drawing lines around who belongs to certain communities and what will be discussed. For some, it has become a part of their beliefs about themselves that they cannot possibly be racist, even when confronted by others who inform them that their actions and words are offensive. More than one fan persisted in contradicting comments like -AngelOfMusic-'s even after multiple explanations detailing how and why the question is offensive. One writes:

> Für mich ist es gerade ein WTF [what the fuck], dass es schon rassistisch sein soll, wenn man jemanden nur fragt, wo er herkommt. Was, bitte, ist daran rassistisch?
>
> [For me it's just a WTF [what the fuck] that it should be racist if one just asks someone where he comes from. What, please, is racist about that?]

Even confronted with explanations of what exactly about the question is racist, this fan's understanding of themselves as not racist, is more important than the many lived experiences of others in the thread. For some fans, it seems as though if one of their comments could be seen as racist, they believe they are being labeled a "racist person" rather than the term being used to describe their comment or question. Fear of being labeled "a Racist" seems to put some fans on the defensive. The fans who defend their right to ask questions like "where do you come from?" also tend to define racism so restrictively that their comments could not possibly fit the definition. That is, comments such as the previous quote seem to suggest that as long as they do not explicitly state that they do not believe a non-white person could be German, the question is not racist.

It is important to remember from the earlier investigation of misogyny online, that inequality has been integral to online communities (Boellstorff 226). Online worlds, just as much as the actual world, have always been and continue to be spaces where dominance, authority, control, and difference remain deeply important. Similar types of control tactics that are used in the actual world appear online (Poland 17). Research shows that many online harassers are more comfortable expressing harmful views or engaging in abuse online when they think they are anonymous rather than anonymity prompting people to express beliefs they do not actually hold. Claiming that anonymous, online views are not real is simply a strategy for avoiding criticism (Poland 23).

In a demonstration of the online culture of *FanFiktion.de*, there are multiple threads on topics of gender and sexuality, however, as of July 2021 when I was researching this chapter, there was only one thread dedicated to the topic of racism. Based on the presence of these threads and fans' discussion of the topics, users on *FanFiktion.de* seem willing to explicitly discuss gender and sexuality. That the thread about racism was started only in 2020 can likewise suggest that sections of wider German-speaking society are more open to discussing gender and sexuality than race and ethnicity. While in the fandom, comment sections on specific fics contain no discussion of skin color or racism directly, we can see fans' views mirrored in certain fics. As one fan comments "der eigene Stil basiert auch auf dem, womit man sich so umgibt" [one's unique style is based on one's surroundings] ("Umfrage zum Thema"). By investigating fics, one can see the role racism and xenophobia play in German-speaking society. After all, conceptualizations of both individual and communal identity are at least partially constructed through an implied contrast with others (Del Negro and Berger, "Identity Reconsidered"136). Inclusion and exclusion are two ways to describe the process of establishing boundaries: in defining who their members are, communities also define who they are not and vice versa. Interpretations of identity are thus constructed within the community by the way fans relate, empathize, and support one another and how they contrast themselves with society at large alongside other groups and communities. Who we like and support can construct identity just as much as who we do not like and exclude.

As briefly noted in the Introduction, the majority of fics within the fandom (63%) had no description of character appearance or a description that was so vague that race/ethnicity could not be determined, such as a simple explanation that a character had brown hair, or that an elderly character had white in their hair. By contrast, 26% of stories contained characters that were described as identifiably white (i.e., either specifically noting that the character had white skin, or describing the character as having blonde hair and blue eyes). There was only one fic out of the 161 where a character was written as an identifiable person of color. The fandom does appear to have an assumption of whiteness. An individual or community's folklore is inevitably determined by the nature of their experiences and surroundings and an investigation of these can show us where communities have progressed and where they still need to go.

Many of the fics that directly state a character had white skin were based on "Snow White" (ATU 709), owing surely to the description in the Grimm tale of "Snow White" being "as white as snow, and red as blood, and her hair was as black as ebony" (187) as well as the 1937 Disney depiction of a very pale, white protagonist. Of particular interest for their depictions of race, however, were fics of "Little Red Riding Hood" (ATU 333) where a description of skin color is not mentioned until Little Red Riding Hood is in danger. In Cela's fic "Little Red Riding Hood" discussed previously (which highlighted men in positions of power taking advantage of their unsuspecting victims), once inside her grandmother's house, Little Red Riding Hood is struck with fear, when she notices the house in disarray. We read:

> Sie erstarrte wie ein verängstigtes Kaninchen und ihr Herz setzte einen Schlag aus. Doch er zögerte nicht. Mit geübten Händen ergriff er mit der Einen ihre Handgelenke und legte die Andere auf ihren Mund [...]. Gierig sog er ihren Duft ein. So süß, wie

> eine Blume—seine Blume [...]. Ihr Brustkorb bebte unter ihrer weißen, weichen Haut. So makellos.
>
> [She stared like a frightened rabbit and her heart skipped a beat. But he didn't hesitate. With practiced hands, he grabbed her wrists with one hand and laid the other over her mouth [...]. Greedily he breathed her scent in. So sweet, like a flower—his flower [...]. Her chest moved under her white, soft skin. So flawless.]

For Cela's fic, this is the first mention of Little Red Riding Hood's skin color, curiously appearing only once she is in a situation in which she must be rescued if she is to live to the end of the tale—only when Little Red Riding Hood is positioned as the damsel in distress. In another fic that follows a similar plot, Bexorcict's "Das arme Rotkäppchen" [The Poor Little Red Riding Hood (accessed 2021),] as the wolf springs on Little Red Riding Hood and is about to attack her, the description of her reads "ihre komplette Haut war nun weiß wie der Schnee" [all of her skin was then as white as snow]. Like in Cela's fic, Little Red Riding Hood's skin color is only mentioned once she is in danger, and is likewise compared to snow which is often associated with purity and innocence. As Ruby Hamad points out, in Western society "only white damsels can be in distress" while women of color are often described as being undeserving of rescue for various reasons depending on racial stereotypes—whether it be that they are too angry, too sexualized, somehow not innocent enough, or not even considered to fall into the "damsel" category (77). With the description of her skin color comes a supposed reassurance of Little Red Riding Hood's innocence as we see with descriptions of her being described as a "rabbit," a gentle "flower," and having "soft" skin. She is a fragile creature in need of rescuing before she is deflowered.

This is not to say that these fics are representative of all fics within the fandom with their depictions of women who are put into horrible situations—which has been shown through various others in which women characters are portrayed as saving themselves or rescuing one another. These versions of "Little Red Riding Hood" do, however, represent something of interest in determining the role of community conceptions of innocence and purity, victimhood, as well as assumptions of whiteness. Not all modern or fan fiction versions of fairy tales can serve emancipatory or liberatory functions as part of a community's folklore, they inevitably also rely on and reinforce social norms. Some fics can even reinforce social norms as well as serve liberatory functions such as the aforementioned passage from Cela's fic. Her fic focuses on the victimization and sexual predation young women experience in Western society and highlights the negative toxicity in this attitude toward women as simply sexual conquests for men. At the same time, the fic likewise reinforces racial stereotypes of purity and innocence, as well as white women needing to be rescued from vicious, animal-like sexual predators. While "Little Red Riding Hood" might be a fairy tale in which the wolf punishes the girl's curiosity, where males determine feminine limits (Bacchilega, *Postmodern Fairy Tales* 59), by emphasizing Little Red Riding Hood's skin color only once she is victimized, it seems that it may in fact only be determining *white* feminine limits.

The only fic with an identifiable person of color is a fic based on "Sleeping Beauty" (ATU 410) filled with the names of celebrities, though most of the celebrities are white German television stars. The evil fairy is described as Mariah Carey, a celebrity whose father was an African American/Venezuelan American. The evil fairy is responsible for cursing Sleeping Beauty and tricking her into pricking her finger on the spinning wheel so that she falls into her death-like slumber (Pterano Dante, "Es ist nun einmal so"). The fic itself is a farcical presentation of the "Sleeping Beauty" narrative. The plot and writing are frivolous and at times even absurd, existing mainly to portray celebrities as characters within a fairy tale. Though the sampling size is too small to allow for any analysis beyond conjecture, this portrayal of the only character who is a person of color in the fandom can show some prejudices that a person of color cannot feature prominently in a story that is not intended to be farcical. Additionally, the only identifiable person of color is also an evil character; as of the time of my writing, there were no identifiable protagonists of color.

On a few occasions, fics invoked stereotypes through characters speaking in Turkish-German dialect. Interestingly, the characters themselves, if they were described physically at all, were written as identifiably white characters. They also only spoke in dialect for a few sentences at a time before slipping back to dialog written in standard High German. Of particular note is that characters only spoke in Turkish-German dialect when angry and were always described as yelling these lines. In DeLullu's

"Rotkäppchens Mission" [Little Red Riding Hood's Mission], a male character begins to stare at Little Red Riding Hood and does not respond when she asks him direct questions. She gets angry at the man and says:

> "Ey, wenn du misch blöd anmachn willst, alda, dann tust an da falschn Adresse sein, eh, alda!" sagte Rotkäppchen in feinsten, akzentfreien Türkisch-Deutsch.
>
> ["Hey, if you want to stupidly come on to me, buddy, you're barking up the wrong tree, hey buddy!"[1] said Little Red Riding Hood in the best, accent-free Turkish-German.]

When he does not stop staring at her, she yells a second time and is described as "nun voll in Rage" [completely in a rage]. That characters only speak in Turkish-German dialect when angry and yelling only builds off of and reinforces stereotypes of the angry, exoticized "other." Likewise, speaking to the leering man in a Turkish-German dialect seems to suggest that he is a person of color since she can be seen as speaking to him in "his" language. She speaks to no other characters in the fic in such a dialect. Although his appearance is not described, we can assume that this character is an object of harmful and racist stereotypes of non-white men who take advantage of innocent white European women.

Investigating folklore such as fan fiction allows us to examine the multiplicity of fairy-tale versions as well as investigate the many voices that are incorporated. They offer a multilayered reflection not just on the fairy tales themselves, but also on social practices and cultural values of which the fans are a part. It is highly unusual to find only one homogenous discourse within a community (Berger and Conrad 2). Like any community, attitudes and beliefs of different members are more accepting in some areas than others. So while we might see areas of great emancipation and challenging of societal norms, due to this multilayered reflection, we also see areas of extreme prejudice such as the portrayal of people of color—most notably people of Turkish or North African descent—or disparaging dialects associated with historically excluded groups.

1 While I have been able to translate the meaning of the words said by Little Red Riding Hood, the phonetic spelling to simulate the Turkish-German dialect was untranslatable.

Narrative not only reflects life but is one of the chief means through which ideas and conceptions of race, class, gender, and other parts of identity are discussed, debated, challenged, and reinforced. The presence of bigotry and intolerance can certainly complicate the archival impulse of folklorists, though ignoring its presence likewise ignores beliefs and behavioral impulses of sometimes large sections of society. This is not to say, of course, that these depictions are not problematic, discriminatory, or should not be addressed. But shying away from the uncomfortable, the muddy, and sometimes the bleakest depictions of human nature does not mean that they are not still present.

Online storytelling provides another opportunity for folklorists to explore the roles of different narratives in folklore as well as personal and community identity. In the stories we tell, people are continually defining the social groups to which they both do and do not belong. Folklore can richly represent a community's various hopes and wishes as well as its fears, anxieties, and prejudices. The stories we tell can foster an "unfolding of the self" (Naidoo 4). The canon tales that individual fans choose and how they change and alter the plots and characters can be empowering in terms of identity construction and be used to verify and explore identity through play or they can reinforce stereotypes and bigoted views. What the story is about—whether chosen consciously or not—depends on the storyteller and how they see the world, and how they want others to see it. There is a continued circulation of these stories where social practices are re-negotiated and examined. These stories serve fans in the process of self-making not only personally, as fans describe the way their stories may be used to explore their personal histories, feelings, and relationships. They also serve as a process by which fans discover their relationships to the world, and the influence of the societal opinions and beliefs from which they come; they reveal deeply situated human behavior.

Fairy tales are both produced and consumed to serve functions in society, working to contextualize, at times problematize, and imbue them with meanings which are situated within their lived realities both personal and social. These stories work in response to the community aesthetics toward power and identity and in turn can come to shape them as new narratives come to be adopted. Through online identity play fans can imagine, explore, and investigate these roles. While many adaptations show evolving cultural attitudes within specific communities toward sexuality and toward imbalances in male and female power, we can likewise investigate these narratives to consider where societies need to grow and develop with respect to inclusion and understanding.

CHAPTER 7

# Renewing the Past through Cultural Memory

In the folklore we tell and retell, there is a constant renegotiation of terms, topics, and ideas which can help to produce a sense of community cohesion and cultural understanding. As I have discussed in Chapter 6, the folklore we choose to tell—as well as how and when we choose to tell it—is placed within the social frameworks of our societies and can both reinforce and challenge its ongoing role within a community. Folklore aids in constituting and solidifying our place within the communities of which we find ourselves a part just as much as they draw attention to communities and groups of which we are not. Importantly, while folklore within specific communities and societies represents a desire to maintain a sense of the "familiar past" (Toelken 39), it does so with an integral influence of the present (Assmann, Aleida 39). Folk stories both reflect and interpret our conceptions of the past and as they are told time and again, they can continually be altered and changed both consciously and unconsciously to reflect thoughts and beliefs of the present. In so doing, they operate on a conception of time which is nonlinear—one where the past and present mutually influence one another.

As described in Chapter 1, the folktale's longevity can be attributed in part to its role within cultural memory. Cultural memory implies a structure of "shared concerns, values, experiences, and narratives" within a group. To claim a part of a group identity, a member must participate in that group's history (Assmann, Aleida 37–38). A major way group members can do so is by telling and listening to their folk stories. By focusing on what folklore lives on in specific groups and communities and which morals and lessons they contain (among other characteristics), we can investigate aspects of its cultural memory and see how a group perceives itself and its own history.

Due to the necessity for cultural memory to remain relevant if it is to continue to be retold, it can be said to have a "presentist" function (Garde-Hansen 7). While cultural memory may evoke past events or calls upon tradition, it not only reconstructs perceptions of the past but simultaneously organizes the experience of the present and expectations of the future (Assmann, Jan 28). Because of this "double-layered structure" and the interaction between perceptions of the past and expectations of the present, cultural memory has an innate potential for ongoing changes, innovations, transformations, and reconfigurations (Assmann, Aleida 44). Cultural memories are continually both reinforced and contested by community members, by new developments and expectations in societies as well as new configurations of who is considered a community member (and likewise: who is not). It is this reevaluation and contestation that keeps cultural memories alive and thriving.

Folk stories show an intricate interplay of intertextual understanding: relying on the adaptability and flexibility inherent in cultural memory to merge the past with present. Though folklore supposedly recalls old-time wisdom, it likewise "grants individuals the freedom to play with [it]" (Bacchilega, *Postmodern Fairy Tales* 5). Folkloric adaptations are not merely made to meet modern expectations, rather these changes also interact with the past as they are performed in the present. In this way they can be said to be "highly charged icons" (Rigney 225) of cultural memory which are adapted and changed to remain relevant to storytellers' and their audiences' lives. Those folk- and fairy tales that continue to be passed on contribute to the replication of stories that form cultural patterns (Zipes, *Irresistible* 5). While it is certainly possible for folktales to be read, seen, and heard in total isolation, they make the most sense when they are analyzed and critiqued alongside various interpretations. If, as Barre Toelken aptly writes, the primary characteristic of folklore is its "dynamic interaction" which helps us to "understand the nature of human cultural history and expression" (31–32), then it should be read, watched, and heard within this context of interdependence and mutual influence.

In this chapter, I focus on the specific role of the folktale as a part of cultural memory as well as both folktale storytelling and digital storytelling as reconceptualizing time as a nonlinear web or, as I will explain below, a "folkloric web of time." Due to the presentist nature of cultural memory, the folktale necessitates a nonlinear relationship between the past and the present. Exploiting the folkloric web of time, folktales exist in a conception of time where both past and present mutually influence each other and where storytellers, readers, viewers, and listeners are tasked with considering both the new adaptation as well as various source media simultaneously. Folkloric retellings both reinforce the role of canonical folktales within the lives of storytellers as well as comment on and critique the canon with respect to the present. After briefly introducing the reliance of folkloric storytelling on a nonlinear conception of time, I investigate how the past was instrumentalized and reinterpreted in "classic" fairy-tale versions such as the Grimms' as well as, undeniably, Disney, to promote and strengthen domestic cultural norms.

Thereafter, I examine the role of specific works of fan fiction and their interaction with cultural memory in versions of "Hansel and Gretel" (ATU 327A) and "Die Gänsemagd"/ [The Goose-Girl] (ATU 923). Fans both update and change canonical fairy tales as well as reinforce the role of these tales in their lives by writing works of fan fiction which exist simultaneously alongside canon versions: ones in which both past and present versions *should be* evoked simultaneously. Fan fiction is a genre which builds upon the folktale's already existing nonlinear conception of time in order to comment on, critique, and reinforce the role of the fairy tales within the lives and communities of "Grimms Märchen" fandom members through negotiations of a tale's true content.

## Instrumentalizing the Past through Cultural Memory

In the West, the conceptualization of time tends to follow a secularized version of the Christian conception of time: one that is rectilinear with the implication that time is irreversible. It is often viewed as a structured process, or a temporal flow with connections to the notion of continual development. Time is then fleeting and destructive of the "here and now" which is continually passing by. It creates distance between the past and present (Lorenz 76–77). We can see this in idioms such as "time marches on," [die Zeit schreitet voran], or that one cannot "turn back the hands of time," [das Rad der Zeit nicht zurückdrehen können] which state that time is continually pressing forward. Time "passes," it "flows," and "marches on" or "forward" but does not circle back and repeat. A linear conceptualization of time seems to make logical sense—World War II ended, and the world will not experience an exact repeat of 1939–1945. We cannot physically return to that moment just as much as I cannot physically revisit my 5th birthday party.

The concept of intertextual relationships, though, and even time itself is subjective in folkloric retellings even in Western cultures that tend to perceive time as linear. When exactly does a folktale take place? Where exactly is the setting? These questions can often only be answered ambiguously. Many may have historical frames, but their settings are largely dependent on social and environmental factors and often set in "homogeneous, empty time" (Anderson 204). These changing factors highlight the dependence of interpretation and meaning on societal beliefs and norms rather than to any sort of ostensibly historical influences or origins. While some aspects of folktales and fairy tales might move to the background of cultural consciousness or fade out of interest, other story elements might be recovered from the periphery and move to become a focal point of social interest (Assmann, Aleida 44).

There are three aspects of the folkloric-storytelling process which may at first seem contradictory: conservatism, dynamism, and fragmentation. *Conservatism* refers to features of content and style in retellings that have been carried over from earlier sources. This is the preservation of the "familiar past." Conversely, *dynamism* refers to the changes which have taken place in each retelling (Toelken 39). A community's folklore is influenced and transformed by social conditions which are constantly changing to account for the ever-shifting realities of life (Abercrombie 215). Folklore may evoke the past, though conservative aspects of folklore can only survive in a community if it remains "alive, effective, and relevant" (Zipes, *The Irresistible* 10) or else it falls out of use and is forgotten. To remain relevant, folklore often undergoes "dynamic" changes. Conservatism and dynamism are interrelated aspects of folkloric retellings which rely on fragmentation (Busse 46). *Fragmentation* emphasizes that tales are a continual part of an ongoing conversation between storytellers and audience members (whether this is an active conversation between individuals or merely a passive, interpretive act in the audience members' reception). All elements are fundamentally important to the folkloric-storytelling process. However, it must also remain recognizable in some form if it is to live on as a part of cultural memory.

Retellings of fairy tales invite readers to reconsider canon tales (Joosen 16), and certainly these adaptations depend on the audience's ability to perceive and interpret the intertextual relationships (Haase, "Introduction" 11). Though more than just a dependence on intertextuality, folklore is a process which "reshapes the shared past to create a shared future" (Wilson 9). Folkloric storytelling does not take a passive approach to the passage of time. It is rather an active, subjective, emotional, and uncertain production of past and present simultaneously (Garde-Hansen 7). In many situations of folkloric storytelling, the storyteller does not simply recall stories or events from the past, but rather can work to keep the memories of people who have come before alive—not just in a fictive way, but at times in a very literal sense for members of different communities where the spirits of those who have passed can temporarily reside with the living while a story is being told on enacted (Niles 82). In folkloric storytelling it is not just the storytellers who make the stories so memorable, rather it is the whole set of people, both living and dead, who share the site of folkloric performance. This is where social dramas are "enacted in a 'time out of time'" (Niles 63). In this folklore conception of space and time, connections are made that can defy what is generally accepted in most Western cultures as the linear progression of time.

Taking the folktale's concept of time as a nonlinear, web-like formation into consideration, I use a modified version of Cristina Bacchilega's fairy-tale web to describe the folkloric web of time. In the fairy-tale web, all versions—be they oral, written, visual, or social—are part of a "web of intertextual relations." This web is not a dialog of fixed meanings, but rather an "intersection of several speech acts and discourses [...] whereby meanings emerge in the process" (*Fairy Tales Transformed* 19). Stories constantly echo other stories, and these echoes add force and understanding to the present story being told. Each story presupposes previous versions and incorporates them. Though how different versions "influence, anticipate, interrupt, take over, or support" one another cannot be fully predicted, even sometimes by the storyteller themselves because of the continual influence of different versions upon others (*Fairy Tales Transformed* 19).

The "fairy-tale web" is helpful in understanding the mutual influences of various source texts and versions across space which "intersect with multiple story-weaving traditions" (Bacchilega, *Fairy Tales Transformed* 20). I see this web formation as likewise representative of the folktale's intersections across time as different retellings converge—as canon versions influence modern interpretations and modern interpretations affect a community's memory of the canon. Using this web as a model demonstrates the fragmentation and intertextuality of the folktale and how past and present versions reflect on one another to enhance understanding, meaning, and critique of each other. Together these influences from past and present form the folkloric web of time. Stories from the past cannot be objectively revisited even if they are preserved in printed anthologies, rather they can only speak and be known through contemporary interpretations.

While each retelling invokes the canon tale, it likewise colors a community's perception of it. How stories and events are recalled by social communities effects changes on interpretations of the shape and meaning of the past (Erll 163). While past events and stories can certainly influence the present, so too can the present affect perceptions of the past. Every time we recall a story, we must reconstruct it and with each reconstruction, the memory of it might be changed—colored by other versions and recollections, increased understanding, new contexts, and inevitably the personal interpretation of the storyteller (Loftus and Ketchum 20). When discussing the "Grimms' fairy tales," especially within popular culture, we are largely not discussing the tales themselves as printed and bound in anthologies throughout the early- to mid-nineteenth century, but rather the various interpretations enabled by them. These interpretations have effectively altered the cultural memories of the tales in many communities; while many might know that certain Grimm tales have depictions of violence, they live on in cultural memories in other forms. The role that these canon tales play in the formation—and at times, even confrontation—of communities with their own sense of representation and understanding, however, is nevertheless important. To discuss how both past and present conceptions and beliefs can mutually influence one another, in what follows I examine two predominant canon influences for the fandom: Jacob and Wilhelm Grimm and Walt Disney Studios.

## Establishing Germanic Cultural Memory

As stories come to be retold, reinterpreted, and passed down through time, they come to serve new functions each time they are told, and they are adapted to the social activities in which they are embedded. These representations claim authenticity by their supposed relationship to the past to promote a continuity between past and present. Encouraged by these motivations, Jacob and Wilhelm Grimm (both knowingly and subconsciously) edited and altered tales within *Children's and Household Tales* to provide a definitive narrative of the past as one which praised the worth and resilience of a Germanic past, but also showed it as having strong and clear connections with the cultural expectations of their nineteenth-century present. It would be far easier for the bourgeois reading public of the Grimms' time to accept and appreciate the Germanic past if it were presented as corresponding strongly with their contemporary nineteenth-century sensibilities.

Changes to cultural memory can and do affect changes in perceived historical reality (Assmann, Jan 74). The Grimms' collection, as an attempted preservation of a cultural memory, is ultimately unconcerned with presenting the past as it really was. What becomes of essential and constituent importance, rather, is *how* the past, present, and future can come to be linked together (Buikema 188). The collection and, later, editing and rewriting efforts of (largely) Wilhelm Grimm were deeply concerned with the present and looked to the past to justify contemporary cultural ideas and customs—using the folkloric web of time to do so. To popularize their collection, they needed to present it in a way that the new and growing reading public would buy and read. The Grimms removed or censored tales or sections of tales which did not live up to their worldviews or were somehow unfitting or uncomfortable topics for the Christian bourgeois norms of the time (Rölleke 49). In this way, the Grimms were likewise participating in a common folktale-storytelling phenomenon. Cultural memory depends on links with the past, yet the past itself "only comes into being insofar as we refer to it" (Assmann, Jan 17). The alterations they made can largely be seen as changes intended to bring a perceived version of the past in conversation with their present.

As an example of some of these changes, one edited tale, "Der Wolf und die sieben jungen Geislein" [The Wolf and the Seven Young Kids] (ATU 123) tells the story of a mother goat who must leave for the day to gather food for her children. She warns them of a wolf who lives in the area who will surely try to trick them to gain access to the house and eat them. The wolf goes to a miller and threatens him in French to help the wolf trick the children. After three attempts, and after the wolf has softened his voice and powdered his paws to make them white (so as to resemble the color of goat hair), the seven little goats open the door and all but one are eaten. The mother returns, hears of what has taken place from her remaining child, and cuts open the belly of the wolf who was sleeping nearby. Her children, unharmed, jump out. She then places rocks in his stomach and due to the weight, he drowns in a well once he awakens.

There are many changes between the 1810 unpublished Ölenberg manuscript and later published editions of the tale. Yet it is the deletion of dialog spoken in French that appears most prominent. As many of their storytellers and collectors were well-educated, they were fluent in French and would have had access to French chapbooks—short, inexpensive, and often abridged versions of popular texts—which were both popular and widespread at the time (Vaz da Silva 403). Likewise, the Grimms acknowledged the source of the tale to be the Hassenpflug family; a family of French Huguenot descent. The Hassenpflug girls gathered their tales from French servants and governesses in addition to those passed down through family narration. A tale told in both languages would have been easily understood by the Grimms' storytellers, as well as the Grimms' bourgeois readership—and yet any mention of French is taken out of the published 1812 version.

Though the removal of French dialog may seem like a slight change, the Grimms situate their collection with claims to the authenticity of stories that have been ostensibly passed down generation by generation from an ancient past. Here the past is instrumentalized to promote and strengthen nineteenth-century intellectual views of a proud and independent German cultural past. Thus through their tales, the Grimms claim a literary link to a cultural memory of the ancient, Germanic past, and present a depiction of a Germany emancipated from the "monopoly of [...] French superiority" (Warner 55). Germanic lands most certainly were not free in 1812 when various regions were occupied by Napoleonic France. The careful editing out of any reference to the French language or heritage reveals an effort to free the folktales in their collection from French and Napoleonic dominance—and, theoretically, the German people as well. It was important for the aims of their collection that the past be reinterpreted and portrayed as free from foreign influences. The Grimms seek to establish a cultural memory of a strong and independent culture with their collection to promote similar feelings in their present when "Germanness" was under attack both literally and ideologically.

The Grimms write that they have stayed true to what they termed to be the "content" (*Inhalt*) of the tales in their collection, not the wording itself; even if they would have been capable of doing so on certain occasions with the patient, repetitive storytelling of individuals like Dorothea Viehmann. By favoring content over wording, they allowed themselves a great deal of freedom and flexibility to interpret and rewrite the tales in a way they deemed necessary—as long as they stayed true to what they had determined to be the overall content; certainly a subjective formulation. Tales which have claims to both age (through the belief that they have been transmitted since ancient times) and newness (continual adaptations to remain relevant to modern readers) show the folktale as an ideal candidate to be changed and updated for the purpose of creating a narrative of cultural cohesion.

We can take as another example the Grimm tale of "Allerleirauh" [Thousandfurs] (ATU 510B) which was first published in 1812 and depicted an incestuous marriage between father and daughter. In this tale, as in so many other Grimm tales, the queen dies in the opening sentences.

Her dying wish is that her husband not marry again unless the woman is as beautiful as she. As the tale progresses and his young child begins to grow older, the king decides that his daughter, a near exact likeness of his late wife, is the only woman who could be considered her beauty's equal. Though for most of the tale she protests and tries to escape, at the end the king and his daughter marry. After this first edition, following criticism and once their collection began to be guided toward an audience of children, the tale was reworked by the Grimms to be a moral lesson in which the king's councilors state "God has forbidden that a father marry his daughter, and no good can come from such a crime [sin]" (251). This tale has become one that illustrates the clear Christian morals of the Grimms' contemporary society. Because of the Grimms' changes, it serves the purpose of instructing children how they should behave and what expectations of them their society has: Christian morality and ethics.

While there were certainly other changes that were made throughout the collection, these two examples illustrate certain aspects that the Grimms wished to emphasize in their depiction of German cultural memory: a proud and free Germanic culture, and nineteenth-century Christian bourgeois morality and ethics. In this effective reinterpretation of the past, their collection was wildly successful. It has been and remains associated with what, in the West, a fairy tale should look and sound like. Fairy tales have been described as a story told "like the Brothers Grimm" wrote in *Childrens' and Household Tales* (Jolles 182). For German-speaking cultures in particular, since the mid-nineteenth century children have learned German from the Brothers Grimm whether they are aware of it or not (Rölleke 12). As likewise mentioned in Chapter 1, the authority of *Children's and Household Tales* as a part of Western cultural memory is certainly secure with the official cataloging of the collection in U.N.E.S.C.O.'s "Memory of the World" project.

The use of the folktale, with its ability to be shaped and transformed, as a cultural object which could have the capability to unite the German people can be seen as a calculated choice. Despite or perhaps even because of these numerous adaptations, folktales still have a claim to authenticity through their supposed ties to the past. As Jan Assmann writes "anyone who [...] fixes his eyes on tomorrow must preserve yesterday from oblivion [...]. This is how the past is reconstructed" (17).

## The Americanization of Cultural Memory

While the publication of ostensibly definitive editions of folk- and fairy tales has produced a means by which anyone may be able to re-read and reference tales that might otherwise have remained out of reach, the privatization of the fairy tale has violated the communal aspects of folk and fairy-tale storytelling cultures (Bacchilega, *Postmodern Fairy Tales* 5). With privatization folktales are influenced by private and market-driven interests and specific versions produced by these private corporations are considered legally "owned commodities," unable to be borrowed and changed without explicit legal permission. A problematic effect of cultural memory is its potential to be claimed and manipulated by media groups which repurpose and restage the past according to either specific marketing strategies or the demands of monetarily dominant private groups rather than a communal whole (Assmann, Aleida 39). The most widely known of these offenders is the international media goliath, Walt Disney Studios.

To examine the role Disney has played in the fairy-tale genre, we can take the film *Snow White and the Seven Dwarfs* as an example. This 1937 production is historically significant since in addition to being Disney's first feature-length fairy-tale production, it is also an early surviving example of an animated feature-length film. This production would set the standards for fairy-tale films for many years to come. The film begins with claims to antiquity, and therefore authenticity, with images of a fairy-tale book's elaborately embellished pages designed in a style reminiscent of medieval illuminated manuscripts. We read a short introduction to the fairy tale—which begins with the formulaic opening "Once upon a time"—before seeing the animated film itself. Once the film begins, we see concrete and overt depictions of how women should behave. In what at first appears to be a rags-to-riches story, Snow White is shown in the beginning clad like a servant, innocent, domestic, and emphatically—white. She quickly—and to all appearances quite happily—assumes cooking and cleaning responsibilities. Though many aspects of Snow White's character remain unchanged from the time of the Grimms, the Disney production puts decidedly more emphasis on Snow White's domestic character by spending significant time showing Snow White cleaning, cooking, and reprimanding the dwarves as if they were small children. Snow White is likewise starkly juxtaposed to her evil stepmother, who we never see performing any domestic duties. As Sandra M Gilbert and Susan Gubar succinctly state, women characters in these productions are portrayed as "a sweet heroine inside the house [...] opposed to a vicious bitch outside" (29). We are presented here with clear examples of what Disney considered to be proper behavior.

Like the beginning, we are reminded again at the end of the film of the authenticity of the story when we see the ancient fairy tale book to finish the frame narrative. Snow White's tale is complete since she has gone from the poor figure in rags, punished by her wicked stepmother to a rich queen who will live in her own castle after marriage. She has been restored to her rightful place in life. Disney relies on the evocation of the past for authenticity to convince viewers of their desire to emulate Snow White's actions, among them, her complacency. This effectively portrays Snow White as a role model for women in 1930s American society: good, white girls should strive for a domesticated life. This has always been so, the production suggests, with its framing of the antique book, and continues in the present. In many Disney versions there is a "deep conservatism that commodifies the fairy tale while promoting apathy and an apolitical acceptance of [the] status quo" (Greenhill and Matrix 6). This status quo promotes conservative gender roles and depictions of the "American fairy tale" being enacted on screen as one available to specifically white audiences. Strikingly absent are any characters of color, showing a very specific depiction of what American society and values should look like according to Disney's perspective of the time.

*Snow White and the Seven Dwarfs* has been rightly hailed as an early cinematic marvel, and after its premiere, Disney received a standing ovation. It was the most successful movie in the United States at the time (Wills 2). If Disney animation and storytelling can be said to be "integral to the formation of American character" by promoting idealism, positivity, and family values (Mollet 110), it is crucially important to determine what exactly that means. "Family values," is often a politically loaded term used to denote the values of a white heteronormative majority. Shortly after its debut, *Snow White and the Seven Dwarfs* was hailed by the *New York Times* as being as "significant cinematically as D. W. Griffith's [film] *Birth of a Nation* [1915]" (Mollet 109). A cinematic landmark, yet racially horrific film, *Birth of a Nation* rewrites the history of the American Civil War, promotes Lost Cause ideology, and portrays the Ku Klux Klan as a necessary, heroic force preserving "American" values. Though *Snow White and the Seven Dwarfs* should certainly not be equated with *Birth of a Nation*, reviews such as these are a reminder of promoted American values of the early twentieth century.

Since this iconic film, the Disney fairy-tale interpretations have been so popular, and saturating Euro-North American culture through market dominance that these versions have become the modern source versions any newer adaptations must engage with (Greenhill and Matrix 7). The tales may lay their claim of authenticity by evoking folkloric roots, yet the production pushes market-driven views and the process changes the tales to portray Disney's definitions of the social roles of present-day men and women. Linda Pershing and Lisa Gablehouse remind us that Disney's "someday-my-prince-will-come" formula has meant that "princesses are big moneymakers for Disney, but their promotion does much more than generate a profit. It also inculcates archaic, patriarchal ideologies in each successive wave of children and reinforces oppressive value systems in older generations" (153).

Character depictions within Disney films have begun to change from the time of *Snow White and the Seven Dwarfs*. A more recent Disney production which shows more progressive depictions of women's roles, *Maleficent* (2014), shows the backstory of the evil fairy in "Sleeping Beauty" (ATU 410) and reveals that it is not a prince who is able to wake Sleeping Beauty with true love's kiss, but rather the evil fairy Maleficent who has grown to love Sleeping Beauty like her own child. Like Disney's *Snow White and the Seven Dwarfs*, *Maleficent* contains what appears to be a rags-to-riches story in the depiction of Sleeping Beauty (in the film named "Aurora"). In an attempt to save her from the evil curse cast upon her at birth, Aurora's father sends her away as an infant to be hidden and cared for until the time of her curse has passed and thus, hopefully, saving her from being forced into a death-like slumber. Aurora is sent to a small cottage in the forest and is unaware of her royal status. At the end of the film, she does not marry a prince to be restored to royalty, but she is crowned as a queen.

Though appearing like "rags to riches" stories, both *Snow White* and *Maleficent* are rather "restoration of status" stories since both Snow White and Aurora were already born into nobility. They have then, in the end, been returned to their rightful places. What is of note is how an actual rags-to-riches storyline is treated within *Maleficent*. The film shows how the fairy Maleficent was not always evil but was corrupted by the betrayal of a man she loved—Stefan. Stefan was a poor orphaned boy who dreamt of one day living in the castle. Through ambition, he worked his way into the king's service. Rather than a positive portrayal, Stefan's desire to rise above his station and eventually become king is shown as the beginnings of evil. He is corrupted by greed and malice and becomes king by betraying his only friend, Maleficent. At the end of the film, though various characters try to appeal to King Stefan's humanity, he has been utterly corrupted by his greed. The development of a true rags-to-riches plot line within the fairy-tale film shows the message that one should not strive to rise above their station as Stefan has done. So while *Maleficent* may produce more positive portrayals of female characters, it still has aspects of "conservatism [...] [that] promot[es] apathy and an apolitical acceptance" (Greenhill and Matrix 6) of socioeconomic position. Aurora remains kind and benevolent even once she has been crowned queen, it seems, because she was royalty to begin with. She has not risen above her station, rather she was restored to it.

There have certainly been advances in Disney productions with the inclusion of non-white heroines in films such as *Pocahontas* (1994), *Mulan* (1998), *The Princess and the Frog* (2009), and *Moana* (2016), and yet the studio's historical preference for white heroes and heroines still remains a source of controversy for the corporation. These more diverse films are not without their problematic depictions however, such as *Pocahontas*'s total rewriting of colonialism in the United States touting the "white savior" in the character of Pocahontas's love interest, colonist John Smith. Despite other welcomed and positive changes in the portrayals of women and the inclusion of characters of color, such as the consultation with Samoan elders and community members for more authentic representation in *Moana* (Grandinetti), the packaged princess dolls which are for sale in Disney Stores largely appear with very made-up faces, "perfect lithe bodies" and lightened skin tones which still encourage a princess "look" and mentality (Wills 118–124).

Even if Disney has begun to produce fairy tale films with stronger female characters such as with *Brave* (2012) and *Frozen* (2013), Disney consumer culture still pushes a princess fantasy showing modern girls and women as proud shoppers and consumers who may no longer worry about playing the bride but rather "about bling, success, and status" (Wills 124). Disney can be said to push a market-driven, capitalistic view of the world (Wills 3), and this can be seen in the history of Disney production—especially in the corporation's aggressive purchasing of competitor brands such as Pixar in 2006. Disney is a dominating figure in the fairy-tale genre, and this has given the corporation a near-monopoly in Western youth culture.

The film *Frozen* specifically has been argued to have shown "progressive, modern Disney at its best" with signs that the corporation might be capable of abandoning outdated values (Wills 129). Though even with its emphasis on the power of sibling love and multiple conversations where characters say that one of the protagonists, Anna, should not marry someone she has just met, the film does focus heavily on Anna's need to be loved and supported by male characters. The development of her romantic relationship with her attempted rescuer, Hans, also plays a significant role. In the end, after she rescues her sister, she realizes that Hans is the man she had been waiting for. While this film might be an example of changes for modern Disney, it is not as progressive as some critics laud it to be.

Disney portrayals have come to be nearly synonymous with the fairy-tale genre which stresses further the importance of the corporation's future decisions on inclusivity and more progressive portrayals of a range of fairy-tale characters. If the Grimms represent a part of the "memory of the world," then Disney might just be "a new religion for the consumer masses" of the West (Wills 30). Echoing the Grimms' ambitions as they sought to reconstruct and recreate a version of the Germanic past to best fit with their present, so too have Disney fairy-tale versions recreated depictions of the past and associations with the fairy tale. Through this undeniable influence, fairy tales in popular media have seen a "petrification" due in large part to Disney productions and its power and influence over the genre (Zipes, "Breaking the Disney Spell" 337). The Grimms may have effectively cultivated their collection to represent the values of the bourgeoisie as always existing at some level within German society: especially with their emphasis on nineteenth-century bourgeois cultural values focused on domesticity and patriarchal authority. Yet with its global reach, the Disney Corporation has been able to solidify its particular interpretations across national borders (Duggan 115).

## Synchronic: Merging of the Past and Present in New Media Storytelling

Thus far, I have discussed that much of the changes made to folktales are due to the tendency of cultural memory to repurpose the past for a more continuous connection to beliefs of specific community's perceptions of the present. Technological changes have likewise played a large role in how these stories get repeated and, ultimately, changed through retelling. The role of new media in the landscape of the twenty-first century has taken on an undeniable role as a medium of cultural remembrance (Rigney 229). As part of the folkloric storytelling culture, fans too have a nonlinear conception of time when writing, reading, commenting on, and editing fics. They wish to (re)introduce more complex aspects to the stories since the world they are familiar with is one which is not so simple. They also seem to recognize themselves as a part of the transformative folkloric storytelling process. Fans actively negotiate interpretations of a tale's true content and repurpose it to serve new functions within the communities in which they are told.

As one fan puts it, in reference to being a fic writer "da hat man dann als Autor die Macht, Unpassendes passend zu machen" [one has then as an author the power to make the unfitting fitting] ("Warum schreibt ihr"). Tales are being adapted according to the social activities and societal perceptions of those who tell them in order to serve as representations of their lived realities in contemporary society. Fans note that they feel they are often paying attention to situations that previous generations "nie groß hintergefragt haben" [never greatly scrutinized] ("Starke Frauen"). Comments such as "Unpassendes passend [...] machen" [making the unfitting fitting] suggest as well that fans subscribe to a similar understanding of staying true to what they have deemed to be the content of the canon rather than that of textual fidelity. This belief bears many similarities to the fashion that the Grimms adopted in their revisions. If folklore is "cut from the marrow of human experience" (Wilson 149) and is likewise "forged in response to present needs" (Wilson 146) by storytellers, then the concept of what a tale's true content may be will continue to be adapted along with it.

One way in which fans authenticate their stories, as noted in Chapter 1, is by adherence to the source text. Fans note time and again that they are cautious not to break canon ("Warum schreibt ihr"). What a "real fairy tale" contains or sounds like is never explicitly defined within the fandom. Regardless, there is certainly a working understanding among fandom members of how this term might be defined, and there is undoubtedly a collective sense of what it means to remain faithful enough to the source material to be considered fan fiction rather than a new creation. These assumptions, however, do not remain static. Just as the members of the community are constantly changing as new writers join and others move away from the site, so too change the expectations of the community and within the fandom, fans actively discuss the role that fairy tales can and should play in their lives. One fan begins with a question that sparks a lengthy comment thread about the role of canonical fairy tales in the lives of children:

> Gerade letzte Woche habe ich mich gefragt, ob es wirklich gut ist, dass Kinder mit Märchen aufwachsen, in denen es ganz klare Schwarz/Weiß-Trennungen [zwischen Gut und Böse] gibt?

> [Just last week I asked myself if it's really good that children grow up with fairy tales where there is a really clear black/white separation [of good vs. evil].] ("Starke Frauen")

Encapsulating much of the discussion is an answer that highlights the importance and influence of stories from the past on the present. Addressed here is the importance of critical reflection on the cultural memory established by editions such as *Children's and Household Tales* by the Grimms:

> Ich habe das Gefühl, es ist besser, ein Kind mit den alten Märchen aufwachsen zu lassen, auch wenn da Sachen drin sind, die heute wohl arg fraglich wären, als ihm nur Geschichten vorzusetzen, die so überarbeitet wurden, dass da alles absolut "politisch korrekt" ist. Wie soll das Kind denn dann noch selber was draus lernen? Bei den alten Märchen (oder überhaupt alten Kinderbüchern) gibt's doch viel mehr Dinge, die das Kind hinterfragen kann. Und daraus dann vielleicht auch so manche Dinge und Änderungen in der Gesellschaft besser verstehen?
>
> [I have the feeling that it's better to let a child grow up with the old fairy tales, even if there are things in them that today would be terribly disputed, rather than to give them stories that have been edited so that everything is absolutely "politically correct." How could the child learn something from them? With the old fairy tales (or in general old children's books) there are so many more things that the child can scrutinize. And through that can maybe better understand some things and changes in society?] ("Starke Frauen")

This discussion illustrates that fans are continually reflecting on canon tales and the role that expectations of the past should and do continue to play in their lives. While writing and participating in various ways within a fandom can certainly be a fun and creative act, it is often simultaneously a place for deep critical reflection. Fans critically reflect on their present and the role the morals of the canon tales play in their lives. They also reinterpret the content of the canon—and with it their community's cultural memory of these tales—in the process. This revisionary work is made easier by the folkloric web of time. If in fan fiction—as a form of folklore—the past and present exist simultaneously alongside one another, then critical reflection and reinterpretation of meaning are inherently a part of that creative endeavor.

While fics may be able to stand on their own as independent stories (and certainly many of the fics mentioned throughout this book could) this is not the point of fic. Fan fiction is ultimately a series of textual entanglements which should not, and indeed cannot, be fully separated from one another. A fic might be understood by readers who are unfamiliar with the source, but fic's very existence assumes constant reflection and comparison with the canon (Jamison 14). Similar to my earlier discussion of the elements of a folktale, fic writing depends on conservatism, dynamism, and fragmentation in order for the past and present to mutually influence one another through a redetermination of what the content of a tale might be. A fic's degree of fragmentation depends on the context of the ongoing conversation within the fandom. Fics rely not just on the canon text(s) and the accompanying cultural memory invoked by them, but also on other fan texts. As discussed in Chapter 3, the essence of fan fiction relies on how they are situated within ongoing discussion in the fandom—they are but a fragmentary part of this conversation. Without this context we can never capture all of what is taking place in a fic. We may get the words themselves, but without an understanding of the interplay of folkloric web of time and conversational context in which they are born, important information goes missing and we are left with, at best, but a snippet.

In what follows I use three fics as examples of the folkloric web of time within fan fiction. I first investigate two different versions of the Grimm tale "Hansel and Gretel" (ATU 327A) and one based on "Die Gänsemagd" or "The Goose-Girl" (ATU 923), all of which utilize the web to offer critiques and new perspectives of the traditional Grimm tales.

## Two Versions of "Hansel and Gretel" and the Folkloric Web of Time

The first example of a fic's dependence on fragmentation, intertextuality, and a folkloric web of time is the Brothers Grimm version of "Hansel and Gretel" and a fic entitled "Inside Grimm: Hänsel und Gretel" by ardara (accessed 2021) which specifically focuses on the distressed state of Hansel after the events of the canon tale. In the Grimm tale, Hansel is continually described as a strong and active character. When he and his sister first overhear the mother's plan to abandon them in the forest, Gretel feels helpless and cries "bitter tears." Hansel quickly replies "Hush, Gretel […] do not distress yourself, I will soon find a way to help us" and when their parents are asleep, he goes outside and finds small, white stones so that they may find their way back home (54). Once the children realize they have been abandoned, Hansel takes charge of the situation and consoles his sister "and when the full moon had risen, Hansel took his little sister by the hand, and followed the pebbles which shone like newly-coined silver pieces, and showed them the way." Even once the children have lost their way, Hansel confidently proclaims that they shall be able to find their way back to their father's house (55).

As the Grimm tale concludes, when the children have finally returned home to their father, it reads that "all anxiety was at an end, and they lived together in perfect happiness" (59). It appears both children are able to forget the chilling events during the tale, their abandonment, capture, and near-death encounter. Though Gretel may begin the tale as a weaker character than her brother, certainly by the end she cannot be described as a "disempowered wom[a]n cower[ing] in fear" like so many other Grimm heroines (Bottigheimer, "Fertility" 50). She takes charge to save both herself and her brother from the evil witch by tricking the witch and shoving her into the oven. Both children eventually confidently work together. By the end, the children are described as simply able to live "happily ever after" since both the evil witch and the evil mother are dead. The tale has concluded, and they are able to move on with their lives in "perfect happiness."

Ardara's fic takes place after the events of the canon in a move that deals explicitly with the psychological condition of Hansel after escaping the witch's hut where certainly "all anxiety" has not come to an end. Her tale reads in its entirety:

> Du bist nicht mehr der Gleiche, seit du aus dem Wald zurückgekommen bist. Ich weiß nicht, was du dort gesehen hast, mein Sohn, aber es hat dich verändert, verstört, zerstört. Deine Schwester hat es auch getroffen, aber bei Weitem nicht so hart wie dich, sie hat Schreckliches durchgemacht, du Unaussprechliches.
>
> Vielleicht ist es leichter für sie, weil sie versucht hat, etwas zu tun, während du gefangen warst und lange nicht verstanden hast, dass das, was SIE mit euch vorhat,

> kein gutes Ende nehmen wird. Du hast einfach nicht verstanden, warum sie dich fressen will, wenn sie doch ein Haus aus Lebkuchen aus dem Boden stampfen kann, warum kann sie sich dann kein Haus aus Kindern hexen, fragst du dich. Immer und immer wieder.
>
> "Ich liebe dich, Papa," sagst du jeden Abend vor dem Schlafengehen, und dann noch: "Du bist mein Traumfänger," es klingt flehend, du willst Erlösung von den Albträumen, die dich heimsuchen, wenn du die Augen schließt, aber du wirst sie nicht bekommen. Die Bilder sind für immer eingebrannt in deine Lider, du siehst sie, wenn du nichts mehr sehen willst, sie sind immer da, rote glühende Szenen, eine schreiende Fratze, lodernde Haare, ein schmelzender Leib.
>
> Schlaf gut, Hans.
>
> [You're not the same anymore since you came back from the forest. I don't know what you saw there, my son, but it changed you, unhinged you, destroyed you. It also affected your sister, but by far not as hard as it affected you, she experienced horror, but you the unspeakable.
>
> Maybe it was easier for her because she tried to do something while you were imprisoned and for a while couldn't understand that what SHE had planned for you wouldn't end well. You simply couldn't understand why she wanted to eat you. If she created a house made of gingerbread out of thin air, why can't she conjure one made of children, you ask yourself. Over and over again.
>
> "I love you, daddy," you say every night before you go to sleep, and then add: "you're my dreamcatcher," it sounds pleading, you want salvation from the nightmares that haunt you when you close your eyes, but you'll never receive it. The images are forever burned into your eyelids, you see her when you don't want to see anymore, they're always there, red glowing scenes, a screaming grimace, hair ablaze, a melting body.
>
> Sleep well, Hans.]

Like other fics explored throughout this book, there is an intensification of emotion as well as a push toward a more nuanced interpretation of events in ardara's tale. Certainly after the horrific events the children endure throughout the canon tale, they would not emerge psychologically unaffected as portrayed in the Grimm version. Here ardara explores the after-effects through a psychological lens. Surely a world in which all cares come to an end cannot exist as easily as the Grimm version suggests.

What is perhaps striking, however, is the use of the folkloric web of time and the degree of prior knowledge required to understand the fic. The tale becomes meaningful only within an interactional context. That is, the canon tale and ardara's fic must be remembered alongside one another for her tale to make sense and it uses this symbiotic relationship to critique the canon as well as to create more depth within the fic itself. Ardara reinterprets the content of the tale not as one about a heroic escape, but one which contextualizes the psychological trauma of two children. This new framing works to repurpose the canon tale without altering the canon tale itself. It is a negotiation of the content though importantly, it is essential to understanding the fic that the fic version does not replace the canon. The canon tale must remain untouched.

Ardara's version is a fragmentation and entirely dependent on the reader to be well acquainted with the canon tale. Without prior knowledge of the canon, the fic makes little sense, and does not even contain a sustainable plot. Here ardara engages with the cultural memory of the canon tale in a fashion which is, perhaps, more obvious than tales discussed in previous chapters. The tale begins with the statement, "ich weiß nicht, was du dort gesehen hast, mein Sohn." [I don't know what you saw there, my son.] The tale assumes that the reader knows that "mein Sohn" [my son] refers to the character of Hansel. Other than the title and the final statement of "schlaf gut, Hans," [sleep well, Hans], there is no mention of names nor does ardara mention that the captor was a witch.

Finally, statements such as "die Bilder sind für immer eingebrannt in deine Lider" [the images are forever burned into your eyelids] and "rote glühende Szenen, eine schreiende Fratze, lodernde Haare, ein schmelzender Leib" [red glowing scenes, a screaming grimace, hair ablaze, a melting body] assume that the reader knows the Grimm ending. Ardara's tale explains none of these details nor does it make any attempt to connect together the events mentioned. The tone of the tale suggests that we (as imagined members of her community) will make the connections. She treats explicit explanation and connection as superfluous.

Folktales as a part of cultural memory "implicate and impact notions of time as particular moments from the past are relationally configured within a specific present for purposeful ends" (French 345). One of ardara's "purposeful ends" seems to be in the emotional impact of the fic with her refocus on trauma and the humanization of the characters. Indeed, the strong emotional pull of the fic relies on the fact that ardara does not explain its background. Her descriptions of the psychological torments of Hansel conjure up images in the reader's mind of the Grimm tale and omits the details themselves to enhance the helpless feeling of a well-intentioned father. Ardara's tale engages with both the past in her fic's reliance on the canon tale as well as the present in its adaptation and rejection of the simplistic way in which the canon tale presents the story of two tortured children. Her version repurposes the Grimm version by giving her readers more context than the canon.

Ardara's dependence on prior knowledge of the canon tale is not only common, but expected, within the realm of fan fiction. Her fic repurposes and recontextualizes the meaning of the canon without replacing it and demands that the reader remember the canon without alteration. This interactional concept of time also draws attention to the fandom, developing clear boundaries around who belongs and who does not. While collections such as the Grimms' *Children's and Household Tales* sought to create new boundaries by excluding foreign influence and making clear connections with the expectations of contemporary readers, fan fiction tales such as "Inside Grimm: Hänsel und Gretel" do so with the expectation of engagement with the canon. Only those who are familiar with the canon, and therefore this community's folklore, will understand her tale, and thus only those who are familiar will belong.

The second fic version of "Hänsel und Gretel" is by elektra121 out of a collection entitled "Grimms Märchen (mit falschem Ende)" [Grimms' Fairy Tales (with False Endings)]. Though the title of her collection might imply that she has rewritten the tales and altered the endings, what her collection actually contains are *only* endings. Like ardara's fic, the audience must be familiar with the Grimm tales to understand her fic series. Her ending simply entitled "Hänsel und Gretel" (accessed 2021) reads in its entirety:

> Im zweiten Frühjahr, als die Teuerung vorbei war, machte sich die Frau des Holzhackers wieder Hoffnung auf ein Kind. Ihr Mann jedoch schaute jeden Abend lange zum Wald, als warte er, dass andere Kinder wiederkämen. Da legte die Frau seine Hand auf ihren Leib, dorthin, wo das neue Leben war.
>
> [In the second spring, when the period of inflation (*Teuerung*) was over, the woodchopper's wife was again expecting a child. Her husband however, watched

> the forest every evening as if he were waiting for other children to come back. The wife then lay his hand on her belly, there, where new life was.]

Elektra121's tale is just three sentences long, but nevertheless prompts a deep critique of and comparison with the canon tale. Similar to ardara's "Hansel and Gretel" version, the lack of background information and the absence of any summary of the Grimm tale can work to intensify the alternate ending. The audience only has their memory of the canon tale as background and must juxtapose elektra121's tale directly with the happy ending of the Grimm version. The fic needs support in explanation, background, and context. For this support, the fic needs to be placed and remembered together with other versions of the tale to reveal a full sense of what it means. The fic repurposes the content of the canon with a confrontational ending, while simultaneously depending on the existence of an unaltered canon tale. Here we are presented with a version in which the children appear to have been eaten by the witch—if we continue the logic and fairy-tale properties of the canon tale. Or, if we interpret the ending in a fashion devoid of magic, perhaps there was no witch and the children were simply abandoned in the woods due to the mother and father's inability to provide enough food for their family (suggested by the tale's mention of the children being abandoned due to a period of inflation).

We are left with an uncertain ending and question the motives of both the father and mother. Were children abandoned out of malice or due to the lack of food? Since the mother is pregnant, we are left to question whether this child will also be abandoned or mistreated, or if it will grow up in a better environment than Hansel and Gretel since the mother and father's economic situation seems to have improved. The fic gives us no answers to these questions. It does, however, call the content of the canon tale into question. We are simply left to question and reflect on the meaning of this ending with respect to the canon tale. Tales such as elektra121's use this interdependence of past and present to defamiliarize and critique canon tales. This type of critique "unsecure[s] the narrative integrity of the classic tales" (Greenhill and Matrix 14) and prompts readers to reflect on the cultural memories of the canon tales. The fic's critique, however, primarily lies in the method of the changes undertaken by fans. The changes undertaken are dependent on the existence of a framework of the familiar, that is, within the framework of the canon tale.

## "Die Gänsemagd" / ["The Goose-Girl"] and the Folkloric Web of Time

My final example of the folkloric web of time in fan fiction is Perscitia's fic "Die Gänsemagd in Sonnenau" [The Goose-Girl in Sonnenau]. The intertextuality of this fic is threefold. The tale itself draws on two canon tales, the Grimms' "The Goose-Girl" (ATU 923) and Astrid Lindgren's fairy tale "Sonnenau," sometimes translated as "The Red Bird." As discussed in Chapter 6, Perscitia's fic is a contribution to Hikari D Tenshi's project to promote creation of more FemSlash. In addition to the two canon tales, Perscitia's tale likewise should not be removed from the context of being part of a larger conversation. It is part of the effort of a group of fans to normalize and expand the number of fairy-tale fics including queer women's relationships since the category of FemSlash is more uncommon than MaleSlash.

The Grimms' "The Goose-Girl" follows the trials of a young princess who is promised to marry a faraway prince. She sets forth on her journey to the prince's kingdom with a talking horse, her chambermaid, and a magical cloth from her mother. After she loses her magical cloth, her chambermaid forces her from her horse and assumes her identity, marrying the prince and condemning the rightful princess to tend the castle's geese. Since the horse has seen what took place and would be able to inform the prince, the chambermaid has him killed—though even this cannot stop him from speaking since the horsehead tells of the chambermaid's betrayal whenever the princess passes by it. Eventually the prince's father, the king, discovers what took place and the chambermaid is tricked into naming her own punishment for assuming the princess's identity and marrying the prince. She is dragged behind horses in a nail-studded barrel, and the prince and rightful princess marry and live happily ever after.

Though her tale, as it progresses, also references Lindgren's "Sonnenau," Perscitia's fic begins with heavy reference to the Grimms' "Goose-Girl." Like the two "Hansel and Gretel" versions discussed above, Perscitia relies on her audience's ability to read her fic alongside the canon tales and offers no summary so she can offer a reinterpretation of the content. The fic begins after the end of "The Goose-Girl" when the princess has married the prince. We read:

> Sie hatte bekommen, was sie wollte, war mit dem wunderschönen Prinzen vermählt, die böse Magd, die ihr die Krone hatte streitig machen wollen, war tot […]." „Sie hat ihr Urteil gewählt," hatte der Prinz ihr schelmisch lächelnd zu gewispert. "Von Pferden in einem Nagelfass totgeschunden werden, ihre Worte. Jetzt wird alles gut, du wirst sehen!"
>
> [She had gotten what she wanted, was married to the wonderfully handsome Prince, the evil maid who wanted to contest her crown was dead […]. "She chose her fate herself," the prince whispered impishly. "To be dragged to death by horses in a nailed barrel, her words. Now everything will be good, you'll see!"]

Perscitia's tale references the events at the conclusion of the Grimm canon tale, but also hints at a significant change that her fic will follow. She describes the prince as "impishly" smiling when he remembers the death of the chambermaid, foreshadowing that the prince and princess perhaps do *not* live happily ever after as the Grimm tale tells us.

The process of change is always guided by specific motives, hopes, and expectations—conscious or not—which come from the referential frame of the present (Assmann, Jan 72). These tales incorporate that which they mean to protest in a continuous reference to the canon. In Perscitia's tale, she uses the folkloric web of time to highlight the Grimms' expectations of women in canonical fairy tales and offers a new interpretation of its content. The Grimms' tale is fleetingly referenced in the beginning so that Perscitia can bring to attention the journey of the princess toward self-discovery—that sometimes obtaining what cultural memory has deemed a stereotypical "happily ever after" can be anything but. In cases such as these, the content must be reinterpreted. As the tale continues, it reads:

> Die Gänsemagd weinte […]. Sie hatte bekommen, was sie wollte […] und […] sie wurde von einer neuen Welle von Schluchzern geschüttelt, so stark, dass sie sich am

> Fensterrahmen des Turmes abstützte, in den sie sich geflüchtet hatte. Geflüchtet aus den warmen Federn des Bettes, das sie sich mit ihrem Prinzen teilte.
>
> [The Goose-Girl cried [...]. She had gotten what she wanted [...] and [...] she was shaken by a new wave of sobs, so strongly that she braced herself against the window frame of the tower she had fled to. Fled to from the warm feathers of the bed that she shared with her prince.]

This scene shows the presentist function of folkloric storytelling: to reshape and retell tales to inform and contextualize contemporary experiences while likewise utilizing the double-layered function of cultural memory to reference and reflect on canon versions. Perscitia highlights the Grimm ending of the tale: after being married, both the Goose-Girl and the prince ruled their kingdom in "peace and happiness" (321), to spotlight another moral. Perscitia's moral shows not just that women are not always happy to be won as prizes for men as they so often are in the canon versions, but that heteronormative relationships should not be celebrated as the only "happily ever after;" that the "someday my prince will come" formula need not always be the case. Perhaps the true content of the canon is then not one which pushes heteronormative expectations, her tale seems to suggest. Perhaps the true content is a journey of self-discovery for the princess. Perscitia's participation in Hikari D Tenshi's project promoting FemSlash likewise shows that other fans see this misrepresentation in the canon tales.

Like the fans who discussed whether canon tales such as the Grimms' should still be read to children, Perscitia's fic uses intertextuality and the folkloric web of time to emphasize how canon tales can and should be questioned, contextualized, and critiqued. This shows a "dialectical interplay" where folkloric storytellers "use the past to interpret the present and the present to interpret the past" (Gongaware 216). This form of storytelling and conception of time shows interpretation though interaction. These revisions are often two-fold. They seek to make the canon fairy tale's complicity with exhausted ideologies visible (such as the expectation of happiness only in heteronormative relationships). They also use the fairy tale's multiple versions to draw attention to topics or themes which have either been forgotten or unexploited in the canon. The fic versions themselves are often based heavily on the impressions left on fans by the canon.

In this way, fans are simultaneously negotiating the influence the canon tales have on the present as well as that they should be repurposed within the fandom's cultural memory.

As we have seen in the changes made by the Grimms and Disney, contrasted with the changes made by online fan fiction writers, the stories we tell and the cultural memories attached to them are often intentionally and even transparently renegotiated to fit with current societal standards and expectations. Likewise, these versions are able to be fully understood and interpreted only in their context of continual conversation with other versions, fans, and the fandom. As highly charged icons of cultural memory, folktales are continually re-invested with meaning where past and present are remembered alongside one another and mutually influence each other to serve a presentist function. Fans continually play with this aspect of the folkloric web of time, reminding us that this is exactly what they are doing—playing with the past canon versions in the present to reimbue it with meaning, as one fan writes:

> Im Gegensatz zu modernen Verfilmungen und/oder Disney nehme ich nicht die Märchenelemente aus ihrem Kontext und versetze sie an einen evtl etwas lustigeren Ort, sondern interpretiere die Elemente [...] und versuche aus ihrer Bedeutung heraus ihre Rolle in meiner Geschichte zu finden.
>
> [In contrast to modern filmic versions and/or Disney, I don't take the fairy-tale elements out of their context and place them in a possibly somewhat funnier location, rather interpret the elements [...] and try to find a role for them in my story based on their meaning.] (Atan)

These fan-fiction tales are not just updating or making the canon more contemporary, rather they involve substantive questioning of narrative construction as well as the societal norms as presented in the Grimm tales as they still survive in cultural memory.

The tales may have moved to a digital medium, but fan writers are participating in a similar negotiation and reevaluation of the past using folkloric storytelling's web of time where past and present coincide for critique and meaning-making. Referencing a fic version of "Snow White" (ATU 709) one fan comments: "Deine Version mutete wie eine vergangene Realität an, aus der der Volksmund dann einen Streit um Schönheit machte."

[Your version seems like a bygone reality out of which folk saying turned into a dispute about beauty] (Rala vom Wald). The folkloric web of time encourages critical reflections of the tales, but also the cultural memory of the past itself. Each folkloric retelling connects the teller and the audience to their social context while reinforcing the story's continued role as a part of cultural memory. Communities learn how to tell their stories by absorbing stories and histories which seem relevant to them, and this is exactly what fan fiction writers are doing. It is the presentist function—of continually focusing on meaning and usefulness in the present—not only of storytelling, but also of digital media to constantly update to retain relevance which in turn shapes the tales, reinterprets content, and determines their role in different communities.

CONCLUSION

# The Role of Folklore in Framing the Present and Future

"Darling, everyone is a storyteller." So responds folksinger Duncan Williamson when asked about his gift for storytelling (Niles 64). Williamson does not say that everyone is necessarily a skilled storyteller, able to enrapture large audiences. Nevertheless, everyone tells stories, even if it is something as small as recounting one's day. While the stories we tell can be personally meaningful, they can also tell us a great deal about the groups and communities to which one belongs, what those communities deem important, and who is considered a member. Folklore's primary existence lies in the actions of people and its roots reside in social and cultural life (Bauman 2). The folk stories we tell helps define us.

Community, in the actual world just as much as online, is a "mixed bag." Not all community associations are good ones, and not all groups and communities serve all of their members well at all times (Avance 67). Despite claims (even amongst fans) that the Internet as a whole is a place that fosters uncivil discourse as outlined in Chapter 2, we can also see that fans consider their communities on *FanFiktion.de* to be places of real community and connection—"eine offene Community" [an open community] for expression and discussion. These places are, for many, more real than connections they may make in the actual world—places where fans feel more freedom in expressing "die eigenen Emotionen und Gefühle" [[their] own emotions and feelings] ("Ist euch Fanfiktion.de") with like-minded others. Throughout comment threads and discussions, comments such as the following appear time and again. This fan had been posting and commenting about her personal struggles with her husband. After another commenter suggests counseling she writes:

> Ich weiß nicht, ob ich mit Fremden darüber reden könnte. Ich kann ja nicht mal offen mit meinen Freundinnen darüber reden.
>
> [I don't know if I could talk about it with strangers. I can't even speak openly with my girlfriends about it.] ("Transgender/Bigender/Androgyn")

Clearly, the community on *FanFiktion.de* and those she is discussing this with are not considered "strangers" in the same sense as she refers to speaking with a counselor and she feels comfortable being emotionally vulnerable with fellow fans—even more so, she notes, than with her actual-world friends.

Fan fiction communities connect fans who might not normally encounter one another, and individuals such as the fan quoted previously, can feel more open to express even the most intimate details of their lives. These connections happen in an environment that creates affordances for communal introspection and change. While this change may begin on the level of individual fandoms, because of their focus on updating and changing stories to fit with present-day goals and expectations, they nevertheless have the potential to change societies through the growth and development of fans themselves. Investigating fandoms' penchant for change, the bottom-up folk archival process of fan fiction websites, and fandoms' focus on adapting media to fit with the present realities of often historically excluded individuals, we can see how they support and maintain diverse subcultures, offering windows into how communities perceive themselves. This highlights both how communities have developed, and pinpoints where they still might have room to grow.

Fan fiction, as continual works in progress, are focused on the presentation of and influence on the here-and-now rather than a potential conceptualization of its lasting effects on future generations. While fan fiction sites such as *FanFiktion.de* certainly have an archival function where texts are stored, these "folk" archives are very different from traditional conceptions of an archive. Rather than a top-down approach, such as the canon folklore editions collected and published by scholars and academics like Jacob and Wilhelm Grimm, these folk archives are a "bottom up" accumulation of writings. These types of archives are created by those whose aims are not to solidify a certain idea of the past for future generations in structured and controlled editions (such as the Grimms'), rather they make the availability and survival of often ignored or censored experiences possible (Baetens et al. 151). This creates a community involvement around the fics where writings and interpretations of these groups are often embraced and encouraged.

Simon J. Bronner writes that

> the old pastoral model of folklore that evoked wisdom of yore being *handed down* by a golden ager may lead us to think that digital culture displaces tradition, but we might instead conceive of digital culture fostering a *handing up* of vernacular knowledge by young, wired wizards with mythic imagination and social ebullience. (32)

The existence of these and other "bottom up" folk archives allows new possibilities for innovation and the presence of previously hidden ideas and perspectives, albeit within communities which are often already accepting of them—or are at least open to being receptive.

Unlike many of the canon tales in various editions of folk stories published in printed editions, fan-fiction websites are capable of being continually updated with little to no trace left behind. Because of this ability for rapid change, fan participation and multiple authorship is something which has become an integral part of the fan fiction writing process. The stories in which fandom members construct their identities are both "multiple and evolving as well as jointly constructed" (Prins 82). Retold stories—stories where basic plot elements are already known—tend to cue more audience involvement and interpretation (Norrick 200). These stories are chosen and retold because of their familiarity, tellability, and often, their portrayal of cultural memory.

Cultural memories are never truly fixed (Assmann, Aleida 44). They have an inbuilt potential for ongoing changes due to their continued reformulation through telling and retelling in different ways across different mediums. Fans take the adaptability and change already inherent in folktales and fairy tales and use it to fuel their diverse adaptations. Evoking several changes that she sees necessary in the canon tales, Zulixe writes with a sense of urgency at the beginning of one of her fics:

> Es geht um Grimms Märchen. Uns ist zu Ohren gekommen, dass dort etwas ganz falsch lief […]. Wir können doch nicht zulassen, dass so viele Kinder Lügen erzählt bekommen.
>
> [It's about Grimms' Fairy Tales. It's come to our attention, that something went really wrong […]. We can't allow that so many children are told lies.]

Our stories and how they live on can work to reshape our cultural memory of traditional tales and affect contemporary ideals for gender roles, gender identity, sexuality, race, and ethnicity, among others.

For Achim von Arnim, Romantic writer, fellow collector, friend, and mentor to Jacob and Wilhelm Grimm, the significance of the folk- and fairy tale was that they inspire invention. If they cannot inspire us, if they do not show us how to tell new stories, the old stories lose both their value and their charm. The value in the folk- and fairy tale lies not in the details of specific versions, and especially not in the preservation of these details—Arnim tells us that stasis is the death of the fairy tale—but to inspire new stories that take them further. He writes that these tales are "neither young nor old" (Jolles 180). As I have shown throughout this book, they are both.

These stories (which as Arnim writes, are the inspiration for new stories) draw on preexisting networks, culture, and beliefs, ensuring not only those elements of cultural identity from the past are carried forward, but also that through adaptation, they continue to remain relevant to the present. What is of importance, indeed of most significance, is that they provide both a sense of continuity and tradition while also allowing ample room for growth. The stories are meant to be told and retold in the present and should make way for new adaptations in the future. These new adaptations may be through new ideas, the addition of new community members, or the influences of other groups entirely.

Comically articulating the need for change, one fan plays with the notion of change for traditional stories to stay alive:

> "Ah, ein junger Edelmann auf seinem Rosse" sagt ich und lächelte ihm zu […]."Na du oh junge Edelfrau …" sie unterbrach mich.
>
> "Sag mal kannst du nicht normal sprechen" fragte sie genervt […].
>
> Ich musste einen Moment überlegen. Eigentlich stand es so in den Büchern, aber …

> "Doch geht auch" sagte ich und ließ mich auf das Sofa fallen.
>
> ["Ah, a young nobleman on his steed" I said and smiled at him [...]. "Well, you oh young noblewoman ..." she interrupted me.
>
> "Hey, can't you just speak normally" she asked, annoyed [...].
>
> I had to think for a moment. This is how it actually was in the books but ...
>
> "Yeah, that works too" I said and let myself fall onto the couch.] (Cakolinchen)

Though Cakolinchen's portrayal might be humorous, in writing their stories and ensuring that fairy tales do not see a death through stasis, fans often explicitly address both the process of change as well as the need for it if the stories will continue to be told.

Fan fiction writers do not see themselves as telling the definitive version of a cultural memory. They are not claiming to tell *the* story representative of the past, but rather *a* story which is a part of a much longer, conversational whole in which differing and even contradictory perspectives are welcomed. While this is certainly a continuation of an age-old practice of communally telling tales (as has been done in human cultures likely since speech first emerged), the shift online offers new opportunities for former audience members to actively participate and make impactful decisions about what is important to their communities. Digital technologies allow this storytelling energy which was already present to move to online spaces and have outreach which was not possible before. The opportunity that fandoms grant to play and experiment with alternative narrative and hierarchy structures opens possibilities for change and discussion to happen outside the rule of established societal hierarchies and rules of conduct.

If we consider fan fiction as a storytelling event as detailed in Chapter 3, it is easy to see why fan fiction itself is inherently focused on the present rather than as a type of preservation or as a part of a definitive or authorized version. Members of the "Grimms Märchen" fan community are pushing the social boundaries of who is responsible for knowledge and what authorship looks like in this online format as they critique, rewrite, and re-envision what the Grimms' tales represent for their community. The fan versions are presented not as stealing an owned commodity by creating new stories from ones which have already been published, but as ones which represent community and exchange. These tale versions are open to conversation with one another, and with the canon versions. As fans note again and again, their writings exist "to enrich" (zu bereichern) the canon, not to replace it ("Warum schreibt ihr").

We have also seen in Chapter 6 that fandom communities are not spared the appearance of racist and bigoted views due to the prejudices fans bring with them from the actual world. Yet it precisely because of the wide range of participation inherent in these online spaces that they can also be a place for introspection and change when fans are faced with new ideas and perspectives. Fans use threads where bigoted comments occur as moments to discuss larger societal problems. They discuss homophobia and respond quickly to comments which either follow clichés or else are thinly veiled homophobic comments such as "Ich bin ja nicht Homophob, aber" [I'm of course not a homophobe, but] / "Ich habe wirklich nichts gegen Homosexualität, aber" [I really don't have anything against homosexuality, but] ("Schwul/lesbisch/bi"). Fan Hellsingel joins a conversation where homophobic remarks begin to occur, pointing out that while this conversation is happening within a fandom community, it highlights larger truths of the overall German-speaking society. Hellsingel writes:

> Das unsere Gesellschaft gerne vorgibt toleranter zu sein, als sie es eigentlich ist, darüber muss man nicht streiten. Allerdings sind es—in meinen Augen—nicht die offen auftretenden Homophoben, die ein echtes Problem sind, sondern die versteckten [...]. Nach dem Motto: Schwule sind mir egal, solange sie sich nicht in der Öffentlichkeit bemerkbar machen. Toleranz und Akzeptanz findet da nur auf geringstem Niveau statt.
>
> [That our society gladly presents itself as more tolerant than it actually is, is something that doesn't need to be argued about. Certainly it's—in my eyes—not the homophobes who openly come forward who are the real problem, rather it's the hidden ones [...]. Following the motto: I don't care about gays as long as they don't make themselves visible. Tolerance and acceptance then are only at the lowest level.] ("Schwul/lesbisch/bi")

Hellsingel, who self-identifies as a member of the L.G.B.T.Q.+ community then sparks a discussion on the hypocrisy inherent in different comments within the thread as well as German-speaking society. While some users get defensive, this prompts others within the comment thread to reflect on themselves, wondering openly if they perhaps belong to the category of "hidden homophobes." Similarly, in a thread covering the topics of racism, sexism, and antisemitism, one fan writes:

> Wenn ich so lese, was als rassistisch angesehen wird, muss ich gestehen, dass ich mich auch schon (unabsichtlich) rassistisch verhalten habe.
>
> [When I read here what's seen as racist, I have to confess that I have also (accidentally) acted racist.] ("Eure Erfahrungen")

This individual then recounts a specific incident which they now realize was an unconsciously racist response, sparking similar comments from others on the thread and providing a space for reflection.

In every community, there will always be those who are unwilling or not yet ready to have their perspectives challenged, but there is also the possibility that fans can grow and learn from one another. Siberianchan writes "Verstand können wir nur denen geben, die ihn auch wollen." [We can only give comprehension to those who also want it.] The Internet makes divisions and bigotry within societies more widely visible. While there are certainly instances where hate is merely fanned online, as I have shown throughout this book, it also creates new opportunities to bring people together and recognize these divisions in order to break them down. Being exposed to others whom fans might not normally encounter, as well as the possibilities of having deep and frank discussions of hard-hitting topics which fans feel more comfortable expressing and sharing within their online communities, provides possibilities for fans to learn and grow from one another and encounter differing perspectives. It can be a great place of learning where fans likewise use characters and situations in the canon media to try and understand things "aus verschiedenen Perspektiven" [from differing perspectives] ("Umfrage zum Thema"). Because of the community rooted within the fandom, there is an established repertoire of respect and understanding between fans. This connection promotes fans to be more invested in having understanding conversations which is often lamented as absent in other private spheres online.

When individuals begin to critique their own perspectives, such as the fan who recounts her unconsciously racist behavior, they begin to reconsider their position in society. This type of reflection and shift allows new stories to emerge as societies change (Naidoo 5). Though the goals of fandoms lie in helping and supporting one another, fandoms have the power to shape cultural attitudes as they help fans grow—especially considering fan fiction's emphasis on community and potentially constant change. Online fandoms are important tools for the support and maintenance of diverse subcultures since they allow social interaction that can often be difficult to maintain in the actual world due to various factors such as geographical location and social power structures. These stories let storytellers work through personal ideas and feelings and imagine seeing the world from other perspectives. They play with narrative to imagine where it is that their communities should continue to grow and highlight what is misdirected, excluded, or contemptible and needs to change. Fans draw attention to what they notice as missing within their communities when it comes to representation. One fan writes: "Nonbinary fehlt. Keine FFs dazu, keine Webcomics, und wo sie vorkommen, da sinds dann nur 'irgendwie androgyn'" [Nonbinary is missing. No FFs to this end, no web comics, and where they exist, there's just "somehow androgynous"] ("Transgender/Bigender/Androgyn"). These stories show not necessarily how their communities actually are, but rather how they see themselves and their potential to both develop and regress.

Despite all the research on the folktale and fairy tale available as of the writing of this book, it can often be difficult to measure exactly how the genre influences attitudes and behaviors of the "folk," to which it actually belongs. The volatile fairy-tale genre can play any role given to it and survive, thrive, and suffer through almost any adaptation and interpretation. Studying fan fiction gives us an additional way to follow the development of folklore and the fairy tale as it grows and adapts with new technologies. As John Miles Foley writes, the Internet and digitization have put to question "our comfortable assumption that ideas [...] can ever truly become immutable items, things, or commodities" (*Oral Tradition* 185)—that the stories within published editions of fairy tales can somehow be owned by an individual. The fairy tale's nearly unprecedented capability for adaptation and change and its ability to hold multiple meanings for multiple individuals and communities is also strangely powerful. In this context, new interpretations are all simultaneously authorized and unauthorized, creating a space for fans to develop multiple means of interpretation and meaning-making depending on the desires and needs of their own as well as their communities.

That all versions can be both authorized and unauthorized gives power back to everyday people rather than media conglomerates or professional collectors to determine which stories move on in the broader horizon of their communities and which interpretations are acceptable or should be silenced. William A. Wilson writes that "it may be true that folklore captures the soul of a people, but it is equally true that the image of that soul reflected in folklore is also a constructed image, a reflection not necessarily of an objective reality but rather of the ideological predisposition of the individual holding the mirror" (147). By embracing that folklore is the study of the living performance of human culture and expression—both for better and for worse—we can begin to see more clearly who is speaking, who is listening and participating, and who is either refusing to engage or even excluded entirely. We can follow which groups are telling the stories and how they are doing so, if there is greater inclusion or exclusion, if communities are pushing back against societal norms and inequalities or reinforcing them. The study of fan fiction as folklore is crucial because it can show how people relate to themselves, each other, and the societies they live in, as well as how the media and texts around them are understood and interpreted. In order to maintain cultural memories, and cultural identities, the stories people tell are continually re-evaluated, reformed, and reinterpreted in order to both reinforce and challenge their views of themselves and their communities. As we have seen, everyone is a storyteller and the story is never definitively, unalterably *told*.

# Bibliography


Abercrombie, Thomas A. *Pathways of Memory and Power: Ethnography and History Among an Andean People*. U of Wisconsin P, 1998.

abyzz. "Der Wolf." <https://www.fanfiktion.de/s/4fb8d12c000132e40c902ee0/1/Der-Wolf>.

Altais. "Das Internet und das 'echte' Leben—so verschieden?" <https://forum.fanfiktion.de/t/7159/1>.

Ahmed, Sara. *The Cultural Politics of Emotion*. Edinburgh UP, 2004.

Anderson, Benedict. *Imagined Communities: Reflections on the Origin and Spread of Nationalism*. Verso, 1991.

"Angela Merkel Calls Trump Twitter Ban 'Problematic.'" *Deutsche Welle*. <https://www.dw.com/en/angela-merkel-calls-trump-twitter-ban-problematic/a-56197684>.

"Anonym unterwegs—Wissen Familie und Freunde von euren Geschichten?" <https://forum.fanfiktion.de/t/4004/1>.

ardara. "Inside Grimm." <https://www.fanfiktion.de/s/5305ecbf00028d3c1386ae61/1/Inside-Grimm>.

Arendt, Hannah. *The Human Condition*, 2nd edn., U of Chicago P, 2018.

Arnim, Achim von, and Clemens Brentano. *Freundschaftsbriefe*, 2 volumes, edited by Hartwig Schultz, Eichborn Verlag, 1998.

Assmann, Aleida. "Re-framing Memory. Between Individual and Collective Forms of Constructing the Past." *Performing the Past: Memory, History, and Identity in Modern Europe*, edited by Karin Tilmans, Frank van Vree, Jay Winter, Amsterdam UP, 2010, pp. 35–50.

Assmann, Jan. *Cultural Memory and Early Civilization: Writing, Remembrance, and Political Imagination*. Cambridge UP, 2011.

Atan. "Kommentar." <https://www.fanfiktion.de/s/4effadb60001ce0806702af8/4/Schneewittchen-Kampf-um-die-Macht>.

attack09. "Auf welchen Fanfiction-Seiten seid ihr sonst noch unterwegs?" <https://forum.fanfiktion.de/t/24814/1>.

"Auf welchen Fanfiction-Seiten seid ihr sonst noch unterwegs?" <https://forum.fanfiktion.de/t/24814/1>.

Aurora Infernalis. "Der Aufreg-Thread." <https://forum.fanfiktion.de/t/1900/1>.

Avance, Rosemary. "Community." *Digital Keywords: A Vocabulary of Information Society and Culture*, edited by Benjamin Peters, Princeton UP, 2016, pp. 63–69.

Bacchilega, Cristina. *Fairy Tales Transformed? Twenty-First Century Adaptations and the Politics of Wonder.* Wayne State UP, 2013.

——. *Postmodern Fairy Tales: Gender and Narrative Strategies.* U of Pennsylvania P, 1997.

Bacon-Smith, Camille. *Enterprising Women: Television Fandom and the Creation of Popular Myth.* U of Pennsylvania P, 1992.

——. *Science Fiction Culture.* U of Pennsylvania P, 2000.

Baetens, Jan, et al. *Digital Reason: A Guide to Meaning, Medium and Community in a Modern World.* Leuven UP, 2020.

Bakardjieva, Maria. "The Internet in Everyday Life: Exploring the Tenets and Contributions of Diverse Approaches." *The Handbook of Internet Studies*, edited by Mia Consalvo and Charles Ess, Blackwell Publishing Ltd., 2011, pp. 59–82.

Barnett, David. "'Oh, What a Big Gun You Have': NRA Rewrites Fairy Tales to Include Firearms." *The Guardian*, May 24, 2016. <https://www.theguardian.com/books/2016/mar/24/nra-fairytales-include-firearms>.

Battles, Paul. "Dwarfs in Germanic Literature: *Deutsche Mythologie* or Grimm's Myths?" *The Shadow-Walkers: Jacob Grimm's Mythology of the Monstrous*, Arizona Board of Regents for ASU and Brepols Publishers, 2005, pp. 29–82.

Bauer, Esther K. "Female Sexuality and Corporeal Agency in Christian Schad's *Zwei Mädchen.*" *Feminist German Studies*, vol. 35, 2019, pp. 53–84.

Bauman, Richard. *Story, Performance, and Event: Contextual Studies of Oral Narrative.* Cambridge UP, 1986.

Berger, Stefan, and Christoph Conrad. *The Past as History: National Identity and Historical Consciousness in Modern Europe.* Palgrave Macmillan, 2015.

Berners-Lee, Tim. "Realising the Full Potential of the Web." *Technical Communication*, vol. 46, no. 1, February 1999, pp. 79–82.

Bexorcict. "Das arme Rotkäppchen." <https://www.fanfiktion.de/s/562d327d0002b8a21c69f69e/1/Das-arme-Rotkaeppchen>.

Black, Rebecca W. *Adolescents and Online Fan Fiction.* Peter Lang, 2008.

Blank, Trevor J. "Introduction: Pattern in the Virtual Folk Culture of Computer-Mediated Communication." *Folk Culture in the Digital Age: The Emergent Dynamics of Human Interaction*, edited by Trevor J. Blank, Utah State UP, 2012, pp. 1–24.

——. "Introduction: Towards a Conceptual Framework for the Study of Folklore and the Internet." *Folklore and the Internet: Vernacular Expression in a Digital World.* UP of Colorado, 2009, pp. 1–20.

Boellstorff, Tom. *Coming of Age in Second Life: An Anthropologist Explores the Virtually Human.* Princeton UP, 2008.

Bottigheimer, Ruth B. "Fertility Control and the Birth of the Modern European Fairy-Tale Heroine." *Fairy Tales and Feminism: New Approaches*, edited by Donald Haase, Wayne State UP, 2004, pp. 37–51.

——. *Grimms' Bad Girls & Bold Boys: The Moral & Social Vision of the* Tales. Yale UP, 1987.

boyd, danah. *It's Complicated: The Social Lives of Networked Teens*. Yale UP, 2014.

Bromseth, Janne, and Jenny Sundén. "Queering Internet Studies: Intersections of Gender and Sexuality." *The Handbook of Internet Studies*, edited by Mia Consalvo and Charles Ess, Blackwell Publishing Ltd., 2011, pp. 270–298.

Bronner, Simon J. "Digitizing and Virtualizing Folklore." *Folklore and the Internet: Vernacular Expression in a Digital World*. UP of Colorado, 2009, pp. 20–66.

Brooks, Ann. *Gender and the Politics of the Public Sphere*. Bristol UP, 2019.

Buchanan, Elizabeth A. "Internet Research Ethics: Past, Present, and Future." *The Handbook of Internet Studies*, edited by Mia Consalvo and Charles Ess, Blackwell Publishing Ltd., 2011, pp. 83–108.

Buikema, Rosemarie. "Literature and the Production of Ambiguous Memory: Confession and Double Thoughts in Coetzee's *Disgrace*." *European Journal of English Studies*, vol. 10, no. 2, August 2006, pp. 187–197.

Burdick, Anne, et al. *Digital Humanities*. MIT P, 2012.

Busse, Kristina. "Intimate Intertextuality and Performative Fragments in Media Fanfiction." *Fandom: Identities and Communities in a Mediated World*, edited by Jonathan Gray et al., 2nd edn., New York UP, 2017, pp. 45–59.

Busse, Kristina, and Karen Hellekson. "Introduction: Why a Fan Fiction Studies Reader Now?" *The Fan Fiction Studies Reader*, edited by Karen Hellekson and Kristina Busse, U of Iowa P, 2014, pp. 1–17.

——. "Introduction: Work in Progress." *Fan Fiction and Fan Communities in the Age of the Internet: New Essays*, edited by Karen Hellekson and Kristina Busse, McFarland & Co. Inc., 2006, pp. 5–32.

Butler, Judith. *Senses of the Subject*. Fordham UP, 2015.

Cakolinchen. "Eine etwas andere Cinderella Story." <www.fanfiktion.de/s/4ce1990d000196c00c902ee0/8/Eine-etwas-andere-Cinderella-Story>.

Calhoun, Craig. "Facets of the Public Sphere: Dewey, Arendt, Habermas." *Institutional Change in the Public Sphere: Views on the Nordic Model*, edited by Fredrik Engelstad, Håkon Larsen, Jon Rogstad, Kari Steen-Johnsen, Dominika Polkowska, Andrea S. Dauber-Griffin, and Adam Leverton, De Gruyter, 2017, pp. 23–45.

Calvino, Italio. *Invisible Cities*. Translated by William Weaver, Harcourt, Inc., 1974.

Captain Lifi. "Ghettokäppchen." <https://www.fanfiktion.de/s/4a9fbd150000e22a0c902ee0/1/Ghettokaeppchen>.

Captain Trips. "Das Internet und das 'echte' Leben—so verschieden?" <https://forum.fanfiktion.de/t/7159/1>.

Casey, Edward S. "Public Memory in Place and Time." *Framing Public Memory*, edited by Kendall R. Phillips, U of Alabama P, 2004, pp. 17–44.

Cela. "Der Wolf und Rotkäppchen." <https://www.fanfiktion.de/s/54ee27570003d2f52f6f4a3c/1/Der-Wolf-und-Rotkaeppchen>.

Cheal, David. *The Gift Economy*, 1988. Routledge, 2016.

Cho, Sumi, et al. "Toward a Field of Intersectionality Studies: Theory, Applications, and Praxis." *Signs: Journal of Women in Culture and Society*, vol. 38, no. 4, 2013, pp. 785–810.

Coppa, Francesca. "Writing Bodies in Space: Media Fan Fiction as Theatrical Performance." *The Fan Fiction Studies Reader*, edited by Karen Hellekson and Kristina Busse, U of Iowa P, 2014, pp. 217–237.

Cosmodius. "Kommentar." <https://www.fanfiktion.de/r/s/5204a89c00033242a27e0003c/date/0/1>.

Countess of Shadow. "Kommentar." <http://www.fanfiktion.de/r/s/4c3f57f7000012c50c902ee0/date/1/>.

Cubé, Caroline. "To Boldly Go: The Hurried Evolution of Star Trek's Opening Narration." *UCLA Library Special Collections Blog*, November 10, 2016. <https://www.library.ucla.edu/blog/special/2016/10/11/to-boldly-go-the-hurried-evolution-of-star-treks-opening-narration>.

Cuccinello, Hayley C. "Fifty Shades of Green: How Fanfiction Went from Dirty Little Secret to Money Machine." <https://www.forbes.com/sites/hayleycuccinello/2017/02/10/fifty-shades-of-green-how-fanfiction-went-from-dirty-little-secret-to-money-machine/#56f536cf264c>.

Daniels, Jessie. "Rethinking Cyberfeminism(s): Race, Gender, and Embodiment." *Women's Studies Quarterly*, vol. 37, nos. 1 & 2, 2009, pp. 101–124.

"Das Internet und das 'echte' Leben—so verschieden?" <https://forum.fanfiktion.de/t/7159/1>.

"Das Internet—zwischen Informationsflut und Schimpftiraden." <https://forum.fanfiktion.de/t/53824/1>.

DasKleineIchBinIch. "Kommentar." <https://www.fanfiktion.de/s/5248523b0002ff3f191269ba/1/Das-Blaukaeppchen-und-der-boese-betrunkene-Wolf-OS->.

Dastagir, Alia E. "Survivor in the Brock Turner Rape Case Has Revealed Her Identity." *USA Today*, September 4, 2019. <https://www.usatoday.com/story/news/nation/2019/09/04/brock-turner-stanford-rape-case-chanel-miller-survivor-emily-doe/2207106001/>.

Dea Tacita. "Im Märchenwald ist die Hölle los." <http://www.fanfiktion.de/r/s/5370deaa0003d4bc340ac223/date/0/1>.

Del Negro, Giovanna P., and Harris M. Berger. "Identity Reconsidered, the World Doubled." *Identity and Everyday Life: Essays in the Study of Folklore, Music, and Popular Culture*, edited by Harris M. Berger and Giovanna P. Del Negro, Wesleyan UP, 2004, pp. 124–157.

DeLullu. "Rotkäppchens Mission." <https://www.fanfiktion.de/s/4cf14db80000fb370c902ee0/1/Rotkaeppchens-Mission>.

Derecho, Abigail. "Archontic Literature: A Definition, a History, and Several Theories of Fan Fiction." *Fan Fiction and Fan Communities in the Age of the Internet: New Essays*, edited by Karen Hellekson and Kristina Busse, McFarland and Co., Inc., 2006, pp. 61–78.

Der Edgerton Bonus. "Das Internet—zwischen Informationsflut und Schimpftiraden." <https://forum.fanfiktion.de/t/53824/1>.

——. "Der Aufreg-Thread." <https://forum.fanfiktion.de/t/1900/1>.

Des-C-Kudi. "Auf welchen Fanfiction-Seiten seid ihr sonst noch unterwegs?" <https://forum.fanfiktion.de/t/24814/1>.

DieLadi. "Habt ihr euch immer schon mal gefragt …" <https://www.fanfiktion.de/s/58407bb90005d145311446dc/13/Habt-ihr-euch-immer-schon-mal-gefragt->.

——. "Habt ihr euch immer schon mal gefragt …" Kommentar. <https://www.fanfiktion.de/r/s/58407bb90005d145311446dc/date/0/1>.

DigiJasmin. "Kommentar." <https://www.fanfiktion.de/r/s/54b2968d0004565a318fd75f/date/0/1>.

——. "Wirsing." <https://www.fanfiktion.de/s/54b2968d0004565a318fd75f/1/Wirsing>.

Drascek, Daniel. "Franz Xaver von Schönwerth und die Oberpfalz—eine interdisziplinäre Annäherung. Vorwort." *Schönwerth—"mit so leisem Gehör gesammelt.": Neue Perspektiven auf Franz Xaver von Schönwerth (1810–1886) und seine Forschungen zur Alltagskultur der Oberpfalz*, edited by Daniel Drascek et al., Verlag Schnell & Steiner GmbH, 2011, pp. 7–10.

dreamycato. "Rotkapp." <https://www.fanfiktion.de/s/562d6d42000333f23704257b/1/Rotkapp>.

Duggan, Anne E. "Gender." *The Routledge Companion to Media and Fairy-Tale Cultures*, edited by Pauline Greenhill, Jill Terry Rudy, Naomi Hamer, and Lauren Bosc, Routledge, 2018, pp. 113–121.

Dunbar, Robin I. M., and Richard Sosis. "Optimising Human Community Sizes." *Evolution and Human Behavior*, vol. 39, 2018, pp. 106–111.

Eagleton, Mary. "Literature." *A Concise Companion to Feminist Theory*, edited by Mary Eagleton, Blackwell Publishing, 2003, pp. 153–172.

elektra121. "Grimms Märchen (mit falschem Ende)." <https://www.fanfiktion.de/s/52bd69e20000112839947d79/1/Grimms-Maerchen-mit-falschem-Ende->.

Enjolras, Bernard, and Kari Steen-Johnsen. "The Digital Transformation of the Political Public Sphere: A Sociological Perspective." *Institutional Change in the Public Sphere: Views on the Nordic Model*, edited by Fredrik Engelstad, Håkon Larsen, Jon Rogstad, Kari Steen-Johnsen, Dominika Polkowska, Andrea S. Dauber-Griffin, and Adam Leverton, De Gruyter, 2017, pp. 99–117.

Erll, Astrid. "Re-writing as Re-visioning." *European Journal of English Studies*, vol. 10, no. 2, pp. 163–185.

Erstad, Ola, and James V. Wertsch. "Tales of Mediation: Narrative and Digital Media as Cultural Tools." *Digital Storytelling, Mediatized Stories: Self-representations in New Media*, edited by Knut Lundby, Peter Lang, 2008, pp. 21–39.

Erzählerstimme. "Ist euch Fanfiktion.de als Hobby peinlich?" <https://forum.fanfiktion.de/t/12676/1>.

"Eure Erfahrungen mit Rassismus, Sexismus, Antisemitismus, etc." <https://forum.fanfiktion.de/t/68516/1>.

"Fan Fiction Terms." <http://www.translationdirectory.com/glossaries/glossary319.php>.

"Fanfiction-Sachbuch im iFuB-Verschlag erschienen." <https://blog.fanfiktion.de/blog/2580/fanfiction-sachbuch-im-ifub-verlag-erschienen/>.

"Fanfiction schreiben—Vergeudung von Talent?" <https://forum.fanfiktion.de/t/16113/1>.

Faraj, Samer, and Steven L. Johnson. "Network Exchange Patterns in Online Communities." *Organization Science*, vol. 22, no. 6, November–December 2011, pp. 1464–1480.

Farfalla91. "Kommentar." <https://www.fanfiktion.de/r/s/5338ab2400013af029236f3d/date/0/1>.

——. "Märchen—Wie es wirklich war." <http://www.fanfiktion.de/s/5338ab2400013af029236f3d/8/Maerchen-Wie-es-wirklich-war>.

Faucher, Kane X. *Social Capital Online*. U of Westminster P, 2018.

feuersalamander. "Kommentar." <https://www.fanfiktion.de/r/s/51da851e0002d99838dcdcd4/date/0/1>.

Fledermaerchen. "Kommentar." <https://www.fanfiktion.de/s/4be1919f00010b430c902ee0/1/Naked>.

Foley, John Miles. *How to Read an Oral Poem*. U of Illinois P, 2002.

——. *Oral Tradition and the Internet: Pathways of the Mind*. U of Illinois P, 2012.

"Forums." <http://forum.fanfiktion.de/f/46>.

French, Brigittine M. "The Semiotics of Collective Memories." *Annual Review of Anthropology* vol. 41, 2012, pp. 337–353.

Garde-Hansen, Joanne, et al. "Introduction." *Save As … Digital Memories*, edited by Joanne Garde-Hansen et al., Palgrave Macmillan, 2009, pp. 1–26.

Garg, Rajiv, et al. "Measuring Information Diffusion in an Online Community." *Journal of Management Information Systems*, vol. 28, no. 2, Fall 2011, pp. 11–37.

Gilbert, Sandra M., and Susan Gubar. *The Madwoman in the Attic: The Woman Writer and the Nineteenth-Century Imagination*, 2nd edn., Yale UP, 2000.

Girlaftermidnight. "Kommentar." <https://www.fanfiktion.de/r/s/54b2968d0004565a318fd75f/date/0/1>.

Goldstein, Kevin. "Nurtured in a Lonely Place: The Wise Woman as Type in 'The Goose Girl at the Spring.' " *Transgressive Tales: Queering the Grimms*, edited by Kay Turner & Pauline Greenhill, Wayne State UP, 2012, pp. 49–67.

Gonçalves, Bruno, et al. "Modeling Users' Activity on Twitter Networks: Validating Dunbar's Number." *PLoS One*, vol. 6, no. 8, August 2011, pp. 1–5. <https://doi.org/10.1371/journal.pone.0022656>.

Gongaware, Timothy B. "Collective Memory Anchors: Collective Identity and Continuity in Social Movements." *Sociological Focus*, vol. 43, no. 3, 2012, pp. 214–239.

Gottschall, Jonathan. *The Storytelling Animal: Stories Make Us Human*. Houghton Mifflin Harcourt, 2012.

Grandinetti, Tina. "Moana Might Be Great for Representation But It's Not All Heartwarming for Hawaii." *The Guardian*, January 12, 2017. <https://www.theguardian.com/film/2017/jan/13/moana-might-be-great-for-representation-but-its-not-all-heartwarming-for-hawaii>.

Gray, Jonathan, et al. "Introduction: Why Study Fans?" *Fandom: Identities and Communities in a Mediated World*, edited by Jonathan Gray, Cornel Sandvoss, and C. Lee Harrington, New York UP, 2007, pp. 1–16.

Greenhill, Pauline. "Folk and Academic Racism: Concepts from Morris and Folklore." *The Journal of American Folklore*, vol. 115, no. 456, *Folklore in Canada*, Spring 2002, pp. 226–246.

Greenhill, Pauline, and Anne Brydon. "Mourning Mothers and Seeing Siblings: Feminism and Place in *The Juniper Tree*." *Fairy Tale Films: Visions of Ambiguity*, edited by Pauline Greenhill and Sidney Eve Matrix, Utah State UP, 2010, pp. 116–136.

Greenhill, Pauline, and Sidney Eve Matrix. "Introduction: Envisioning Ambiguity: Fairy Tale Films." *Fairy Tale Films: Visions of Ambiguity*, edited by Pauline Greenhill and Sidney Eve Matrix, Utah State UP, 2010, pp. 1–22.

Grimm, Jacob, and Wilhelm Grimm. *Grimm's Complete Fairy Tales*. Translated by Margaret Hunt, Canterbury Classics, 2011.

——. *Kinder- und Hausmärchen Gesammelt durch die Brüder Grimm: Vollständige Ausgabe auf der Grundlage der dritten Auflage (1837)*, edited by Heinz Rölleke, Deutscher Klassiker Verlag, 1985.

"Gründe fürs Wegklicken." <https://forum.fanfiktion.de/t/4986/1>.

Gunnell, Terry. "Daisies Rise to Become Oaks. The Politics of Early Folktale Collection in Northern Europe." *Folklore*, vol. 121, no. 1, April 2010, pp. 12–37.

Haase, Donald. "Feminist Fairy-Tale Scholarship." *Fairy Tales and Feminism: New Approaches*, edited by Donald Haase, Wayne State UP, 2004, pp. 1–36.

——. "Introduction." *The Reception of Grimms' Fairy Tales: Responses, Reactions, Revisions*, edited by Donald Haase, Wayne State UP, 1993, pp. 9–23.

——. "Preface." *Fairy Tales and Feminism: New Approaches*, edited by Donald Haase, Wayne State UP, 2004, pp. vii–xiv.

——. "Response and Responsibility in Reading Grimms' Fairy Tales." *The Reception of Grimms' Fairy Tales: Responses, Reactions, Revisions*, edited by Donald Haase, Wayne State UP, 1993, pp. 230–249.

Habermas, Jürgen. "The Public Sphere." *Media Studies: A Reader*, edited by Sue Thornham, Caroline Bassett and Paul Marris, Edinburgh UP, 2009, pp. 45–51.

——. "Warum Nicht Lesen?" *Warum Lesen: Mindestens 24 Gründe*, Suhrkamp Verlag, 2020, pp. 99–123.

Hachiko. "Kommentar." <https://www.fanfiktion.de/s/4a9fbd150000e22a0c902eeo/1/Ghettokaeppchen>.

Hamad, Ruby. *White Tears/Brown Scars: How White Feminism Betrays Women of Color*. Catapult, 2020.

Hamilton, David. "Twitter CEO Defends Trump Ban, Warns of Dangerous Precedent." *AP News*, January 13, 2021. <https://apnews.com/article/jack-dorsey-twitter-defend-trump-ban-843c3e5fb72c0cfb89c1fd1132a525d8>.

Hammond, Heidi. "Social Interest, Empathy, and Online Support Groups." *The Journal of Individual Psychology*, vol. 71, no. 2, Summer 2015, pp. 174–184.

Hellekson, Karen. "A Fannish Field of Value: Online Fan Gift Culture." *Cinema Journal*, vol. 48, no. 4, 2009, pp. 113–118.

Hellekson, Karen, and Kristina Busse. "Fan Fiction as Literature." *The Fan Fiction Studies Reader*, edited by Karen Hellekson and Kristina Busse, U of Iowa P, 2014, pp. 19–25.

——. "Fan Identity and Feminism." *The Fan Fiction Studies Reader*, edited by Karen Hellekson and Kristina Busse, U of Iowa P, 2014, pp. 75–81.

——. "Introduction: Why a Fan Fiction Studies Reader Now?" *The Fan Fiction Studies Reader*, edited by Karen Hellekson and Kristina Busse, U of Iowa P, 2014, pp. 1–17.

Himmelgrau. "Kommentar." <https://www.fanfiktion.de/r/s/4fb8d12c000132e40c902eeo/date/1/1>.

Hinck, Ashley, and Amber Davisson. "Fandom and Politics" [editorial]. In "Fandom and Politics," edited by Ashley Hinck and Amber Davisson, special issue, *Transformative Works and Cultures*, no. 32, 2020. <https://doi.org/10.3983/twc.2020.1973>.

"Internet World Statistics." <https://internetworldstats.com/>.

Isabella1994. "Kommentar." <http://www.fanfiktion.de/r/s/52a58006000031a6912b9a317/date/1/1>.

"Ist euch Fanfiktion.de als Hobby peinlich?" <https://forum.fanfiktion.de/t/12676/1>.

Jackson, Bruce. *The Story Is True: The Art and Meaning of Telling Stories*. Temple UP, 2007.

Jamison, Anne. *Fic: Why Fan Fiction Is Taking Over the World.* Smart Pop, 2013.

Jarvis, Shawn. "Trivial Pursuit? Women Deconstructing the Grimmian Model in the *Kafeterkreis*." *The Reception of Grimms' Fairy Tales: Responses, Reactions, Revisions*, edited by Donald Haase, Wayne State UP, 1993, pp. 102–126.

Jenkins, Henry. "Afterword: The Future of Fandom." *Fandom: Identities and Communities in a Mediated World*, edited by Jonathan Gray, Cornel Sandvoss, and C. Lee Harrington, New York UP, 2007, pp. 357–364.

——. *Convergence Culture: Where Old and New Media Collide*. New York UP, 2006.

——. "Fandom, Participatory Culture, and Web 2.0—A Syllabus," 2010. <http://henryjenkins.org/blog/2010/01/fandom_participatory_culture_a.html>.

——. *Textual Poachers: Television Fans & Participatory Culture*. Routledge, 1992.

Jenkins, Henry, and Sangita Shresthova. "Up, Up, and Away! The Power and Potential of Fan Activism." *Transformative Works and Cultures*, vol. 10, 2012. <https://doi.org/10.3983/twc.2012.0435>.

Jensen, Klaus Bruhn. "New Media, Old Methods—Internet Methodologies and the Online/Offline Divide." *The Handbook of Internet Studies*, edited by Mia Consalvo and Charles Ess, Blackwell Publishing Ltd., 2011, pp. 43–58.

Jolles, André. *Simple Forms*. Translated by Peter J. Schwartz, Verso, 2017.

Jones, Steven Swann. "The Innocent Persecuted Heroine Genre: An Analysis of Its Structure and Themes." *Western Folklore*, vol. 52, no. 1, *Perspectives on the Innocent Persecuted Heroine in Fairy Tales*, 1993, pp. 13–41.

Joosen, Vanessa. *Critical and Creative Perspectives on Fairy Tales: An Intertextual Dialogue between Fairy-Tale Scholarship and Postmodern Retellings.* Wayne State UP, 2011.

KaLiBeYT13. "Kommentar." <https://www.fanfiktion.de/r/s/58407bb90005d145311446dc/date/4/1>.

KathaXD. "Kommentar." <https://www.fanfiktion.de/s/5248523b0002ff3f191269ba/1/Das-Blaukaeppchen-und-der-boese-betrunkene-Wolf-OS->.

Katzelin. "Ist euch Fanfiktion.de als Hobby peinlich?" <https://forum.fanfiktion.de/t/12676/1>.

Kendall, Lori. "Community and the Internet." *The Handbook of Internet Studies*, edited by Mia Consalvo and Charles Ess, Blackwell Publishing Ltd., 2011, pp. 309–325.

Kohm, Steven, and Pauline Greenhill. "Little Red Riding Hood Crime Films: Critical Variations on Criminal Themes." *Law, Culture and the Humanities*, vol. 10, no. 2, 2014, pp. 257–278.

Kumar, Krishan, and Ekaterina Makrova. "The Portable Home: The Domestication of Public Space." *Sociological Theory*, vol. 26, no. 4, December 2008, pp. 324–343.

Kustritz, Anne. "Fan Fiction." *The Routledge Companion to Media and Fairy-Tale Cultures*, edited by Pauline Greenhill, Jill Terry Rudy, Naomi Hamer, and Lauren Bosc, Routledge, 2018, pp. 508–514.

——. "Fandom/Fan Cultures." *Routledge Companion to Fairy Tale Cultures and Media*, edited by Pauline Greenhill, Jill T. Rudy, Naomi Hamer, and Lauren Bosc, Routledge, 2018, pp. 245–251.

——. "'They All Lived Happily Ever After. Obviously': Realism and Utopia in *Game of Thrones*-Based Alternate Universe Fairy Tale Fan Fiction." *Fairy Tale and Its Uses in Contemporary New Media and Popular Culture*, special issue of Humanities, edited by Claudia Schwabe, vol. 5, no. 43, doi:10.3390/h5020043.

Langellier, Kristin M., and Eric E. Peterson. *Storytelling in Daily Life: Performing Narrative*. Temple UP, 2004.

Lau, Kimberly J. "A Desire for Death: The Grimms' Sleeping Beauty in *The Bloody Chamber*." *Transgressive Tales: Queering the Grimms*, edited by Kay Turner and Pauline Greenhill, Wayne State UP, 2012, pp. 121–139.

Lea-Iruka. "Kommentar." <http://www.fanfiktion.de/r/s/4aff147a00011 72c0c902eeo/date/7/1>.

Lexila. "Das Internet und das 'echte' Leben—so verschieden?" <https://forum.fanfiktion.de/t/7159/1>.

Limette02. "Das verlorene Königskind." <https://www.fanfiktion.de/s/4ce2ce7400016c950c902eeo/1/Das-verlorene-Koenigskind>.

Liptak, Adam. "Can Twitter Legally Bar Trump? The First Amendment Says Yes." *New York Times*, January 9, 2021. <https://www.nytimes.com/2021/01/09/us/first-amendment-free-speech.html>.

LittleChi. "Urban Fairytales." <https://www.fanfiktion.de/s/4f6da9b00001e5ea0c902eeo/1/Urban-Fairytails>.

Liu, James H., and Denis J. Hilton. "How the Past Weighs on the Present: Social Representations of History and Their Role in Identity Politics." *British Journal of Social Psychology*, vol. 44, 2005, pp. 537–556.

Loftus, Elizabeth, and Katherine Ketcham. *Witness for the Defense: The Accused, the Eyewitness, and the Expert Who Puts Memory on Trial*. St. Martin's P, 1992.

Loges, Natasha. "How to Make a 'Volkslied': Early Models in the Songs of Johannes Brahms." *Music and Letters*, vol. 93, no. 3, August 2012, pp. 316–349.

Lord, Albert Bates. *Epic Singers and Oral Tradition*. Cornell UP, 1991.

Lorenz, Chris. “Unstuck in Time. Or: The Sudden Presence of the Past.” *Performing the Past: Memory, History, and Identity in Modern Europe*, edited by Karin Tilmans, Frank van Vree, and Jay Winter, Amsterdam UP, 2010, pp. 67–102.

Lüders, Marika. “Why and How Online Sociability Became Part and Parcel of Teenage Life.” *The Handbook of Internet Studies*, edited by Mia Consalvo and Charles Ess, Blackwell Publishing Ltd., 2011, pp. 452–469.

Lundby, Knut. “Introduction.” *Digital Storytelling, Mediatized Stories: Self-representations in New Media*, edited by Knut Lundby, Peter Lang, 2008, pp. 1–17.

*Maleficent*. Directed by Robert Stromberg, *Walt Disney Studios Motion Pictures*, 2014.

Maribelle 28. “Kommentar.” <https://www.fanfiktion.de/r/s/5370deaa0003d4bc340ac223/date/0/1>.

——. “Schneeweißchen und Rosenrot.” <http://www.fanfiktion.de/s/5370deaa0003d4bc340ac223/1/Aus-alt-mah-neu-Maerchen-mal-anders>.

McNeill, Lynne S. “Digital: ‘Blood and Glitter’: Fairy Tales as Text, Texture, and Context in Digital Media.” *The Routledge Companion to Media and Fairy-Tale Cultures*, edited by Pauline Greenhill, Jill Terry Rudy, Naomi Hamer, and Lauren Bosc, Routledge, 2018, pp. 376–388.

Meehan, Johanna. “Communicative Ethics.” *A Companion to Feminist Philosophy*, edited by Alison M. Jaggar and Iris Marion Young, Blackwell Publishers, 1998, pp. 411–419.

Megele, Claudia, and Peter Buzzi. *Online Identity, Digital Citizenship and Boundaries*. Bristol UP, 2018.

Melina Evergreen. “Kommentar.” <https://www.fanfiktion.de/s/53deb492000012c5fb2a16e/1/Dornroeschen-oder-der-Wert-des-Fleisses>.

“Memory of the World: Programme Objectives.” *UNESCO*. <http://www.unesco.org/new/en/communication-and-information/flagship-project-activities/memory-of-the-world/about-the-programme/objectives/>.

Miller, Kent D., et al. “Strategies for Online Communities.” *Strategic Management Journal*, vol. 30, no. 3, March 2009, pp. 305–322.

Miller, Michelle D. “The Psychology of Computing.” *Teaching Effectively with Technology*, Harvard UP, 2014, pp. 42–63.

moe-rikyou. “Kommentar.” <https://www.fanfiktion.de/r/s/4e5cc0af0000e0010c902ee0/date/0/1>.

Mollet, Tracey. “‘With a Smile and a Song …’: Walt Disney and the Birth of the American Fairy Tale.” *Marvels & Tales*, vol. 27, no. 1, 2013, pp. 109–124.

MonaGirl. “Warum schreibt ihr Fanfiktion [Umfrage].” <https://forum.fanfiktion.de/t/53036/1>.

Naidoo, Marilyn. “So, What’s Your Story?—The Role of Storytelling in Nurturing Inclusive Congregational Identity.” *HTS Teologiese Studies/Theological Studies*, vol. 74, no. 4, 2019. <https://doi.org/10.4102/hts.v75i4.5448>.

Narai, Ria. "Female-Centered Fan Fiction as Homoaffection in Fan Communities." "Queer Female Fandom," edited by Julie Levin Russo and Eve Ng, special issue, *Transformative Works and Cultures*, no. 24, 2017. <http://dx.doi.org/10.3983/twc.2017.1014>.

Nashima no ryuu. "Kommentar." <https://www.fanfiktion.de/s/4a9fbd150000e22a0c902ee0/1/Ghettokaeppchen>.

Negt, Oskar, and Alexander Kluge. "'The Public Sphere and Experience': Selections." Translated by Peter Labanyi, *October*, vol. 46, Alexander Kluge: Theoretical Writings, Stories, and an Interview, Autumn 1988, pp. 60–82.

Nikolajeva, Maria. *Power, Voice and Subjectivity in Literature for Young Readers*. Routledge, 2010.

Niles, John D. *Homo Narrans: The Poetics and Anthropology of Oral Literature*. U of Philadelphia P, 1999.

Nin, Anaïs. *Seduction of the Minotaur*. Swallow P, 1961.

Nisbett, Gwendelyn S. "Don't Mess with My Happy Place: Understanding Misogyny in Fandom Communities." *Mediating Misogyny: Gender, Technology and Harassment*, edited by Jacqueline Ryan Vickery and Tracy Everbach, Palgrave Macmillan, 2018, pp. 171–188.

NoBelieveNoTrust. "Cinderella—Was wäre wenn .....?" <https://www.fanfiktion.de/s/505b4daa000299e206702af8/1/Cinderella-Was-waere-wenn->.

Norrick, Neal R. "Twice-Told Tales: Collaborative Narration of Familiar Stories." *Language in Society*, vol. 26, no. 2, June 1997, pp. 199–220.

"Nutzungsbedingungen." <www.fanfiktion.de/p/terms-of-service/0>.

Nymis. "Auf welchen Fanfiction-Seiten seid ihr sonst noch unterwegs?" <https://forum.fanfiktion.de/t/24814/1>.

Ong, Walter J. *Orality and Literacy: The Technologizing of the Word*. Methuen & Co. Ltd., 1982.

PanicMoon. "Aschenputtel mal anders." <https://www.fanfiktion.de/s/5e80e3240005c2d631042b81/1/Aschenputtel-mal-anders>.

Panthera. "Ist euch Fanfiktion.de als Hobby peinlich?" <https://forum.fanfiktion.de/t/12676/1>.

Papacharissi, Zizi A. *A Private Sphere: Democracy in a Digital Age*. Polity P, 2010.

Penley, Constance. "Future Men." *The Fan Fiction Studies Reader*, edited by Karen Hellekson and Kristina Busse, U of Iowa P, 2014, pp. 177–191.

Perrault, Charles. *The Complete Fairy Tales*. Translated by Christopher Betts, Oxford UP, 2009.

Perscitia. "Die Gänsemagd in Sonnenau." <https://www.fanfiktion.de/s/5ab140cf0004e73117703a4f/4/Die-Gaensemagd-im-Sonnenau>.

Pershing, Linda, and Lisa Gablehouse. "Disney's Enchanted: Patriarchal Backlash and Nostalgia in a Fairy Tale Film." *Fairy Tale Films: Visions of Ambiguity*, edited by Pauline Greenhill and Sidney Eve Matrix, Utah State UP, 2010, pp. 137–156.

Phillips, Whitney, and Ryan M. Milner. *The Ambivalent Internet: Mischief, Oddity, and Antagonism Online*. Polity P, 2017.

Plant, Sadie. *Zeros and Ones: Digital Women and the New Technoculture*. Fourth Estate, 2016.

Poland, Bailey. *Haters: Harassment, Abuse, and Violence Online*. U of Nebraska P, 2016.

Prins, Jacomijna, et al. "Telling the Collective Story? Moroccan-Dutch Young Adults' Negotiation of a Collective Identity through Storytelling." *Qual Sociol*, vol. 36, 2013, pp. 81–99.

"[Projekt] Märchen Female-Slash [Fanfiction, Freie Arbeiten]." <https://forum.fanfiktion.de/t/39291/1>.

Pterano Dante. "Es ist nun einmal so …: Rosalie Dorn--die schlafende Schöne." <https://www.fanfiktion.de/s/5a4836bd000035d32dc91a1e/3/Es-ist-nun-einmal-so->.

——. "Rumpelstilzchen." <https://www.fanfiktion.de/s/5a4836bd000035d32dc91a1e/1/Rumpelstilzchen>.

Rala vom Wald. "Kommentar." <https://www.fanfiktion.de/s/4effadb60001ce0806702af8/4/Schneewittchen-Kampf-um-die-Macht>.

"Rapefics—Solange der Täter gut aussieht, ist alles okay!?" <https://forum.fanfiktion.de/t/34643/1>.

RavenclawGirl. "Auf welchen Fanfiction-Seiten seid ihr sonst noch unterwegs?" <https://forum.fanfiktion.de/t/24814/1>.

Reagle, Joesph M. *Reading the Comments: Likers, Haters, and Manipulators at the Bottom of the Web*. MIT P, 2015.

"Rechtlinien." <http://www.FanFiktion.de/p/ageadvice/0>.

Rigney, Ann. "The Many Afterlives of Ivanhoe." *Performing the Past: Memory, History, and Identity in Modern Europe*, edited by Karin Tilmans, Frank van Vree, and Jay Winter, Amsterdam UP, 2010, pp. 207–234.

Rissi-chan. "Kommentar." <http://www.fanfiktion.de/r/s/4aff147a0001172c0c902ee0/date/7/1>.

Rölleke, Heinz. "Kommentar". *Kinder- und Hausmärchen Gesammelt durch die Brüder Grimm: Vollständige Ausgabe auf der Grundlage der dritten Auflage (1837)*, Jacob and Wilhelm Grimm, edited by Heinz Rölleke, Deutscher Klassiker Verlag, 1985, pp. 1151–1189.

Rölleke, Heinz, and Albert Schindehütte. *Es war einmal … Die wahren Märchen der Brüder Grimm und wer sie ihnen erzählte.* Eichborn AG, 2001.

Sadiqi, Fatima, and Moha Ennaji. “The Femininzation of Public Space: Women’s Activism, the Family Law, and Social Change in Morocco.” *Journal of Middle East Women’s Studies*, vol. 2, no. 2, Spring 2006, pp. 86–114.

Sandvoss, Cornel. “The Death of the Reader? Literary Theory and the Study of Texts in Popular Culture.” *Fandom: Identities and Communities in a Mediated World*, edited by Jonathan Gray et al., 2nd edn., New York UP, 2017, pp. 29–44.

Schneider, William. “Oral History in the Age of Digital Possibilities.” *Oral History and Digital Humanities: Voice, Access, and Engagement*, edited by Douglas A. Boyd and Mary A. Larson, Palgrave Macmillan, 2014, pp. 19–33.

“Schwul/lesbisch/bi.” <https://forum.fanfiktion.de/t/16283/1>.

Sefira. “Kommentar.” <https://www.fanfiktion.de/r/s/5370deaa0003d4bc340ac223/date/0/1>.

Siberianchan. “Dornröschen—oder der Wert des Fleißes.” <https://www.fanfiktion.de/s/53deb492000012c5fb2a16e/1/Dornroeschen-oder-der-Wert-des-Fleisses>.

Siegel, Alan. “Get a Life! What a ‘Saturday Night Live’ Sketch from 1986 Can Teach Us about the Ongoing Battle between Superfans and the People Behind the TV and Movie Franchises That They Love.” *The Ringer*, January 31, 2018. <https://www.theringer.com/movies/2018/1/31/16947436/saturday-night-live-william-shatner-star-trek-snl-nerds-star-wars-last-jedi>.

Sionon Klingensang. “Das Internet—zwischen Informationsflut und Schimpftiraden.” <https://forum.fanfiktion.de/t/53824/1>.

——. “Umfrage—Was ist für euch Fanfiction?” <https://forum.fanfiktion.de/t/62186/1>.

“Slash.” *Fanlore*. <https://fanlore.org/wiki/Slash>.

*Snow White and the Seven Dwarfs*. Directed by Ben Sharpsteen et al., RKO Radio Pictures, 1937.

Stanko, Taryn Lyn, et al. “Navigating an Identity Playground: Using Sociomateriality to Build a Theory of Identity Play.” *Organization Studies*, 2020, pp. 1–23, doi: 10.1177/0170840620944452.

Starkeeper. “Auf welchen Fanfiction-Seiten seid ihr sonst noch unterwegs?” <https://forum.fanfiktion.de/t/24814/1>.

“Starke Frauen.” <https://forum.fanfiktion.de/t/6223/1>.

Stein, Louisa Ellen. “‘This Dratted Thing’: Fannish Storytelling Through New Media.” *Fan Fiction and Fan Communities in the Age of the Internet: New Essays*, edited by Karen Hellekson and Kristina Busse, McFarland & Co. Inc., 2006, pp. 245–260.

Stein, Louisa Ellen, and Kristina Busse. “Limit Play: Fan Authorship between Source Text, Intertext, and Context.” *Popular Communication*, vol. 7, no. 4, pp. 192–207.

"The Strange New World of the Internet: Battles of the Frontiers of Cyberspace." *Time*, vol. 144, no. 4, July 25, 1994. <http://content.time.com/time/magazine/0,9263,7601940725,00.html>.

Stromer-Galley, Jennifer, and Alexis Wichowski. "Political Discussion Online." *The Handbook of Internet Studies*, edited by Mia Consalvo and Charles Ess, Blackwell Publishing Ltd., 2011, pp. 168–187.

Stroud, Scott R., and William Cox. "The Varieties of Feminist Counterspeech in the Misogynistic Online World." *Mediating Misogyny: Gender, Technology and Harassment*, edited by Jacqueline Ryan Vickery and Tracy Everbach, Palgrave Macmillan, 2018, pp. 293–310.

Sturmklang. "Once Upon a Bloody Time." <http://www.fanfiktion.de/s/50c3554600024b1f0c902ee0/3/Once-Upon-A-Bloody-Time>.

——. "Reviews." <www.fanfiktion.de/r/s/50c3554600024b1f0c902ee0/date/3/1>.

Sumpex. "Ist euch Fanfiktion.de als Hobby peinlich?" <https://forum.fanfiktion.de/t/12676/1>.

TamSang. "Anonym unterwegs—Wissen Familie und Freunde von euren Geschichten?" <https://forum.fanfiktion.de/t/4004/1>.

Tatar, Maria. *The Hard Facts of the Grimms' Fairy Tales*, 2nd edn. Princeton UP, 2003.

Thompson, Stuart A., and Charlie Warzel. "They Used to Post Selfies. Now They're Trying to Overturn the Election." *New York Times*, January 14, 2021. <https://www.nytimes.com/2021/01/14/opinion/facebook-far-right.html>.

Thorne, Steven L. "Community Formation and the World as Its Own Model." *The Modern Language Journal*, vol. 95, no. 2, Summer 2011, pp. 304–307.

Thorne, Steven L., and Rebecca Black. "Identity and Interaction in Internet-Mediated Contexts." *Identity Formation in Globalizing Contexts*, edited by C. Higgins, Mouton de Gruyter, 2011, pp. 257–278.

Thoronris. "Auf welchen Fanfiction-Seiten seid ihr sonst noch unterwegs?" <https://forum.fanfiktion.de/t/24814/1>.

Tintenstreuner. "Was wäre, wenn …?: Dornröschen." <https://www.fanfiktion.de/s/567ab6550000be2b11a98ef8/2/Was-waere-wenn->.

Toelken, Barre. *The Dynamics of Folklore: Revised and Expanded Edition*. Utah State UP, 1996.

"Transgender/Bigender/Androgyn." <https://forum.fanfiktion.de/t/32494/1>.

Turk, Tisha. "Fan Work: Labor, Worth, and Participation in Fandom's Gift Economy." *Transformative Works and Cultures*, vol. 15, 2014. <http://dx.doi.org.ezproxy.wlu.edu/10.3983/twc.2014.0518>.

Turner, Kay, and Pauline Greenhill. "Introduction: Once Upon a Queer Time." *Transgressive Tales: Queering the Grimms*, edited by Kay Turner and Pauline Greenhill, Wayne State UP, 2012, pp. 1–24.

"Umfrage—Was ist für euch Fanfiction?" <https://forum.fanfiktion.de/t/62186/1>.

"Umfrage zum Thema Fanfiktion und Identität." <https://forum.fanfiktion.de/t/38671/1>.

Van Eeden-Moorefield, Brad, et al. "Same-Sex Relationships and Dissolution: The Connection between Heteronormativity and Homonormativity." *Family Relations*, vol. 60, no. 5, 2011, pp. 562–571.

Vaz da Silva, Francisco. "The Invention of Fairy Tales." *Journal of American Folklore*, vol. 123, no. 490, Fall 2010, pp. 398–425.

"Verbote und Einschränkungen." <http://www.FanFiktion.de/p/rules-and-regulations/0>.

Vickery, Jacqueline Ryan. "This Isn't New: Gender, Publics, and the Internet." *Mediating Misogyny: Gender, Technology and Harassment*, edited by Jacqueline Ryan Vickery and Tracy Everbach, Palgrave Macmillan, 2018, pp. 31–49.

Vickery, Jacqueline Ryan, and Tracy Everbach. "The Persistence of Misogyny: From the Streets, to Our Screens, to the White House." *Mediating Misogyny: Gender, Technology and Harassment*, edited by Jacqueline Ryan Vickery and Tracy Everbach, Palgrave Macmillan, 2018, pp. 1–27.

Warner, Marina. *From the Beast to the Blonde: On Fairy Tales and Their Tellers.* Farrar, Straus and Giroux, 1994.

——. *No Go the Bogeyman: Scaring, Lulling, and Making Mock.* Farrar, Straus and Giroux, 1998.

——. *Once Upon a Time: A Short History of Fairy Tale.* Oxford UP, 2014.

"Warum schreibt ihr Fanfiktion [Umfrage]." <https://forum.fanfiktion.de/t/53036/1>.

"Warum wird FemSlash seltener geschrieben als MaleSlash?" <https://forum.fanfiktion.de/t/15820/5>.

Weissman, Jeremy. *The Crowdsourced Panopticon: Conformity and Control on Social Media.* Rowman & Littlefield, 2021.

Wertsch, James V. *Voices of Collective Remembering.* Cambridge UP, 2002.

Willis, Ika. "Keeping Promises to Queer Children: Making Space (for Mary Sue) at Hogwarts." *Fan Fiction and Fan Communities in the Age of the Internet: New Essays*, edited by Karen Hellekson and Kristina Busse, McFarland and Co., Inc., 2006, pp. 153–170.

Wills, John. *Disney Culture.* Rutgers UP, 2017.

Wilson, William A. The *Marrow of Human Experience: Essays on Folklore*, edited by Jill Terry Rudy and Diane Call, Utah State UP, 2006.

Winsor, Morgan, et al. "4 Dead after US Capitol Breached by Pro-Trump Mob during 'Failed Insurrection.'" <https://abcnews.go.com/Politics/capitol-breached-protesters/story?id=75081629>, January 7, 2021.

Wolfspirat. "Kommentar." <https://www.fanfiktion.de/r/s/51f2a1a20000eff82c46791a/date/1/1>.

Wynssa Fel. “Kommentar.” <http://www.fanfiktion.de/r/s/4d8f5730000126c90c902eeo/date/1/1>.

——. “Partycrashing für Fortgeschrittene.” <http://www.fanfiktion.de/s/4d8f5730000126c90c902eeo/1/Partycrashing-fuer-Fortgeschrittene>.

yumichan18. “Rotkäppchen—oder ‘Eine schreckliche Realität.’ ” <https://www.fanfiktion.de/s/504648c800013f660c902eeo/1/Rotkaeppchen-oder-quot-Eine-schreckliche-Realitaet-quot->.

Zhang, Juwen. “Chinese American Culture in the Making: Perspectives and Reflections of Diasporic Folklore and Identity.” *Journal of American Folklore*, vol. 128, 2015, pp. 449–475.

Zipes, Jack. “Breaking the Disney Spell.” *The Classic Fairy Tales*, edited by Maria Tatar, Norton, 1999, pp. 332–352.

——. “The Changing Function of the Fairy Tale.” *The Lion and the Unicorn*, vol. 12, no. 2, December 1988, pp. 7–31.

——. *Fairy Tales and the Art of Subversion*. Routledge, 2012.

——. *The Irresistible Fairy Tale: The Cultural and Social History of a Genre*. Princeton UP, 2012.

——. “The Struggle for the Grimms’ Throne: The Legacy of the Grimms’ Tales in the FRG and GDR since 1945.” *The Reception of Grimms’ Fairy Tales: Responses, Reactions, Revisions*, edited by Donald Haase, Wayne State UP, 1993, pp. 167–206.

——. *Why Fairy Tales Stick: The Evolution and Relevance of a Genre*. Routledge, 2006.

Zulixe. “Die verlorene Seite der Märchen.” <https://www.fanfiktion.de/s/59942fbd00059a2f1fbb013a/1/Die-verlorene-Seite-der-Maerchen>.

# Index

# German Studies in America

Edited by
Celia Applegate, Gail Hart, Kai Evers, Susan Gustafson, Peter Meilaender

*German Studies in America* publishes research across the field of German studies in the broadest sense, from literary criticism to cultural studies. The editors welcome scholarly work that takes an innovative approach to German, Swiss, or Austrian history, literature, politics, philosophy, national identity, religion, popular culture, film, music, and/or visual art. We are also eager to consider projects that adopt interdisciplinary and intersectional approaches as well as studies with theoretical approaches including psychoanalysis, gender studies, feminism, Marxism, critical race studies, etc. We publish scholarly monographs, translations and edited volumes of essays in both German and English. This series adheres to the highest academic standards and is peer reviewed.

STUDIENREIHE ZUR GERMANISTIK

*Germanic Studies in America:*

Vol. 1 Nordmeyer, Rubaijat von Omar Chajjam. 2. ed. 104 pages, 1969.
Vol. 2 Richards, The German Bestseller in the 20th Century. A complete Bibliography and Analysis. 276 pages, 1968.
Vol. 3 Germer, The German Novel of Education 1792-1805. A complete Bibliography and Analysis. 280 pages, 1968.
Vol. 4 Gerlitzki, Die Bedeutung der Minne in «Moritz von Craun». 132 pages, 1970 Vol. 5 Bowman, Life into Autobiography. A Study of Goethe's «Dichtung und Wahrheit». 162 pages, 1971.
Vol. 6 Putzel, Letters to Immanuel Bekker from Henriette Herz, S. Pobeheim and Anna Horkel. 108 pages, 1972.
Vol. 7 Geldrich, Heine und der spanisch-amerikanische Modernismo. 304 pages, 1971.
Vol. 8 Friesen, The German Panoramic Novel in the 19th Century. 232 pages, 1972.
Vol. 9 Novak, Wilhelm von Humboldt as a Literary Critic. 142 pages, 1972.
Vol. 10 Shelton, The Young Hölderlin. 282 pages, 1973.
Vol. 11 Milstein, Eight Eighteenth Century Reading Societies. A Sociological Contribution to the History of German Literature. 312 pages, 1972.
Vol. 12 Schatzberg, Scientific Themes in the Popular Literature and the Poetry of the German Enlightenment. 1720-1760. 350 pages, 1973.

Vol. 13 Dimler, Friedrich Spee's «Trutznachtigall». 158 pages, 1973.
Vol. 14 McCort, Perspectives on Music in German Fiction. The Music-Fiction of Wilhelm Heinrich Riehl. 154 pages, 1974.
Vol. 15 Motsch, Die poetische Epistel. Ein Beitrag zur Geschichte der deutschen Literatur und Literaturkritik des achtzehnten Jahrhunderts. 218 pages, 1974.
Vol. 16 Zipser, Edward Bulwer-Lytton and Germany. 232 pages, 1974.
Vol. 17 Rutledge John, The Dialogue of the Dead in Eighteenth-Century Germany. 186 pages, 1974.
Vol. 18 Rutledge Joyce S., Johann Adolph Schlegel. 322 pages, 1974.
Vol. 19 Gutzkow, Wally the Skeptic. Novel. A translation from the German with an Introduction and Notes by Ruth-Ellen Boetcher Joeres. 130 pages, 1974.
Vol. 20 Keck, Renaissance and Romanticism: Tieck's Conception of Cultural Decline as Portrayed in his «Vittoria Accorombona». 120 pages, 1976.
Vol. 21 Scholl, The Bildungsdrama of the Age of Goethe. 80 pages, 1976.
Vol. 22 Bartel, German Literary History 1777-1835. An Annotated Bibliography. 230 pages, 1976.
Vol. 23 Littell, Jeremias Gotthelf's «Die Käserei in der Vehfreude»: A Didactic Satire. 122 pages, 1977.
Vol. 24 Carels, The Satiric Treatise in Eighteenth-Century Germany. 168 pages, 1976.
Vol. 25 Lensing, Narrative Structure and the Reader in Wilhelm Raabe's «Im alten Eisen». 118 pages, 1977.
Vol. 26 Profit, Interpretations of Iwan Goll's late Poetry with a comprehensive and annotated Bibliography of the Writings by and about Iwan Goll. 202 pages, 1977.
Vol. 27 Hollyday, Anti-Americanism in the German Novel 1841-1862. 212 pages, 1977.
Vol. 28 Horwath, Der Kampf gegen die religiöse Tradition. Die Kulturkampfliteratur Österreichs, 1780-1918. 295 pages, 1978.
Vol. 29 Pantle, Die Frau ohne Schatten - By Hugo von Hoffmansthal and Richard Strauss. An Analysis of Text, Music, and their Relationship. 256 pages, 1978.
Vol. 30 Leckey, Some Aspects of Balladesque Art and their Relevance for the Novels of Theodor Fontane. 114 pages, 1979.
Vol. 31 Thomas, Ordnung und Wert der Unordnung bei Bertolt Brecht. 141 pages, 1979.
Vol. 32 Emmel, Weltklage und Bild der Welt in der Dichtung Goethes. Zweite, durchgesehene Auflage, 223 pages, 1979.
Vol. 33 Stern, Hilde Domin: From Exile to Ideal. 93 pages, 1979.
Vol. 34 Gellinek, Herrschaft im Hochmittelalter. Essays zu einem Sonderproblem der älteren deutschen Literatur. 180 pages, 1980.
Vol. 35 Weeks, The Paradox of the Employee. Variants of a Social Theme in Modern Literature. 160 pages, 1979.

Vol. 36 Mittelmann, Die Utopie des weiblichen Glücks in den Romanen Theodor Fontanes. 125 pages, 1980.

Vol. 37 Manyoni, Langzeilentradition in Walthers Lyrik. 128 pages, 1980.

Vol. 38 Helbig, G.E. Lessing: Die Erziehung des Menschengeschlechts. 77 pages, 1980.

Vol. 39 Schrader, A Method of Stylistic Analysis Exemplified on C.M. Wieland's «Geschichte des Agathon». 240 pages, 1980.

Vol. 40 Whiton, Der Wandel des Polenbildes in der deutschen Literatur des 19. Jahrhunderts. 208 pages, 1981.

Vol. 41 Fairy Tales as Ways of Knowing. Essays on Märchen in Psychology, Society and Literature, ed. by Michael M. Metzger and Katharina Mommsen. 200 pages, 1981.

Vol. 42 Beckett, The Reception of Pablo Neruda's Works in the German Democratic Republic. 251 pages, 1981.

Vol. 43 Wiswall, A Comparison of Selected Poetic and Scientific Works of Albrecht von Haller. 432 pages, 1981.

Vol. 44 Cervantes, Struktur-Bezüge in der Lyrik von Nelly Sachs. 144 S., Lwd., 1982. Vol. 45 Guthke, Erkundungen: Essais zur Literatur. 432 pages, 1983.

Vol. 46 Remak, Novellistische Struktur: Der Marschall von Bassompierre und die schöne Krämerin (Bassompierre, Goethe, Hofmannsthal). 130 pages, 1983.

Vol. 47 Laane, Imagery in Conrad Ferdinand Meyer's Prose Works. Form, Motifs, and Functions. 258 pages, 1983.

Vol. 48 Schaffner, The Apprenticeship Novel. A Study of the «Bildungsroman» as a Regulative Type in Western Literature with a Focus on Three Classic Representatives by Goethe, Maugham, and Mann. 178 pages, 1984.

Vol. 49 Gellinek, Pax optima rerum. Friedensessais zu Grotius und Goethe. 153 pages, 1984.

Vol. 50 Lewis, Eugene O'Neill, The German Reception of America's First Dramatist. 211 pages, 1984.

Vol. 51 Brüggemann, Drei Mystifikationen Heinrich von Kleists, Kleists Würzburger Reise - Kleists Lustspiel mit Goethe - Aloysius, Marquis von Montferrat. 220 pages, 1985.

Vol. 52 Weisstein, Links und links gesellt sich nicht. Gesammelte Aufsätze zum Werk Heinrich Manns und Bertolt Brechts. 517 pages, 1986.

Vol. 53 Allen, The Faust Legend. Popular Formular and Modern Novel. 178 pages, 1985.

Vol. 54 Hertling, Theodor Fontanes Irrungen, Wirrungen: Die 'Erste Seite' als Schlüssel zum Werk. 77 pages, 1985.

Vol. 55 Vogt, Vision und Revision: A Study of Inspiration in Thomas Mann's Fiction. 168 pages, 1987.

Vol. 56 Gillespie, Garden and Labyrinth of Time. Studies in Renaissance and Baroque Literature. 326 pages, 1988.

Vol. 57 Shirer, Difficulties of Saying 'I' The Narrator as Protagonist in Christa Wolf's Kindheitsmuster and Uwe Johnson's Jahrestage. 274 pages, 1988.

Vol. 58 Ammerlahn, Aufbau und Krise der Sinn-Gestalt: Tasso und die Prinzessin im Kontext der Goetheschen Werke. 170 pages, 1990.

Vol. 59 Bernhardt, Goethe's Römische Elegien: The Lover and the Poet. 220 pages, 1990.

Vol. 60 Neue Tendenzen der Arnimforschung, herausgegeben von Roswitha Burwick und Bernd Fischer. 320 pages, 1990.

Vol. 61 Markolin, Eine Geschichte vom Erzählen. Peter Handkes poetische Verfahrensweisen am Beispiel der Erzählung «Langsame Heimkehr». 268 pages, 1991.

Vol. 62 Clouser, Love and Social Contracts. Goethe's Unterhaltungen deutscher Ausgewanderten. 310 pages, 1991.

Vol. 63 Cicora, From History to Myth, Wagner's Tannhäuser and its Literary Sources, 217 pages, 1992.

Vol. 64 Denham, Visions of War, Ideologies and Images of War in German Literature Before and After the Great War. 197 pages, 1992.

Vol. 65 Velardi, Techniques of Compression and Prefiguration in the Beginnings of Theodor Fontane's Novels, 202 pages, 1992.

Vol. 66 Stoehr, Beyond the Zeus Principle: Two Hundred Years of Love and Politics in the Novel. 399 pages, 1993.

Vol. 67 Mommsen, Goethe und Diez: Quellenuntersuchungen zu Gedichten der Divan Epoche. 401 pages, 1995.

Vol. 68 Whaley, Johann Wolfgang von Goethe's Poems of The West and The East «West-Eastern Divan»–«West-Östlicher Divan»: Bi-Lingual Edition of the Complete Poems. Verse translation by John Whaley, with an introduction by Katharina Mommsen. 490 pages, 1998.

Vol. 69 Mommsen, Lebendige Überlieferung, George, Hölderlin, Goethe. 406 pa- ges, 1999.

Vol. 70 Brüggemann, Makarie und Mercurius, Goethes Wilhelm Meisters Wanderjahre ls hermetischer Roman. 158 pages, 1999.

Vol. 71 Hertling, Bleibende Lebensinhalte, Essays zu Adalbert Stifter und Gottfried Keller. 142 pages, 2003.

Vol. 72 Hertling, Adalbert Stifters Essays *Wien und die Wiener* (1841–1844) als verhaltenspsychologische „Studien" impressionistischen Kolorits. 128 pages, 2005.

Vol. 73 Moore, The Eye and the Gaze. Goethe and the Autobiographical Subject. 269 pages, 2015.

Vol. 74 Gustafson and Becker Malett, *Stella: A Play for Lovers* (1776) by Johann Wolfgang von Goethe. 118 pages, 2018.

Vol. 75 Meilaender and Rindisbacher, Writing Switzerland. Culture, History, and Politics in the Work of Peter von Matt. 288 pages, 2019.

Vol. 76 Pfeiffer and Tschepik, Meanings of Modern Work in Nineteenth- and Twenty-First-Century German Literature and Film. 182 pages, 2020.

Vol. 77 Roots, Fannish Folklore: Feminist Fan-Fiction Retellings of Germanic Fairy Tales. 256 pages, 2022.

www.ingramcontent.com/pod-product-compliance
Lightning Source LLC
Chambersburg PA
CBHW071513110726
47908CB00003B/826

* 9 7 8 1 8 0 0 7 9 3 3 3 0 *